PANTHERS RISING

HOW THE *CAROLINA PANTHERS* ROARED TO THE *SUPER BOWL* —AND WHY THEY'LL BE *BACK*

SCOTT FOWLER

TRIUMPH
BOOKS

This book is available in quantity at special discounts for your group or organization. For further information, contact:

Triumph Books LLC
814 North Franklin Street
Chicago, IL 60610
(312) 337-0747
www.triumphbooks.com

Printed in the United States of America
ISBN: 978-1-62937-312-6
Design and editorial production by Alex Lubertozzi
All photos courtesy of the Charlotte Observer

*To two wonderful families—my own and
the larger family of Panthers fans. Thank you for reading
my stories and supporting my work for all these years.
Keep Pounding!*

CONTENTS

PART IV

The Stumble: January to Early December 2014

PART V

The Recovery: Mid-December 2014 to January 2015

PART VI

The Rise: The 2015 Season

PART VII

The Super Bowl…and Beyond: 2016 and a Bright Future

FOREWORD

by Eugene Robinson

THE CAROLINA PANTHERS are the real deal. They aren't pretenders. They will be back in the Super Bowl before long. I'm telling you that there is something special going on in the Carolinas with this team.

But how did it happen? Yes, the Panthers are rising, and they are deserving of this book by my friend and *Charlotte Observer* sports columnist Scott Fowler that chronicles that rise. But why are they rising? This book will tell you, and I will give you my opinion right here.

Before we get into all the players who make a difference, though, you have to start with coach Ron Rivera. I played in the NFL for 16 years, and there is just something about a coach who was an NFL player. It resonates in the locker room. That coach realizes the rigors that a player goes through. He is the head coach, but he has also walked the same path as a player. Coach Rivera did that. The same thing goes for Mr. Richardson—the team's owner and founder walked in those same shoes. You know that those guys know football. So a player can't use that old comeback: "Well, you've never played the game." They did! As a player, you have an automatic affinity with them.

Coach Rivera can be stern but he is also relatable, and that's a hard balance to achieve. He has assembled a great coaching staff and kept it together, which also isn't easy. He's authoritative. He's an imposing presence. All those kinds of optics, they go into it, too. And it turns out he's very honest. He's transparent.

Sometimes I'm thinking, *Dude, do you have to be that transparent? Do you have to tell everybody what we're doing?* He is like an open book with X's and O's. But it's not really like he's telling you a secret. Some people think you have to keep everything a secret. What you put out there, though, is displayed, and everyone gets a chance to see it. He understands that. And everyone appreciates honesty.

Again, before we get to the players, you have to think about Dave Gettleman—*Coach* Gettleman. He's not a coach, but I call him that out of respect. He has given Coach Rivera and his staff the tools they need to do their jobs. He has had his hands full with free agents and the draft, and he's found all sorts of guys. Think of someone like Mike Remmers. On a practice squad in St. Louis, now Remmers is a mainstay here at right tackle. Or Michael Oher. Tennessee thought he was done. Now he comes in here and solidifies left tackle. And Coach Gettleman has drafted so well, even in the middle and lower rounds—guys like Tre Boston and Bene Benwikere, who will be great players in this league.

Now you can have all the good coaches you want, but you also have to have players who are going to ball out on offense and defense to win a Super Bowl. In my Super Bowl year, it was Brett Favre, Reggie White, LeRoy Butler, Keith Jackson, Mark Chmura, Edgar Bennett, Dorsey Levens—we had all the ingredients. But all of that doesn't mean anything unless you have Brett Favre pulling the trigger.

The Panthers have their own Brett Favre in Cam Newton, and a lot of what is happening now is due to him. People don't realize how good that young man is. He got labeled a running quarterback when he came in, and rightfully so. He had 14 rushing TDs as a rookie in 2011. That was unheard of. But we all know as football players that you don't win at the quarterback position by running. You win throwing that rock. And Cam can throw!

Spreading the Wealth

One of the best things that ever happened to Cam Newton was Kelvin Benjamin going down in the 2015 training camp. He was throwing to Kelvin or Greg Olsen all the time. Now it was, "Cam, you do what you do. Just throw it to whoever is open." I was an NFL free safety and I still think like one. I can tell you that Cam doesn't get enough credit for how he can move the free safety to one side of the field with his eyes or shoulders and then throw it to the other side like it was nothing. To get an interception off this cat now, you about need a tipped ball. Cam has become a combination of Randall Cunningham, Steve Young, and John Elway.

I remember a few games during this rise for the Panthers in particular. One was during the 7–8–1 season in 2014, when we went into New Orleans and beat them 41–10. There was a scuffle during that game. Guys were shoving each other. It was like, "Yeah, we're in your house. Yeah, we ain't going nowhere. And yeah, we are beating the stink out of you. What are you going to do about it?"

Not many people can do something about it, though, because this Carolina offense really is that good, and its defense is exceptional. It's hard to believe now that, when the Panthers were 1–3 in 2013, people were calling for Coach Rivera's job. Remember that? And then it got rolling. That win in 2013 at Miami was huge, converting on a fourth-and-10 play on the game-winning drive. And the win at home versus New England. Suddenly, winning was contagious.

I know a little something about defense, and I can tell you that you can't win in the NFL without a good one. Ours is better than good. Our defensive team speed is insane. And Kawann Short? He told me once he wanted to be a defensive end to get sacks. He stayed at defensive tackle and got them anyway. He really can't be blocked. Luke Kuechly and Thomas Davis at linebacker? Wow. They are just so fast and so good.

So if you put any quarterback in this system with these players, yeah, we're competitive. But Cam? That makes such a huge difference. He is, hands down, just that good. And he knows it. And that's what you want. I want him to know he's that good. That's what makes him dangerous.

I'm fortunate to be part of this whole deal, and I don't take my job lightly. I give thanks to Mr. Richardson and everyone else who's been involved for allowing me to do it. I never knew that people liked my voice. I hate my voice! I don't like the way I sound. But I absolutely love this team. I only played here one year, but I've been broadcasting the Panthers for 14 more.

When I went back to Seattle to be an honorary captain for a game in 2015, a lot of people asked me if I still felt like a Seahawk since I played there 11 years. I told them I feel much more like a Panther. I rub shoulders with these guys every single day. And I try to break down film like I'm still playing.

Super Bowl Miscues

Now in the Super Bowl, let's be real. When you have chances to make plays, you have to make them. When you misjudge it, mistime it, or whatever, it invariably comes back to get you, because the other team is just too good. I know that firsthand.

Once while I was with Atlanta playing Denver, I was guarding Rod Smith on a post route in the Super Bowl. I cut in front of him, thinking, *I'm going to intercept this ball*. But John Elway had thrown a ball with a higher trajectory than I thought he would. All I could do was try to tip it away. I missed it by a few inches, and Smith scored on an 80-yard touchdown.

In the Carolina-Denver Super Bowl, there were some plays to be had by the Panthers. If Jerricho Cotchery had caught the ball cleanly the first time on that juggling catch the officials later said wasn't a catch, the free safety was out of position, so Cotchery might have gone a long way. We were about to blow that game open. Instead, no catch, and then the sack-fumble by Von Miller for a Denver TD right after that. Dude, that could have been a 14-point swing! And then on a swing pattern, Cotchery was being covered by Von Miller. Cam made one of his best throws all day, and it got dropped inside the Denver 5. You can't recover from that. And I'm not saying any of that to impugn Cotchery. Denver's defense was a beast! I get it.

But in the Super Bowl, you can't get away with that. In the regular season, yes. In the first round of the playoffs, yes. But not in the Super Bowl.

Here Comes the Magic

The good news is we're going back to the Super Bowl. Absolutely, we'll be back. And going back soon—maybe next year, maybe the year after, but soon! I still consider myself a football player. I realize what the Panthers have in that locker room. Do you?

The Panthers went to the promised land, got a taste, and were denied. You know how hungry these cats are going to be now? They are about to call roll and take some names. I know people say I'm a homer, and yes, I know I work for the Panthers. But I'm speaking as a football player who had 62 interceptions, not as a fan or even a member of the media here. Football is what I do. These guys are that good!

There's a dude in Charlotte named Cameron Jerrell Newton, and that dude is the real deal, and there are a lot of other great players too. There is in the Carolinas one of the most sensational players in the NFL—Luke Kuechly—lurking on the defense. He is a player that the league has never seen before. He is the best middle linebacker in the game, his football IQ is unmatched. His infectious passion and his ability to make plays—I've got no words for it.

This team is stacked head to toe with talent and experience. To omit any of these names—Thomas Davis, Kawann Short, Jonathan Stewart, Greg Olsen, Ryan Kalil, Michael Oher, Ted Ginn Jr.— would border on criminal. And they are hungry!

Then you have Coach Rivera doing what he does and Coach Gettleman giving him the tools to do it. So get ready. Houdini, David Copperfield—whatever magician you want to name—it's going to be on par with that. You can just sit back and watch the magic, Panthers fans. Because it's coming.

*   *   *   *

Eugene Robinson played 16 years in the NFL as a safety. He participated in three Super Bowls and made the Pro Bowl three times. Robinson played for Seattle, Green Bay, Atlanta, and Carolina during his stellar career. Including the playoffs, Robinson posted 62 career interceptions. He also won a Super Bowl ring in 1996 as a starter on a Green Bay team that included Brett Favre and Reggie White.

Robinson finished his playing career with Carolina in 2000, settled in Charlotte with his family, and soon began working for the Panthers' official radio team. Robinson has served as the Panthers' primary radio color analyst since 2002, broadcasting more than 250 Panthers games and both of the team's Super Bowls.

Introduction

THE GOLDEN ERA OF
THE CAROLINA PANTHERS

AS THE CAROLINA PANTHERS have risen to unprecedented heights in their franchise history, they have followed two commandments above all others:

1. Keep Pounding
2. Keep Your Personality

What has resulted? A roar heard across the NFL.

After never making the playoffs in back-to-back years for their first 18 seasons, the Panthers have finally married consistency to charisma. They made the playoffs by winning the NFC South every season from 2013 to 2015, and at the end of the 2015 season found themselves with an astonishing 17–1 record and a place in the Super Bowl for the second time ever.

Carolina lost that Super Bowl, of course, as Denver's defense simply outplayed the Panthers. But that 24–10 loss in Santa Clara, California, wasn't the end for Carolina. That was the beginning. The NFL's golden game—it was Super Bowl 50, the golden anniversary of the championship—served as a reminder that we are all living smack in the middle of the Panthers' golden era.

Ever since the Panthers played their first-ever season as an expansion team in 1995, I have covered the team for their hometown newspaper, the *Charlotte Observer*. Back then Bank of America Stadium wasn't even built yet, the Panthers' home games were 140 miles away at Clemson, South Carolina, and Sam Mills was known only for being the team's undersized star inside linebacker.

Much water has flowed under the bridge and into Lake Norman since then. I have written for the newspaper about a regular season when the Panthers went 1–15. I have written about a regular season when they went 15–1. I have covered four Panthers head coaches, two Carolina Super Bowls, and one murder trial.

After more than two decades of experience watching the Panthers, I can tell you with certainty that the version of the team being fielded each Sunday these days is different. More so than any previous incarnation, these Panthers have sustainability.

Never before have the Panthers boasted both an NFL Most Valuable Player (quarterback Cam Newton) and an NFL Defensive Player of the Year (linebacker Luke Kuechly) on the same team, each in their prime and each anchoring one side of the ball.

Never before have the Panthers had a head coach who has known firsthand what it feels like to win the Super Bowl as a player and has grown into his first head-coaching job so seamlessly as Ron Rivera. Never before have the Panthers had a tight end who makes as many big catches as Greg Olsen or a defensive tackle with the sacking prowess of Kawann Short.

Those are just a few of the building blocks of a joyful Panthers team that has dazzled its fan base over three straight playoff seasons and the prospect of many more. The Panthers have shown the world it was possible to enjoy life thoroughly in the "No Fun League" that the NFL too often turns into. Rivera constantly counsels the players to "keep your personality"—he played on the 1985 Super Bowl–champion Chicago Bears, after all, who filmed their famous "Super Bowl Shuffle" video before their own regular season had even ended.

So, within reason, Rivera allows his players to enjoy themselves as long as they also put in the work. Turn the end zone into their own dabbin' dance club? Sure. Pose for team photos while the game was still going on? Absolutely. Act like they *hadn't* been here before? No doubt about it.

And what's wrong with that? Absolutely nothing. Led by Newton, whose athletic exuberance became this team's calling card, Carolina led the NFL in scoring in 2015 for the first time ever (31.25 points per game) and also led the league in takeaways and interceptions.

Newton spoke for the team on the eve of his first Super Bowl when he talked about how he wasn't going to tamp down his on-field celebrations for anybody. "When I look in the mirror, it's me, you know what I'm saying?" Newton said. "Nobody changed me. Nobody made me act this certain type of way. And I'm true to my roots. And it feels great."

"The Mindset of Our Team"

But the Panthers are not all about dabbing and dancing. The Panthers' historic run over the past several seasons was constructed on the cornerstone of the phrase "Keep Pounding," the sweaty motto that Mills injected into the team when he was battling cancer during the 2003 season. Mills—a beloved linebacker and then an assistant coach with the Panthers who died of cancer in 2005— told the team before a playoff game against Dallas that to "Keep Pounding" was the key when life got tough. Those two words are now sewn into the collar of every Panthers jersey.

"Sam Mills was the originator of that quote, and now it's the mindset of our team," Kuechly said. "No matter the situation, no matter what's going on, you've got to keep playing. Keep pounding. It's worked for us. Whether we're up or whether we're down, we play until the game's over."

Part of the reason the Panthers are now a perennial contender in the NFL is talent. They have more of it now than they have ever had before, and a lot of that is due to the evaluating acumen of general manager Dave Gettleman. He had given up on ever getting a GM job, but got this one a month shy of his 62nd birthday and has put together a playoff team every year since. But part of it is also the camaraderie that makes the work feel not so much like work—the way Carolina's players play for each other and try so hard not to let each other down.

Newton and Kuechly have an unofficial contest many week-nights during the season to see which of them can leave Bank of America Stadium the latest and study the most film before they go. Dozens of players routinely come in on Tuesdays, traditionally the day off for NFL players during the regular season, to put in extra time in preparation for the next week's opponent. And veterans teach the younger players that doing the minimum is not enough if you are shooting for greatness.

So when the lights are off at the stadium late at night during the week, that doesn't mean no one is home. Generally, if you peek inside the darkened rooms, you will find a number of men watching game film, searching for an edge.

The Fight—and the Aftermath

When Sunday comes, though, and the stadium lights are on? It's showtime.

"Both the '85 Bears and this team have the propensity to stay true to our personality," Rivera said. "We don't get uptight about the little things." Rivera decided early on that, while he did want to shape his players on the field, he wouldn't try to turn them into robots. He let them breathe. He let them celebrate.

"We don't care about the outside world looking in, the scrutiny, the trash-talking about our dancing, or how much fun we're having," Panthers fullback Mike Tolbert said late in the 2015 season. "I mean, if you don't want us to have fun, stop us."

Rivera allows Newton to celebrate every first down like it was the first one ever made and every touchdown as if the quarterback had just learned to fly (and sometimes, it looked like he just had).

Rivera learned a lesson early in his head-coaching career that to curb a player's flamboyant personality too much would often take away some of the bravado that was an essential part of who the player was. In that case, the player was former Carolina corner-back Josh Norman—who left Charlotte for a huge contract with Washington in April 2016—but in Rivera's mind the application of that lesson was universal. "Keep your personality," he would say, "but also make sure you do your job."

Of course, sometimes big personalities crash into each other. That's what happened on one of the most critical days of the last few years for the Panthers. The incident occurred on August 10, 2015, during a heated team practice in Spartanburg, South Carolina.

At that point in their careers, the team's star quarterback and Norman, the team's star cornerback, never had a lot to say to each other. But they habitually made it a point to try to outdo each other in practice. On a hot summer day, a pot was about to boil over. In an hour-long interview I conducted exclusively for this book, Norman talked about the fight in detail (recounted in chapter 27) and also remembered his relationship with his quarterback before it occurred.

"Cam's a good guy, but we didn't really talk," Norman said. "We had an admiring respect. A respect, like, a sniffing kind of respect. You know when two dogs sniff and they know what's good and then they go their different ways? And don't really play with each other? Like that. I just wanted to one-up him, and he just wanted to one-up me."

So on that day at training camp, Norman intercepted a pass from Newton and then started showboating as he tried to return it for a touchdown. Rather than simply getting out of the way as quarterbacks are taught to do in team drills—this was a controlled team scrimmage where no one was supposed to hit the ground—an irritated Newton chased down Norman and tried to tackle him. Norman stiff-armed the quarterback. Newton's helmet came off.

The two got into each others' faces and started yelling. Suddenly, Newton threw Norman to the ground and fell on top of him.

All this happened about 15 yards in front of me, as I stood on the Panthers sideline. It was the weirdest, most surreal 30 seconds of practice I had ever seen. It quickly became full-scale chaos, as players piled onto each other, trying to separate the star quarterback and cornerback. "Mayhem!" as Norman called it.

Fortunately, no one was hurt. But it turned out that those 30 seconds released a pressure valve for the Panthers. And ultimately, after the fight, the team drew closer. Said Norman just before Super Bowl 50 as he looked back on the incident, "Both guys are aggressive in their approach and they want to be great. And when you have two guys going at each other like that—one throws a touchdown, the other one comes back and intercepts the ball—it's hard. They both have a super high level of competition to the point where they get a little heated. Sparks start to fly. And once those sparks start to fly, they released our greatness."

Newton and Norman both had the best years of their careers after that fight. Norman parlayed his season into a $75 million, five-year contract with Washington in 2016 after the Panthers rescinded the franchise tag they placed on him; Newton's resulted in the first-ever NFL Most Valuable Player award given to a Panther.

And Rivera—who shortly after the fight thought that he was going to have to give a "we have to get past this" speech to avoid a year-long rift between the offense and defense—instead had to do very little. "I'm all set to give this great speech about teamwork and togetherness and family and what we're trying to build inside the locker room," Rivera said. "And then Ryan Kalil, Thomas Davis, Greg Olsen, Charles Johnson, and Luke Kuechly, basically all of the captains [except for Newton, since he was involved in the scuffle], came up and said, 'Coach, we got this. We'll take care of it. We're good.' So I never talked to the team."

Another Super Bowl? Absolutely

The Panthers have become very good at adapting and overcoming. In 2014 the team started 3–8–1 and didn't win a game for two months. Then, just as they were being written off, they ran off five straight victories (including the team's first playoff victory in 10 years—a home win over Arizona). Then, despite losing wide receiver Kelvin Benjamin during the 2015 training camp, Carolina's offense had the sort of crazy-good season no one could have foreseen.

The Panthers' defense has ranked in the top 10 every year since 2012—which, not coincidentally, was the year Kuechly got drafted. It is fueled in the middle by linebackers Kuechly and Davis, who played in the Super Bowl despite a broken arm. The Panthers secondary proclaimed its section of the locker room "Thieves Avenue" in 2015 and led the NFL in interceptions.

What will the future hold for the Panthers? No one truly knows. Injuries are the NFL's great unknown. But I believe the Panthers have finally transformed themselves into a consistent winner, a team that has taken its seat among the NFL elite and won't be leaving that table anytime soon.

I wrote this book to explore how that occurred—and to figure out what happens next. *Panthers Rising* covers the five-year time period between the 2–14 season of 2010 and the rise to the Super Bowl in great depth, as well as casting an eye on what the future holds for Carolina.

To write this book, I conducted a number of new interviews with key current and former Panthers players, as well as lengthy sit-down conversations with Rivera and Gettleman. I asked 16-year veteran Eugene Robinson—the Panthers' radio analyst since 2002—to write what turned out to be an extremely insightful foreword (thanks, Eugene!) And I threaded together my own research and observations based on chronicling Carolina on a day-to-day basis since the team was a baby taking its first steps.

Now the Panthers are in their early twenties. Like everyone in their early twenties, the Panthers are full of promise and trying to make good decisions that will set them up for a lifetime of sustained success.

I will tell you this. Based on what I have seen on a day-to-day basis, the Carolina Panthers are closer to winning a Super Bowl than they have ever been. Sometime, in the next several years, the Panthers will earn their way back to the biggest of all games. And this time, the Panthers are going to win it.

PART I

THE FOUNDATION

2010–2012

1

2–14, JIMMY CLAUSEN, AND ROCK BOTTOM

IF YOU ARE going to make a dramatic climb, at some point you must start at rock bottom.

In terms of on-the-field performance, the Carolina Panthers have had two rock-bottom seasons in their history. In 2001 the Panthers went 1–15. Two years later, they made it to the Super Bowl before losing to New England.

But that team gradually faded, as players grew older and draft picks didn't work out. By 2010 the Panthers were a shell of the team that had made the playoffs in 2003, 2005, and 2008. By 2010 the Panthers and coach John Fox no longer saw eye to eye. Fox was a lame-duck coach, widely (and correctly) assumed to be playing out the string before he moved onto another head-coaching job. Owner Jerry Richardson didn't want to renew Fox's contract at that point, and the Panthers were basically purging a lot of big salaries from the books, which meant they were playing more for the future than for that season.

Ultimately, that worked out okay. If not for going 2–14 in 2010, the Panthers would never have been in a position to draft Cam Newton with the No. 1 overall pick of the 2011 draft. But Panthers fans first had to endure some serious scars from that 2–14 season. That went for writers that covered the team, too.

In my 20-plus years covering the Panthers, the 2010 season was the only time I ever dreaded going to work to cover the team. They were just so boring. So inept. So predictable. That 2010 team set a number of dubious team records, chief among them that it scored only 17 touchdowns in 16 games. One of those was an interception return TD by cornerback Captain Munnerlyn, so the offense only scored 16—one TD per game.

If you are a Panthers fan, do you remember how awful it felt for Carolina to only score one TD in all of Super Bowl 50? The 2010 Panthers played like that most of the time. They had 10 points or fewer in half of their games and averaged 12.25 points per game, easily the fewest in the NFL. Compare that to the 2015 Panthers, who scored 59 TDs and averaged 31.25 points per game—most in the NFL. In five years, the Panthers went from worst to first in NFL scoring.

Quarterback, Personnel Problems

The 2010 Panthers team actually had some talent. Running backs Jonathan Stewart and DeAngelo Williams joined wide receiver Steve Smith on offense. The defense featured Munnerlyn, linebacker Jon Beason, and end Greg Hardy, and saw one of the best individual seasons of Charles Johnson's career—the defensive end had 11½ sacks.

But the quarterback play was awful all season, and that's what most people still remember. It didn't start out with Clausen. After Jake Delhomme had a bad season in 2009, the Panthers decided to fire the quarterback who had started eight playoff games for them and at that time was the best QB in the team's history. Panthers general manager Marty Hurney and Fox pulled the plug in March 2010, releasing Delhomme, who said he was "blindsided" by the move.

Carolina was shedding salary left and right at this point. The Panthers also lost Julius Peppers before the 2010 season when they declined to use the franchise tag on him for the second straight year (it would have cost $20 million for a single year to do so). Peppers quickly signed with Chicago. And the Panthers parted ways with a half-dozen other key veteran players, as they decided to go young and cheap.

All this would rankle Fox, who didn't like to play rookies as a general rule. During the 2010 season, he once got snippy when asked whether the Panthers would spend money on a veteran replacement for an injured player, saying the reporter would have to contact the "personnel department" for the answer. Several times the coach implied in interviews that the players he had been given simply weren't good enough to win. (Oddly enough, in 2015, Fox would be the Chicago Bears coach and would start Clausen—briefly—again. It worked out just as badly as it did the first time.)

Owner Jerry Richardson would say in a rare press conference in early 2011 that part of the reason for going young that season was his belief that firing the veterans was the only way to force Fox to play the young players. Richardson would also say in that press conference that a lack of consistency was the key reason he decided to let Fox's contract expire after employing the coach for nine years.

"The facts are in nine years we had three winning seasons," Richardson said, "but we failed to have two winning seasons back-to-back."

Carolina decided to go with Matt Moore as its starting quarterback in 2010, but that became apparent as a mistake very quickly. In a Week 1 loss, Moore threw three end-zone interceptions in the same game and lost a fumble before leaving with a concussion. He was cleared to return the next week and committed two more turnovers.

By Week 3, Fox had decided to throw Clausen—the team's second-round draft pick out of Notre Dame in 2010—to the sharks. "We've got to spark our offense—and in particular our passing game—so we're going to start Jimmy Clausen this week," Fox said before the Week 3 game against Cincinnati.

But Clausen—who was not helped by a spotty offensive line—was woefully overmatched. He would go 1–9 as a starter that season, with his specialties being the three-yard dump-off pass and the "scramble to the right and heave it out of bounds" throwaway.

His list of problems was long. Richardson would later tell my *Charlotte Observer* colleague, sports columnist Tom Sorensen, that the owner nicknamed Clausen "Doughboy" in 2010 owing to the quarterback's unimpressive physique.

Clausen was battered and jittery. His windup was too long. He got too many passes batted to the ground. He went down too easily in the pocket. He threw three touchdown passes in the entire *season*—that's about one good game's worth for most starting quarterbacks—and nine interceptions while finishing with the worst quarterback rating in the league. He never had a 200-yard passing game. He never threw a TD pass to a wide receiver. It was historically awful.

On the plus side, Clausen never blamed his teammates for his issues, was a nice guy, and tried hard. That was about it.

"Permanent Sucker License"

As the Panthers' losses mounted in 2010, so did the fans' frustrations. Due to the PSL concept invented by the Panthers and their early-years marketing guru Max Muhleman, the "permanent seat license" holders have to renew their season tickets every year or else lose the PSL entirely and also the right to resell it at a future date.

Because of that, the Panthers are almost guaranteed to officially sell out every game. But one fan told me in 2010 that PSL really stood for "permanent sucker license."

While the Panthers never officially lost their home sellout streak, they had to work hard to maintain it. For group sales, they sold some of the $52 tickets in the upper deck for $32 that season. In a 31–10 loss to Atlanta in December 2010, perhaps 25,000 people were really in the stands. And they felt like suckers on that cold rainy day, when Carolina dropped to 1–11 and trailed 14–0 before nine minutes had elapsed. "It doesn't totally surprise me," Fox said of the 50,000 empty seats the team played in front of that day. "I can hardly blame our fans."

After one game, Clausen apologized to Beason for playing so badly. "I don't feel that I'm playing to my level of capability that I expect from myself," Clausen said later of his apology. "I thought that was the right thing to do."

When told of Clausen's apology, Smith—who was frustrated all year that Clausen couldn't get the ball to him—noted that Beason plays defense. "I'm the last guy to tell anybody to be apologizing," Smith said. "But if you're going to apologize, you should apologize to people who're in the huddle with you. But he has a lot to learn. He ain't at Notre Dame anymore, that's for sure."

So 2010 was rock bottom, and that fact was exacerbated by a few other factors. Much of the city of Charlotte had an air of discontent in 2010. Charlotte is one of the biggest banking hubs in America, and as such it was hit harder than many places by the recession when the banking industry began melting down in 2008. It didn't recover as quickly as some other places in the country, either. Charlotte needed an escape from its real-world problems, and the Panthers were not providing one.

Richardson issued a statement to the *Observer* in 2010 about the lost season, apologizing to the team's fans. "It has not worked out the way anyone hoped, and I accept full responsibility," he wrote in the statement. "I apologize to our fans who have supported us so well. Bringing a championship to the Carolinas has always been our goal, and that will continue."

A championship seemed very far away at the end of 2010. The playoffs seemed very far away. A winning season seemed very far away. But two rays of hope were about to beam over the horizon. In a period of four months in 2011—four of the most important months in the team's history—the Panthers would hire Ron Rivera as head coach and draft Cam Newton with the No. 1 overall pick.

2

RON RIVERA GETS HIS SHOT

ON HIS NINTH TRY, Ron Rivera finally hit paydirt.

Rivera got the break he needed in January 2011, when the Panthers hired him to be the fourth head coach in franchise history. Little did they know they were hiring a man who would be voted the NFL's Coach of the Year in both 2013 and 2015.

At the time, Rivera was known as a fine defensive coordinator who had won a Super Bowl as a reserve linebacker for the Chicago Bears in the 1980s. Owner Jerry Richardson had grown tired of head coach John Fox and hadn't renewed Fox's contract at the end of the dreadful 2–14 season of 2010.

Richardson was in the market for a head coach and had previously shown a strong predilection for hiring first-time head men who were former NFL defensive coordinators—both Dom Capers, the team's first head coach, and Fox had fit that description. So Rivera—who had directed successful defenses in Chicago and San Diego—had that going for him. But as the Panthers started over in early 2011, trying to rebuild a team that had crumbled to dust, the 49-year-old Rivera was no sure thing. He had already interviewed for eight NFL head-coaching jobs and had been turned down every time.

General manager Marty Hurney and team president Danny Morrison interviewed three other current defensive coordinators for Carolina's head-coaching job, too—the New York Giants' Perry Fewell, San Francisco's Greg Manusky, and Cleveland's Rob Ryan. Rivera, whose Chargers defense had ranked No. 1 in the NFL in fewest yards allowed in 2010, aced his first interview, though, and was the only man the Panthers asked to come back in for a second interview. "I think we spent six hours with Ron, and it felt like an hour and a half," Morrison said shortly after Rivera was hired. "He was just so focused."

Said Richardson of Rivera the day he was hired, "His approach, his demeanor, his style, his experience, the fact that he's been a former player, seemed to me to be perfect for us at this particular point in time."

Rivera had been focused in those six hours because he didn't want to get beaten again. In his 0-for-8 run interviewing for head-coaching jobs before Carolina, he had lost out on previous jobs to coaches who would go on to great NFL success, like Green Bay's Mike McCarthy and Pittsburgh's Mike Tomlin.

But Rivera had also been beaten out by coaches who quickly flamed out as head coaches, like Atlanta's Bobby Petrino, Miami's Cam Cameron, and St. Louis's Scott Linehan. Each time he was passed over, Rivera tried to learn from the experience and make his presentation more organized and efficient. But until he got the Carolina job, he never knew for sure if he would get to run his own team.

Telling the Truth

Rivera had long understood the concept of a chain of command and longed to be at the top of one. His father, Eugenio Rivera, was a Puerto Rican–born, commissioned Army officer. Ron was the third of Eugenio and Dolores Rivera's four sons, growing up mostly in California. The four boys were close and considered each other "the first teammates each of us ever had," as Rivera said— although that didn't mean everything was equal. When they had to clean up the yard every Saturday morning, his older brothers always picked the best jobs first and stuck Ron with whatever they didn't want to do. Ron got his revenge by growing to 6'3"—the other three brothers never topped 5'10".

A second-round draft choice in 1984 after an All-America career at Cal, Rivera played nine years with the Chicago Bears. He was a reserve on the Bears' 18–1 Super Bowl–champion team of 1985 and had a front-row seat as that volatile, entertaining team blitzed the competition with stars like Walter Payton, Mike Singletary, and Jim McMahon. Talk about confident—the '85 Bears filmed the "Super Bowl Shuffle" music video while the regular season was still going on! That year would influence the coach greatly when the Panthers began exhibiting their own fiery, joyful personalities on the field during his tenure.

Rivera was all business at his first press conference as Carolina's head coach, barely cracking a smile as he laid out his plans for the future in front of the cameras. I remember walking out of that press conference thinking to myself, *Geez, this guy is intense, and he's not going to be much fun at all to cover.*

The first part of that was true. The second part was not.

Rivera has turned out to be the most honest, straightforward, and successful head coach the Panthers have ever had. If you ask him a question, be ready for a real answer. Rivera has a few pet phrases he uses when he doesn't want to talk about something in depth—"And we'll go from there," is a favorite deflection tool. But generally the coach doesn't deal in cliches or generalities. And with his players, he tries to always tell the unvarnished truth.

"Coach [Mike] Ditka was very blunt, too," Rivera said, speaking of his own coach with the Bears in the 1980s. "And I really appreciated it. That's probably the best way you can be with players, because all they really want to do is know the truth."

Rivera also has a playful sense of humor and an adventurous spirit, frequently attending cultural, charitable, and sporting events in and around Charlotte with his wife, former WNBA assistant coach Stephanie Rivera. The Riveras have a grown son, Christopher, and a daughter, Courtney, who works for the team's social media department. Half Puerto Rican and half Mexican, Rivera also is the second Hispanic head coach in the NFL (after Oakland's Tom Flores) to get his team to a Super Bowl. He is lauded everywhere—inside and outside Bank of America Stadium—for being a genuinely nice guy in a profession that isn't exactly bulging with them.

Said tight end Greg Olsen, "In this league, everyone just assumes that in order to be a football coach you have to be standoffish, secretive, and a little bit of a prick. You don't. You can demand guys' respect and their ear by the way you treat people. Ron is the perfect example. He treats guys like men. He has high expectations. His standards are through the roof, and guys take a lot of pride in upholding those standards. They don't want to disappoint him."

Younger Brother Blues

When Rivera was hired, he understood the Panthers had just finished 2–14 and were an NFL bottom-feeder. As the coach told me in our first major interview before his first training camp with the Panthers in 2011, "Right now we're the younger brothers. We're going to get beat up and stuff. Pushed around. But younger brothers grow up. I've got an older brother who's a police officer. When we were growing up, he would smack me around. Now I'm about five inches taller and 50 pounds heavier—so we do grow up."

In Rivera's first two seasons—2011 and 2012—it often looked questionable whether he would make it to Year 3. He made some notable mistakes on the field—ultraconservatism in key moments was a recurrent theme—and some quieter ones off of it. For instance, Rivera says now, since he was a first-time NFL head coach he should have had someone on his staff who had previously held a head-coaching job in the league.

"I didn't hire a guy who had previous NFL head-coaching experience," Rivera said. "So I didn't have a guy I could talk to when something happened. That would have helped."

Hurney Gets Fired

Hurney, who had more to do with hiring Rivera than anyone else, got fired by Richardson after the Panthers started 1–5 in 2012. At that point, Rivera was 7–15 in his first 22 games with the Panthers. And dating back to the beginning of that nasty 2010 season, Carolina had won fewer games (nine) than any other team in the NFL in that 38-game period.

Richardson told Rivera that the Panthers had to be "trending upward" for him to be coaching the team again in 2013. Rivera seemed calm for a man whose job was on the line. Then again, he said, he was used to living with that sort of uncertainty.

"I always feel like I'm coaching for my job," Rivera said in 2012. "It's just like when I was a player. I was drafted in the second round in 1984. For nine years, I came into that facility in Chicago, wondering if I was going to get cut. This is no different. I come to work like I did as a player, and that's to do the best I can."

Rivera also had learned from his father that panic was an unseemly quality for a man in charge. As he once told me, "One of the things I learned from my dad, with him being in the military, is that when all hell is breaking loose, they are going to look to their commanding officer. And you have to maintain a certain decorum. Because they are all looking to you."

The Panthers did trend upward at the end of 2012, going 6–4 after Hurney got fired, to finish with a record of 7–9. Rivera still had to conduct an awkward press conference the day after the season ended—he and Richardson hadn't had their postseason meeting yet, so he didn't know whether he was going to get fired. Richardson waited six days to make a decision on Rivera and whether he would return for a third year. Rivera said the owner told him, "I don't want to make an emotional decision. I want to be able to take my time and think about things."

So on the Saturday after the season, the two met at the stadium. If Richardson had fired Rivera then, everything would have changed.

"It was just the two of us," Rivera said. "We sat down. I brought my book of the 2012 season in review. We went over it page by page and discussed the direction we were headed. When we finished, he looked at me and said, 'I'd like you to stay and be our head coach.'"

Rivera Meets with His Leaders

When Rivera got that news, he decided since he had another year he needed some suggestions from some of his leaders. He had once brought in a group of retired military personnel to speak to the Panthers, and one thing they had told him about debriefing after a mission had stuck with him. The military guys had told Rivera that they would sit around a table, literally take their ranks off their uniforms, and tell everyone to speak freely.

"So that's where I came up with my idea to take my group of leadership guys to dinner," Rivera said. "And so Stephanie [Rivera's wife] and I took those guys and their wives....We went to Del Frisco's and got a private room, sat down, and had dinner. After dinner Stephanie took the ladies into another room for coffee and dessert. And then I said, 'All right, guys, let's take the rank off. What's going on? What did I miss? What do you like? What don't you like?'"

This plea was met by utter silence for a moment. "At first," Rivera said, "nobody wanted to talk. And then they started talking and saying, 'I didn't like how this went, this guy did this or that.' And I said, 'You know? F— you guys.'"

Rivera wasn't really angry, but he did want the veterans to understand that silence wasn't a good option. "It's my fault because I'm the head coach and I should know these things and I didn't," Rivera told the group. "But for not telling me, you're almost as guilty as me. I said, 'Guys, I need the open dialogue. I need the help.' And that's where it all started."

As a result, Rivera created a second, smaller office near the locker room so players could come see him without having to go on the elevator to the second floor and walking in front of a number of front-office people to get there. He started being more visible, walking around the locker room or weight room. John Madden had told him he had to have a few "go-to guys" on the team who would tell him what was really going on, so Rivera cultivated that sort of relationship with veterans like DeAngelo Williams, Ryan Kalil, and Thomas Davis.

All that was good. But what Rivera needed most for his job security was to win consistently, with some better results in close games. He was 2–12 in 2011 and 2012 in games decided by seven points or fewer. Some of that fell on him. Some of it fell on his defense. But some also fell on the quarterback that Rivera had wedded his head-coaching career to almost from its first moments.

In one of our first interviews, I asked Rivera what percent a quarterback's play accounts for an offense's success or lack of it. He came up with an incredibly specific number: 55 percent.

The quarterback bearing that 55 percent load from Rivera's very first game as the Panthers coach was undeniably talented, emotional, petulant, dazzling, joyful, and one-of-a-kind. From the moment he was drafted, everything about the Panthers was different.

His name was Cam Newton.

3

THE NOISE AROUND CAM NEWTON

WHEN CAM NEWTON showed up in Charlotte, he first wanted to wear the No. 2.

That, after all, had been his number at Auburn. And with the Tigers, he had maxed out his one season—a 14–0 record, a national championship, and a Heisman Trophy. Despite the fact Newton only played there for one year, Auburn was so grateful for that season that it would soon erect a statue of Newton (he's running the ball, not throwing it) in front of its football stadium.

So Newton wanted No. 2. But the problem was that No. 2 was already spoken for, by second-year quarterback Jimmy Clausen, who was still on the roster. Instead, the Panthers assigned Newton No. 1. And now it is hard to imagine Newton with any other number because he has accomplished so many firsts.

First No. 1 overall draft pick for Carolina. First NFL Most Valuable Player in Panthers history. First player to win 17 games in a single season for Carolina. First to lead the Panthers to multiple playoff appearances in a row, and on and on and on.

But in the spring of 2011, none of that was a certainty. Fans know that "hindsight is 50-50," as Newton has memorably said on several occasions. So with the passage of time it seems that it was always a given that Newton would end up in Charlotte and ultimately thrive.

That's not true, however. If you read this chapter closely—it concentrates on the weeks and days just before Newton was drafted—you will know that Newton was not considered the consensus

No. 1 pick by everyone in the same way that Andrew Luck was one year later.

A Dose of Luck

Indeed, the Panthers would have almost certainly taken Luck themselves had the Stanford quarterback entered the NFL Draft early in 2011, as he was eligible to do. At the end of the 2010 season, more than a few Panthers fans at Bank of America Stadium were literally praying for Luck. One Carolina fan at a December 2010 loss in Atlanta had even worn a bag on his head and printed upon it: "We want Mr. Luck."

But while Luck's college head coach Jim Harbaugh bolted for the NFL and the San Francisco 49ers, Luck loved college and decided to stay at Stanford one more year. (He has said several times since that the fact the Panthers would have likely taken him No. 1 had nothing to do with his choice.)

Luck's call left the Panthers scrambling a little. The NFL had thrown them a lifeline as it does to all teams who finish worst in the league—the No. 1 pick the following year —and Carolina couldn't afford to mess it up.

The Panthers badly needed a quarterback, for anyone could see already that Clausen wasn't going to be an elite signal-caller. But was Newton the right choice? In April 2011, *Sports Illustrated* published a cover story that seems laughable now but accurately caught the tenor of the times. The cover showed three soon-to-be NFL rookie quarterbacks standing together along with a headline that read: "You Choose: Jake Locker? Cam Newton? Blaine Gabbert? Toughest Call in Football."

There were plenty of Newton naysayers. One of the most well-known, Nolan Nawrocki, was a former Illinois college player who had become known for writing the annual draft book published by *Pro Football Weekly. PFW* was a relatively small publication, but it was well-respected inside the league and owned a reputation of catering to NFL junkies.

Nawrocki, who would later admit he had never met Newton personally, nevertheless torched him in his review. Then he doubled down on that criticism in a nationwide conference call, saying that he had heard the words "fraud," "narcissist," and "con artist" mentioned when discussing Newton with scouts.

Wrote Nawrocki in that 2011 review that went viral online, "Newton has a track record as a non-dependable, non-trustworthy, fake rah rah leader at a very key leadership position....He could really struggle to win a locker room. He projects as a top-15 pick in this year's draft, but he is still very much a project. In five years, don't be surprised if he is looking for another job."

In five years, of course, Newton was actually the NFL MVP.

In case that wasn't enough, Nawrocki also wrote under the "negatives" section for Newton: "Very disingenuous—has a fake smile, comes off as very scripted, and has a selfish, me-first makeup. Always knows where the cameras are and plays to them. Has an enormous ego with a sense of entitlement that continually invites trouble and makes him believe he is above the law—does not command respect from teammates and will always struggle to win a locker room....Lacks accountability, focus, and trustworthiness— is not punctual, seeks shortcuts, and sets a bad example. Immature and has had issues with authority. Not dependable."

"An Entertainer and Icon"

There were others, mostly unnamed NFL scouts who echoed some of the same concerns, albeit in less vitriolic ways. And Newton didn't help himself when he told *Sports Illustrated*'s Peter King shortly before the 2011 scouting combine and less than three months before the draft: "I see myself not only as a football player, but an entertainer and icon." He would be all three of those things eventually, of course, but it was a quote that would have been best kept to himself at the time.

ESPN.com columnist Gene Wojciechowski would write the night that Newton was drafted that the Panthers had overreached by picking him. "I wouldn't have touched him at No. 1 with a goalpost," Wojciechowski wrote then. "Newton is a walking red flag....I question his past. I question his future."

Newton did have to answer questions about his past before the 2011 draft, that was for sure. He had attended three colleges, starting at the University of Florida (where he was a barely used backup behind Tim Tebow). He left Florida after a 2008 arrest involving a stolen laptop worth $1,700 that was seen in his room and which he allegedly threw out of the window when police came, an act that was widely lampooned. The charges were later dropped when Newton completed a pretrial intervention program for first-time offenders.

Newton brought up the incident on his own in a Charlotte press conference in November 2015 and used it as an example of how to recover from a mistake. Said Newton then, "You're talking about a person, what, six or seven years removed from a stolen laptop, things that people don't really want to talk about. A person that had to go to junior college. There's athletes in junior college right now asking, 'Am I going to make it? Am I going to get a scholarship?' But I did all that, and look at who I am today. I'm not saying that to brag or boast....We all make mistakes. But yet it's all about how you rebound from that mistake rather than giving up."

The Thank-You Note

After leaving Florida, Newton went to Blinn College for a single year in Texas and won a national junior-college championship. He was a man playing among boys, sometimes accounting for as many as seven touchdowns in a single game. That year made him a hot commodity again, recruited all over the place by the top schools.

Then came the next misstep. Documents related to an NCAA investigation that were released in 2011 showed that Cam's father, Cecil Newton, and a former Mississippi State player named Kenny Rogers sought between $120,000 and $180,000 for Cam Newton to sign with Mississippi State when he was transferring from Blinn.

Newton instead signed with Auburn and led the Tigers to that national championship and an undefeated season in 2010. He was also judged by the NCAA not to have known about the pay-for-play scheme.

Cecil Newton told ESPN in 2014 that he "willfully fell on his sword for my son," taking the blame in a case where both Cam Newton and Auburn were exonerated. The pay-for-play scandal hung over much of his one year there, though he never missed a game. But it certainly made headlines, and the Panthers were well aware of both it and the laptop incident. They asked Newton all sorts of questions about it and came away convinced that he was telling the truth about not being involved.

The Panthers had Newton into Charlotte for a visit, where the quarterback impressed everyone. Newton would later write Richardson a three-page thank-you note about the visit. Whether Newton knew it or not, one of Richardson's go-to customer service moves has long been the personalized thank-you note, so that handwritten note from Newton struck a major chord in the Panthers' owner. (It also didn't hurt that Newton had no tattoos or body piercings—while Richardson has hired and paid many players who have them, he prefers young men not to have them, and he and Newton had a discussion about it.)

That was far from the only research the Panthers did, though, as they tried to figure out whether Newton was worth the risk. "Oh, we did everything," Panthers head coach Ron Rivera said in his interview for this book. "The first bit of tape I watched was Auburn versus Alabama [when Newton led the Tigers from a 24–0 deficit to a 28–27 win in Tuscaloosa], and the second half was phenomenal. I went right over to [then GM] Marty Hurney's office and said, 'This is our guy.' Marty told me to calm down, but he felt pretty much the same way....I watched all of his throws from that season. And I watched all of his runs. Surprisingly, most of them were called runs. We broke it down, and Blaine Gabbert actually scrambled more than Cam Newton that season, that's a fact."

Besides several trips to Auburn made by various coaches, Rivera, and Hurney, Rivera decided he wanted to see Newton in his home environment. So he flew to Atlanta on a Saturday morning. "I rented a car and met Cam and his younger brother for breakfast at some southern dive they took me to," Rivera said. "Then I went to the home. I talked to the mother first, then to Cecil Jr. and Sr. (Cam's older brother, Cecil, is an offensive lineman who has come close to making a 53-man NFL roster several times.) We had a great conversation. I got a good sense of how he was raised."

Rivera was so excited when he got back to his rent-a-car that he telephoned Hurney right away. "I couldn't wait to call him," Rivera said. "I called him, and excuse my language, but I said, 'You'll not f—ing believe this.'" Rivera then described everything he liked about the trip and Newton's family and said, "Marty, I'm more sure now than ever that he's our guy."

As for Newton on the field, anyone could see his ridiculous arm strength and his size—at around 6′5″ and 250 pounds, Newton and Panthers tight end Greg Olsen are basically the same size.

Because of Newton's up-and-down collegiate pattern, however—three colleges in four years—the Panthers were not sure if giving him millions of dollars would change him. But they were about to find out.

4

CAM ARRIVES— EVERYTHING CHANGES

I REMEMBER the first time I met Cecil Newton, Cam's father. It was the day before the 2011 NFL Draft began. Cam was taking part in an NFL event in New York that involved him happily quarterbacking a couple of groups of kids about 10 to 12 years of age. Cecil was standing and watching two of his sons—his youngest, Caylin, was on the field too as part of the event—when I approached him and asked to talk.

Cecil Newton was genuinely curious that day about what the mood in Charlotte was like after the Panthers' 2–14 season, and I was genuinely curious about his son. It was an interesting conversation, full of quotes from Cecil that look somewhat prescient in hindsight. Among the things Cecil Newton said that day were these:

On Newton's soon-to-be NFL impact—"It's not just going to be an immediate impact. You're not going to go straight into the Super Bowl and start winning. The advancement process is going to be somewhat slow for Cam."

On his son's personality—"He's kind of a fun-loving guy who lives to laugh to a great extent, but who is an intense competitor and puts his all into the competitive process. Great person to be around. Doesn't have a real big social life. Lives simply."

On his son's competitiveness—"He's a guy who loves comedy. Kind of a fun-loving guy who lives to laugh to a great extent but who is an intense competitor, puts his all into the competitive process....Knowing him the way I know him—and I've coached him at home since he was eight—he's built for the process."

On his son's leadership—"A leader is not always someone who's pounding on the table and always has to rally the troops in the huddle and forcing them to listen. A leader is going to be contributing to the winning process, the change-of-attitude process, when nobody else is paying the price to do that. That's on a Saturday, that's on a Sunday, that's on a Monday night, that's throughout the week, paying your debts to get other people to rally around you."

By then, the Panthers had made up their mind to draft Newton. It turned out to be one of the most talent-laden drafts in NFL history at the top with, including Newton, five possible Pro Football Hall of Famers among the first 11 picks. Denver selected outside linebacker Von Miller No. 2—he and Newton would face off in the Super Bowl five years later. (Like Newton, Miller also wanted to be selected No. 1, but Carolina knew it had to solve the quarterback position.) Cincinnati picked wide receiver A.J. Green at No. 4, Atlanta took wide receiver Julio Jones at No. 6, and Houston grabbed defensive end J.J. Watt at No. 11.

I was covering that draft in New York and for Newton's selection was seated inside Radio City Music Hall, which was more well-known for being the home of the Rockettes than the NFL Draft. Just before the draft, though, Newton's lightning-rod status was on full display. The NFL introduced the top 25 prospects in attendance about 30 minutes before the draft began.

Newton not only got the most boos, he also got the most cheers. It reminded me of covering NASCAR races at Charlotte Motor Speedway when Dale Earnhardt Sr. was introduced. "The Intimidator" always drew the most boos as well as the most cheers from fans, and seemed to revel in both. Like Newton, Earnhardt understood and embraced the spotlight. Earnhardt once told me the only time he would worry about fans' reactions would be when he generated no reaction at all. Like Earnhardt, no one was apathetic about Newton.

"My Own Category"

Ultimately, the Panthers wasted no time on draft night. They believed that the player to stake their future on—and that of their rookie head coach, too—was Cameron Jerrell Newton. They had seen him at Auburn. They had seen him in Charlotte. They had seen him at his family's home in Georgia. They wanted to see a lot more.

So the Carolina Panthers, on one of the most auspicious and important days in their history, picked Newton with the No. 1 overall pick on April 28, 2011. Although they had 10 minutes to turn in a card with Newton's name on it as their draft pick, Carolina took only 10 seconds.

Newton, in New York for the draft with his mother, father, and two brothers, quickly pulled on a Panthers hat that clashed with his pink tie. He high-fived his family and strode onstage to hold up a Panthers jersey alongside NFL commissioner Roger Goodell. It was foreshadowing of the most obvious kind. The jersey Newton held up was No. 1, which he would later wear. The loudspeakers in Radio City Music Hall blared "Cat Scratch Fever," one of the Panthers' longtime anthems in Bank of America Stadium. And Newton soaked it all in with a thousand-watt smile that would become very familiar to Panthers fans. The only thing missing was the "Superman" celebration, but Newton hadn't invented that yet.

"My No. 1 priority is to get with this organization and get going," Newton said backstage at Radio City. "I am moving to Charlotte ASAP."

Newton also began a theme on draft night that he would echo over and over throughout his career: Don't compare me to anyone else, because you've never seen the likes of me before.

He does this now whether he's compared to Hall of Famers like Steve Young or other running quarterbacks who have had very successful careers. On draft night, someone asked him about his similarities to Vince Young, who also led a national championship team at the University of Texas but who later had a spotty NFL career.

Said Newton then, "I'm my own man. I'm my own athlete. I shouldn't be compared to anybody because the attributes I bring to this game is something I haven't really worked out. That's what I work at, and what I work to be— my own category."

"He Puts Butts in Seats"

While there were some predictions of failure for Newton, there were also some predictions of grandeur in the days immediately before that 2011 draft. Former NFL running back Eddie George, now a broadcaster, told me the day before the draft, "Cam is a beast. He's got that Magic Johnson smile, and his athleticism speaks for itself. But now the biggest test comes, because everybody is going to want to ride his coattails, to be in his entourage. How will he handle that? Is he studying film, or is he out in the clubs? Because if he focuses on his craft and hones his skills, he could one day be the best quarterback in the NFL."

Deion Sanders, the hall of fame cornerback, predicted to me 24 hours before the draft that the Panthers would take Newton and that Newton in turn would eventually take the Panthers to the Super Bowl. "First of all, it's what they need," Sanders said of the Panthers' impending selection of Newton. "Second of all, he puts butts in seats."

Remember, this was a major concern for the Panthers in the spring of 2011, too. They had seen their stadium two-thirds empty at some home games (although the games had been officially "sold out" thanks to the permanent seat license concept). Team owner Jerry Richardson would say later he could feel that the fans had lost hope during that 2–14 season. And when the fans don't come, the merchandise doesn't get sold, and the concession stands are empty, and the sponsorships eventually dry up. So "butts in seats" was a nice byproduct of Newton's selection.

I asked Sanders during that interview the day before the draft, will Cam Newton win a Super Bowl at Carolina? "In due time, yes," Sanders said. "He can do it, man. I think he has *it*."

A First-Game Revelation

The off-season before Newton's rookie year was sabotaged by the NFL lockout, which basically short-circuited every team's off-season work while the players and the owners reached another labor agreement. So Ron Rivera didn't see his team in full until training camp in Spartanburg in late July, and that's when Newton met a lot of his teammates for the first time, too. There was even some question at the time, remarkable as it seems now, as to whether Clausen would hold onto the starting job or if Newton would start on 2011's opening day in September as a rookie.

Newton had a very average first preseason, but the Panthers were ready to start the rebuilding process with Newton at the helm. Rivera named Newton his starter before the season-opening game at Arizona and hoped for the best.

For you fantasy football players out there, it is probably hard to imagine a fantasy league now where Newton is not a very high draft pick. This is how different it was in 2011. Newton mostly went undrafted in fantasy leagues. Yahoo! Sports would report that Newton was owned in only 12 percent of fantasy leagues just before the 2011 season began—he was the rookie quarterback for an offense that had averaged one TD per game the year before.

Arizona has appeared in the role of "key opponent" several times in Newton's career. (He has beaten the Cardinals twice in the playoffs and had a terrible performance against them in the 2013 regular season that served as a catalyst for Carolina's turnaround.) Newton's first-ever game would be the first time Arizona was on the other side of the ball.

The Cardinals decided to try to make Newton beat them with his arm, frequently stacking the tackle box with eight defenders and daring Newton to find the right receiver and throw the ball into tight windows.

The result was unsurprising in one way: Carolina lost 28–21.

But it was stunning in another respect: Newton threw for 422 yards.

Was his coach surprised? "Pleasantly, yes," Rivera said. "Did we expect him to have great flashes? We did. But he had a whole bunch in a row....Did he exceed our expectations? Yes, that's probably the best way to put it. He surprised a lot of people who didn't believe in him."

Panthers fans who had gotten used to Clausen's three-yard dump passes got to experience the thrill of Newton's downfield passing for the first time. The quarterback completed eight passes of more than 20 yards. The Panthers had averaged a measly 1.9 pass plays per game over 20 yards the year before, so that first Sunday literally constituted a month's worth of big pass plays for the 2010 team.

Newton made some mistakes, too—he threw an interception into double coverage and drew a 15-yard penalty for excessive celebration after his first NFL rushing TD. (He hadn't yet figured out what he could do in the end zone that wouldn't be penalized.) And, in what would become another recurring theme, he was very upset that the Panthers didn't win. They ultimately were beaten by Patrick Peterson's 89-yard punt return and the fact that Newton couldn't get the offense into the end zone with five plays at or inside the Arizona 11 in the closing minutes.

"The last time I lost a game was Navarro Junior College," Newton said afterward, referring to a game he had played in junior college for Blinn nearly two years before in 2009. "What do you want me to say, it feels great? It is not a comfortable feeling for me."

But the 422-yard passing performance kicked the NFL hyperbole machine into full gear. A few days later, Green Bay coach Mike

McCarthy would compare Newton's ability to "Big" Ben Roethlisberger, who had already led Pittsburgh to two Super Bowl wins.

An ESPN.com writer compared Newton's debut to some of the all-time best debuts of anybody ever, rating it better than Harper Lee's *To Kill a Mockingbird* and LeBron James' 25-point debut as a rookie, but behind The Beatles and their American debut on *The Ed Sullivan Show*.

On Yahoo! Sports, more than 75,000 fantasy football players picked Newton up as a free agent in 24 hours, meaning he was now on about half the teams in those fantasy football leagues.

Former NFL MVP Kurt Warner had questioned Newton right after Carolina drafted him, saying on the air, "Franchise quarterbacks have to be able to play in the pocket. He's a long way from that right now." Warner wrote on Twitter shortly after Newton's first game: "Big enough man to admit when wrong: Cam Newton is impressing me today! Said he wouldn't be ready, but sure looks like he is to me!"

The truth was somewhere in the middle between Nawrocki's pre-draft analysis and the breathless hype. "It's only one game," said wide receiver Steve Smith, who caught 178 yards worth of passes and scored twice in the Arizona game. "So you can't throw a parade. But it's something to build on."

Build Newton did. In his second game, at home against Green Bay, the Panthers lost again, 30–23, but the quarterback threw for a staggering 432 yards. It was extraordinary, really—and seems even more so in retrospect. The only two 400-yard games of Newton's first five seasons came in his first two games.

By then, the pattern had emerged. Carolina was losing close games despite its rookie quarterback, who was playing brilliantly for long stretches. The Panthers too often were undone by a suspect defense and special teams—they would give up 28 or more points nine times that season.

But Newton was amazing everybody, including Jon Gruden.

The Trouble with "36"

Gruden won a Super Bowl as head coach for Tampa Bay before graduating to become one of the most well-known broadcasters in the NFL, working in prime time every fall as the lead analyst on *Monday Night Football*.

Known as a quarterback specialist as a coach, Gruden also filmed a series of specials for ESPN each year with college quarterbacks about to enter the NFL Draft. He would quiz them, watch them throw, and critique them. The questions were usually softballs related to football rather than off-the-field comportment. Pretty harmless stuff, but entertaining because Gruden is such a natural on TV.

But Newton's critics had seized upon one moment when Newton was the special guest on Gruden's *QB Camp* show for ESPN—a show that aired repeatedly before the April 2011 draft. During one filmed segment, Gruden asked Newton to call an Auburn play aloud as the two sat together in a room. "Give me something," Gruden said to Newton. "What's an Auburn play sound like?"

Newton hesitated before answering, saying Gruden was putting him "on the spot." Finally, the quarterback said that an example of an Auburn play call would be, "Thirty-six." It was awkward, because football plays usually sound much more complicated than that and have about six or eight more words to them, like the example Gruden used on the same show of, "Flip right, double-X, Jet, 36-counter, naked waggle, X-7, X-quarter."

That number—36—was then brought up all the time in conversation about Newton. It was seen by some as evidence that Auburn's offense was so simplistic that it must have been tailored for a player who would never be able to fully understand the pro game with all its verbiage and pre-snap variables. The unspoken thought was this: maybe Newton was just not smart enough to play NFL quarterback and Auburn had hid that fact well enough behind his athleticism to win the national championship.

I broached that subject to Gruden in an interview in 2011.

"We need to quash that right now," Gruden said, "and I'm sorry if that's what anyone took away from the show. That's not Cam's fault that he's in a no-huddle offense. He's not the offensive coordinator. He's just the performer. That's just the communication system they used. It was all in an express, no-huddle system....He called a few signals to see what the defense was playing and then he called a play numbered in a simple way."

Gruden quickly became one of Newton's staunchest supporters. Well before Newton's rookie season was over, he said it was "absolutely jaw-dropping" as to what Newton had been able to do.

"I'm in total shock and awe about him," Gruden said. "The fact that he's had two 400-yard games already—and one of them against the Packers?! I'm not sure any quarterback has ever started out better....I knew it would happen for him, but I didn't know it would happen this quickly. But Cam has a certain degree of magic."

Yes, he did. Opponents realized it, too, and some tried to get him out of the game. According to an NFL investigation, Newton was targeted with a bounty on his head by the New Orleans Saints that season in 2011. Said the NFL in a press release, "The investigation showed bounties being placed on four quarterbacks of opposing teams—Brett Favre, Cam Newton, Aaron Rodgers, and Kurt Warner. Multiple sources have confirmed that several players pledged funds toward bounties on specific opposing players."

The Saints didn't hurt Newton that season, and he started every game. He set an NFL record for most rushing touchdowns by a quarterback (14, a total he has never achieved since) and was also named the Associated Press Offensive Rookie of the Year after throwing for 4,051 yards.

"Drag Dudes through the Mud"
Newton accounted for a rookie-record 35 TDs overall, since he also had 21 passing TDs. And once he got to a defense's second

level, he was frequently bigger than the players trying to bring him down. As Herm Edwards, a former NFL player and coach for 30 years who is now an ESPN analyst, told me once about the linebackers and defensive backs who had to tackle Newton, "There are guys out there in the back half of NFL defenses making business decisions at that point. They're going, *I don't really want to tackle this guy*. Cam is a whole different sort of cat. His athleticism is just like, 'Really?! Really?!'"

But Newton's rookie season wasn't perfect. Far from it. The Panthers went 6–10, tripling their win total from a season before but still coming nowhere near the playoffs. And Newton was a sulky loser, often staring into space at his locker for many long minutes after games while everyone else was getting dressed. He once snapped at Olsen when the tight end tried to console him after a loss. Respected veteran offensive linemen Jordan Gross and Ryan Kalil took it upon themselves to pull Newton aside late in the season and tell him he had to be more upbeat when things weren't going well, reminding him that he wasn't the only one on the team who didn't like to lose.

Newton also created some internal waves with what he told an *ESPN The Magazine* interviewer during the season about the Panthers when they were beaten. "The house that I'm in is somewhat of a tarnished house where losing is accepted," Newton said, adding that some of his teammates did not take losses seriously enough.

Well, he was only 22. And teammates could see how badly he wanted to be victorious every Sunday, so they lived with the rest of it and tried to help him grow up a little at a time. "He has a huge drive to win," Smith said of Newton, "and not just to win by three points, but to drag dudes through the mud. It's that mentality. I relate to that very well."

The Panthers didn't have enough of those players, though. There wasn't enough talent on the defensive side of the ball, in particular.

And so in 2012, in a move that was second only to drafting Newton in terms of importance to the Panthers' long-term success, Carolina found itself a linebacker named Luke Kuechly.

5

L-U-U-U-U-U-U-UKE

IN APRIL 2012, the *Charlotte Observer* sent me to New York again to cover the NFL Draft. I did this occasionally when the Panthers had a top-10 pick, starting way back when I covered Kerry Collins being picked No. 5 overall in 1995 and then interviewed him in the back of the plane on the flight to Charlotte.

In 2011 my trip to New York for the draft had worked out well for the newspaper. Cam Newton had been picked No. 1 and had provided a lot of juicy material in his two-day stay in New York. So we decided to try it again, although this time there was a lot of uncertainty about who the Panthers would pick at No. 9.

Then the Panthers picked Luke Kuechly at No. 9 overall. And although I liked the pick very much, my heart sank about my immediate assignment. The trip to New York had been a waste. Of all the players the Panthers might have picked in the first round in 2012, Kuechly was the only one who was not in New York.

This was an early sign of what Panthers fans would come to love about Kuechly. If there's a hypefest somewhere and he's not obligated to participate in it, count on Kuechly staying as far away as possible. If there's a tackle to be made, however, or film to be studied, or an autograph to be signed, count on Kuechly to be there.

The NFL routinely provides about 15–25 of the best players in the draft a free trip for themselves and their immediate family to New York for the selection show. It makes for a better TV show for the draft pick to actually be there, holding up his new jersey beside the NFL commissioner, and very few turn down an all-expenses-paid trip to the Big Apple. Andrew Luck and Robert Griffin III, who went No. 1 and No. 2 in that 2012 draft, were there that night, as were a dozen or so other high-profile would-be selections.

Kuechly was not there, however. He watched the draft with his family and friends on a couch in his basement in Cincinnati. In the afternoon before the draft, while many NFL players were making final adjustments to their custom-made suits, Kuechly was playing Wiffle ball with his friends in the backyard of the family home.

"With all the stuff going on, flying around to different places, I was just ready to hang out," Kuechly explained later.

Kuechly leads a relatively simple life, mostly based on football, family, friends, and more football. No one watches more film. The instinctive feel that Kuechly has for the game has always been augmented by an incredible amount of work. He loves the mental part of football, the pre-snap adjustments that pit him against the opposing team's quarterback in a battle of wits. I wrote about him for the newspaper on Kuechly's first full day as a Panther in 2012: "Listening to him in his press conference Friday, I was occasionally reminded of the way the late Sam Mills used to talk about football—with a glint in his eye and an obvious mastery of the chess-piece aspect of the game."

Little did I know at the time that Kuechly would actually turn out to be better than Mills; that would have been considered heresy then. But I'm sure Mills would have loved to have coached Kuechly and, given Sam's self-deprecating nature, said exactly the same thing.

Everyone knows how good Kuechly is now, of course, and how essential he has been to the Panthers' rise. In 2012, though, fans were still learning how to spell and pronounce his name (it's KEEK-lee). The Panthers' annual Fan Fest is a free annual event before each season that combines a Carolina practice and autograph session and draws tens of thousands to Bank of America

Stadium every year. Kuechly's name was misspelled on the back of his practice jersey—it read "KUECHLEY"—for his first Fan Fest in August 2012.

Kuechly didn't care. He was just trying to keep quiet and fit in at that point on a team that temporarily appeared to be overcrowded with linebackers. Both Thomas Davis and Jon Beason were stars on the defense—albeit ones who were returning from serious injuries—and the Panthers also had another solid linebacker in James Anderson. My good friend and fellow *Charlotte Observer* sports columnist Tom Sorensen spoke for a number of fans when he wrote right after Kuechly was picked, "I don't understand taking Boston College linebacker Luke Kuechly with the ninth overall pick. Kuechly might be a sensational middle linebacker, but the Panthers already have one. Do you really ask Jon Beason to slide over to accommodate a rookie?"

The Tackle Machine

Eventually, the Panthers would do just that and more. General manager Dave Gettleman would ultimately trade Beason, a three-time Pro Bowler at middle linebacker, away in October 2013 for a late-round draft pick. By then, everyone knew Kuechly was never leaving the middle of the Panthers defense unless he got hurt. He was just too good. The chant of "L-u-u-u-u-uke" had started to spring up organically every time Kuechly made a tackle in a home game.

Although all of that seemed to happen very quickly, in reality Kuechly had been training for this moment for many years. The middle son of Tom and Eileen Kuechly, Luke was a lightly recruited, 210-pound safety-linebacker hybrid coming out of St. Xavier High in Cincinnati. He was low-maintenance and high production, much like he is now. But Ohio State and Notre Dame (the Fighting Irish might have been his No. 1 choice) never showed a lot of interest. Kuechly was also a lacrosse star and could have gone somewhere on a lacrosse scholarship, but he was more interested in football.

Because Kuechly's grades were good, the schools that wanted him were places like Northwestern, Duke, Stanford, and BC. He ultimately picked Boston College and became a revelation.

Kuechly racked up eye-popping tackle statistics for three straight years from 2009 to 2011, leading the ACC in tackles every season he played and averaging 14.0 tackles per game over his career (an NCAA record). He once had 23 tackles in a game against Duke. Because he wore wire-rimmed glasses off the field, he looked something like Clark Kent, which led to the nickname "Superman" (shades of Cam Newton).

In his sophomore and junior years, Kuechly flew to Charlotte after each season because he was named as a finalist for the Bronko Nagurski Award, given by the Charlotte Touchdown Club to honor the national collegiate defensive player of the year. Kuechly lost out to Ndamukong Suh the first time and then won the award on his second try.

Kuechly turned pro after his junior year and first met Newton at the IMG Academy in Florida when both were working out before the 2012 season. Newton at first thought Kuechly was a tight end and, even after finding out otherwise, was impressed by his hands.

So when Panthers general manager Marty Hurney picked Kuechly at No. 9 in 2012, Newton quickly got hold of the linebacker and invited him to dinner. What followed became one of the most famous dinners in Charlotte history—a three-person meal that sure would have been a lot of fun for you if you had gotten the fourth seat at the table.

The MJ Dinner

On his first night in Charlotte after the Panthers drafted him, Kuechly waited outside his hotel in the dark. Newton had said he was going to pick him up for dinner. A Ferrari pulled up. Kuechly figured that's the kind of car a starting NFL quarterback would drive and reached for the passenger door. It was locked. And then the driver-side door opened, and Michael Jordan stepped out.

An embarrassed Kuechly introduced himself. Jordan, commonly considered the best basketball player of all time and now the owner of the Charlotte Hornets franchise, said he was glad to meet him and that he would be joining the two Panthers for dinner. Newton had in the meantime pulled behind Jordan's car, and so Kuechly got in the car with Cam and the three drove to Selwyn Pub, which is one of Jordan's favorite haunts when he is in Charlotte.

What transpired after that? MJ and Cam talked, and Luke stayed as quiet as a mouse. He had had a Jordan poster on his bedroom wall in Cincinnati, and he had no idea what to say to one of his sports idols. He watched the latter rounds of the NFL Draft on one TV, a baseball game featuring the New York Yankees on the other, and "just kept my mouth shut," as Kuechly would say months later.

Kuechly waited to make his noise on the field. His impact was immediate, even though he began the season playing out of position at weak-side linebacker. In a preseason game against the New York Jets, Kuechly made so many tackles so quickly that TV analyst Cris Collinsworth, who was broadcasting the game, said on the air that Kuechly was "already one of the best players on this team."

An Incredible First Step

Kuechly's first few games were not without their "welcome to the NFL" moments, however. He lined up on the wrong side of the middle linebacker on his very first snap of his first preseason game. He tried to charge around all over the place and make every tackle for weeks, and sometimes his over-exuberance made him miss. His pass coverage wasn't as good as he wanted it to be, although it was already better than most NFL linebackers.

The Panthers had had a terrible defensive season in 2011, allowing franchise highs in points (429), touchdowns (50), and yards

(6,042). Kuechly helped all of that immediately. But the linebacker really took off after Beason went down for the season with shoulder and knee injuries, forcing the Panthers to move Kuechly to middle linebacker. (Interestingly, when Rivera first watched film of the Panthers when preparing for his coaching interview, he thought Beason was not a natural middle linebacker and believed he would be better on the outside).

By the end of his rookie year, Kuechly would lead not only Carolina but the entire NFL in tackles. He became the NFL's Defensive Rookie of the Year. Rivera, a former NFL linebacker himself, was amazed at Kuechly's first step. It was almost always toward the line of scrimmage and in the direction where the ball would end up, which meant Kuechly and the ball intersected constantly.

Kuechly missed his family and Cincinnati's Skyline Chili, but he quickly made a home for himself as a rookie in Charlotte. Already, he seemed to be an integral part of the foundation Carolina was building. Newton was asked so many times about Kuechly's ascendance that he assumed a pose of mock indignation when asked one too many "How great is Luke?" questions.

"I'm not going to just keep rubbing batter on the cake," Newton said.

The only thing that really got Kuechly frustrated in his first year as a Panther was the lack of winning. In Kuechly's last year of college, BC finished 4–8. In his first year as a pro, the Panthers started 1–5.

Hurney, who was responsible for drafting both Newton and Kuechly as well as making the trade that brought in Greg Olsen, was then fired in midseason. Rivera worried that he was next to go. The Panthers would finish 7–9 in 2012, going 6–4 after Hurney got canned but missing the playoffs for the fourth straight year. Panthers owner Jerry Richardson ultimately retained Rivera, although it took the owner six days after the season to make sure.

Patience was a virtue in that case. With their head coach, their
quarterback, and their middle linebacker all firmly entrenched, the
team was about to embark on the most successful sustained run of
its history. And as that run began, a recent Panthers tradition called
the "Sunday giveaway" began to gain national momentum.

6

THE SUNDAY GIVEAWAY

THE MOST BELOVED and photogenic tradition the Carolina Panthers share with their supporters is handing the football they just scored a touchdown with to a fan in the stands—usually a child standing in the front row. That tradition has been named, shepherded, and popularized by Cam Newton, who not only has given his own TD footballs away by the dozens in his career but has also persuaded many of his teammates to do so as well when they score.

What is less widely known is that Newton actually didn't come up with the tradition on his own, and he didn't start it in his first NFL game, either. But it has grown as the Panthers have grown, and it is now as indelible a part of the team as the phrase "Keep Pounding." Like that phrase, it cannot be underestimated as part of the reason for the Panthers' rise, for it has helped to cement the bond between the fans and the team.

Shula's Big Idea

Let's start at the beginning. The first real TD Newton scored himself was a one-yard plunge in his first game, against Arizona. His TD celebration at the time was raw and unrefined—he had the "Clark Kent becomes Superman by Ripping Off His Shirt" thing down already. But he also dropped to one knee and mimicked a few Pete Townshend–type guitar licks on the football, and that cost him a 15-yard penalty for getting on the ground to celebrate.

As for the football, Newton simply left it on the ground. An offensive lineman had to retrieve it for him. He came off the field patting his chest and telling his teammates, "My bad," for getting penalized in a close game.

By October of 2011, though, Newton had refined his celebration. He wasn't drawing penalties, and he was drawing out the "Superman" celebration more slowly and vividly. TV cameras knew by then to stay focused on him every time he scored.

But Mike Shula, then the Panthers quarterback coach and later their offensive coordinator, had an idea of how to make those moments better. Instead of keeping all the attention on Newton, Shula (the father of three daughters himself) thought that if his quarterback spread the warmth of that TD feeling—especially at home games—he could get the stadium roaring even more.

Shula broached the subject before the game, but he also had an "in" with Newton that no one else in the stadium did when Newton scored standing up on a 16-yard run against Washington on October 23, 2011. Shula's voice was being piped directly into Newton's helmet headset—a standard NFL practice to allow play calls to get from the coaches to the quarterback more easily.

So, as Newton recounted shortly after the game: "He [Shula] says when you celebrate, it's not a celebration unless you give back. He says, 'You do all that riff-raff, whatever you do, but at the end you give that football to a little kid. You find a little kid.' So after I did whatever I did, I heard [Shula] in my headset saying, 'Give it to a little kid! Give it to a little kid!' I looked and there was this kid just gleaming from ear to ear, so I gave it to him."

Shula has routinely declined to be interviewed about this subject ever since and tries to deflect all the credit for what Newton calls "the Sunday giveaway" to his quarterback. As he told me once: "That's all Cam. He has made that tradition his own."

The very first Sunday giveaway was a handoff from Newton to 10-year-old Law Waddill of Raleigh, North Carolina. His reaction turned out to be typical of what many of the "Cam Football Kids" would feel like when they were part of the Sunday giveaway.

"I was shaking and sweating," Law said. "There were tears in my eyes. It was really weird. Here was this Heisman Trophy winner, giving me a ball that he scored with."

Law and his 10-year-old cousin Nathan Guptill—who lives in Charlotte and was right behind Law when Newton handed up the ball—decided to share custody of the football. They would each keep the football in their respective rooms for a few weeks until they saw each other again and switched it up.

Incidentally, Newton has not been fined hundreds of thousands of dollars for giving away the footballs, contrary to a persistent but incorrect Internet rumor that rears its head every couple of years. If an NFL player throws a ball randomly into the stands, that does indeed constitute a fine of more than $5,000 because of the crowd-control issue. In such situations, people can get hurt in those kinds of *Lord of the Flies* scenarios where everyone is fighting for the same football and only the strongest—or the one with the most dubious ethics—gets it. Once, after the Panthers scored what turned out to be the game-winning TD in a thrilling game against New England in 2013, Newton flung the ball 16 rows into the Bank of America stands. For that one, he was fined $5,250.

But handing a prized football to an individual fan is quietly encouraged by the NFL—Newton isn't even charged the cost of the football.

A "Football Kids" Reunion

Near Christmastime in 2013, I embarked on a fun project at the suggestion of Mike Persinger, my longtime sports editor at the *Charlotte Observer*. By then the Sunday giveaway was well-established, and cameras would always follow the Panthers players when they handed the balls into the stands. Normally the ball was handed off, the child who got it grabbed a few precious seconds of airtime, and then everyone went their separate ways.

Mike's idea was to get as many of Cam's football kids as we could find together under one roof for a picture and an interview. The ideal scenario would be for Newton to then be the surprise guest at the photo shoot and take a photo with the kids, although we knew that was not a sure thing. Newton is quite difficult to get one-on-one for interviews or photos, although he does make an occasional exception. For most of the regular season, though, the Panthers limit the times he talks publicly to the media to Wednesday during the week and Sundays after the game. Most NFL quarterbacks operate under similar limits, although a number of them speak three times a week to the media rather than two.

Finding the kids wasn't easy. The Panthers kept no list of them. We had photographed some and interviewed a couple over the years, and most of them had briefly been on TV. But many times we had no names to attach to faces.

Gradually, though, I started to compile a list. In my newspaper column and in other places online, I asked people to contact me if they had a ball from Newton. I followed a couple of other vague leads. And over the course of several weeks, I eventually found 16 kids who had made that connection with Newton. Then we got permission from the Panthers to use a room at Bank of America Stadium for the photo shoot. Of those 16 children, 15 were able to come—the only exception was one who was out of town.

In part because Newton chooses the children so randomly, they had all sorts of stories. Some slept with their footballs. Some took them to school. One 12-year-old girl—Hannah Garthright of Charlotte—had written him a letter.

"You gave me a football and I wanted to say thank you," she wrote. "I have hearing aids and ADHD, and when I see the Panthers get a touchdown, it makes me think that I can do that too—only a little bit different, because I play basketball. You inspire me by letting me know that I can do anything. P.S.—I like your smile."

"You're Sleeping with a Pig!"

I wasn't completely sure whether Newton was going to show up that day in late 2013 for the photo shoot. He had played a game the day before and won it, but he had gotten hit a lot and obviously was going to need some time in the training room.

But the quarterback did come. Not only that, he brought his parents. And not only that, while I had asked him for five minutes of his time, he stayed for 30, charming the kids all over again.

To see Newton around children is to understand him more fully. While he can strike people as overly celebratory or as a sore loser (see the Super Bowl news conference for the most striking example), he is at his best with kids. Well-versed in communicating with younger people in part because he has his own younger brother, he is genuine and charismatic with children of all ages. Newton is never at a loss for something to say whether he is talking to a very sick cancer patient or a shy four-year-old or an aspiring high school football player.

This is a trait that has been noticed nationally. Newton signed up for an off-season project in 2016, after his fifth NFL season as the host of a Nickelodeon network show called *All In with Cam Newton*. In the reality-based series, he takes kids on dream-fulfilling journeys.

On this day in 2013, he teased the children who told him they slept with their footballs. "You know what a football is made of?" he asked. "That's an ol' dead pig right there. You're sleeping with a pig!"

In my favorite picture from the shoot, the kids reenacted Newton's Superman pose with him. "Listen now, this might be the only time you'd be able to scream," Newton told them. "Because when I do it, I scream, because a lot of excitement comes out. So on the count of three, we're going to do it, and we're going to scream at the camera."

A few of the kids laughed at that idea.

"I don't laugh when I do it now," Newton said, putting on a fake stern face. "This ain't no joke. This is the real deal. Superman! Right here! All right. You ready? Everybody ready?...One. Two. Three!!!!"

The resulting screams still echo at Bank of America Stadium, where the tradition also continues in full force. Some teammates like tight end Greg Olsen usually give the ball to Newton to hand to someone in the crowd. Running back Jonathan Stewart and wide receiver Ted Ginn Jr. usually give their TD balls away themselves.

In 2015 the Panthers gave away 42 touchdown footballs to fans during the most successful season in team history—at least that's how many USAToday.com counted that included video evidence. The balls went to fans young and old, but all were delighted. The website also ranked the best reactions among those 42 fans, and I'd have to agree with its choice for No. 1. Isabella Bottomley, who was eight years old at the time, had on a pink toboggan cap and looked like she was about to lift off with utter excitement when she got a football during Carolina's playoff win over Seattle in early 2016.

"A Life of Its Own"

But there were many others besides Isabella whose lives have been touched by the tradition. Colin Toler, for example. Colin, six, was from Virginia and was taken to the Panthers game against Green Bay on November 8, 2015, by his two grandfathers. His father had died of a heart condition a month earlier. He never would have gotten a ball except that, after Newton scored, the former Panther Julius Peppers peevishly picked up the ball and, instead of handing it back to Newton, tossed it to the sideline. Newton retrieved it, found Colin and his smile, and handed the ball up to him.

Those sorts of stories are repeated every Sunday during the give-aways. As the Panthers start getting closer to the end zone, kids who aren't seated in the front row but are in the lower section begin to sneak down to the railings, hoping to get lucky.

"It just took [on] a life of its own," Newton said of the giveaway in 2015. "Now you see kids rushing down [the stands to get a football]....As a matter of fact, when we get closer in the red zone, we can see more kids moving down. That's the sight to see right there."

It is a sight to see, for sure, and one of the best current traditions the Panthers employ. It will undoubtedly be part of the team's future for many years to come.

But to better understand what that future may hold, you need to understand what the past was like. The Panthers' rise has been so dramatic in part because they were so inconsistent for most of their history. Part II of this book provides a brief overview of that history. It is not a season-by-season recitation, but an anecdotal look at some of the Panthers' most dramatic moments from 1995 to 2009 during Carolina's "B.C." (Before Cam) era.

PART II

THE EARLY YEARS
1995–2009

7

SAM MILLS AND "KEEP POUNDING"

HE WAS FUNNY. He was bright. He played linebacker a lot like Luke Kuechly does now, with instincts and smarts and sheer talent all wrapped into a ferocious package on the field and a gentle one off of it.

While Sam Mills' fight with cancer inspired the Panthers' team motto "Keep Pounding," don't make the mistake of defining Mills solely by that battle. Mills was much more than that—a husband, a father, a leader, a Pro Bowl linebacker for Carolina and New Orleans and a player who was "short, balding, and can't see very well," as he told me with a wry grin many times over the years.

That statue of Mills outside Bank of America Stadium? That was placed there in 1998, five years *before* Mills was diagnosed with intestinal cancer. Team owner Jerry Richardson put Mills in the Panthers' Hall of Honor simply because from 1995 to 1997, in Mills' three years as a player for Carolina, Mills became the example of what every Panther should aspire to be. As of this writing, he remains the only player to have ever actually played a down for Carolina who has made it into in the Hall of Honor. (It may as well be called the Closet of Honor at the moment, but that's another story.)

After Mills retired at age 38 following the 1997 season, he became a valued Panthers assistant coach. And it was in that role that he came up with the phrase "Keep Pounding" in a speech to the team the night before Carolina played a home game against the Dallas Cowboys. No video is known to exist of the speech. It was no longer than 10 minutes, according to several men who were there.

In a lengthy 2004 interview we did that remains my personal favorite time with Mills, we sat for three hours over lunch at a Charlotte restaurant about a year before Mills died. Mills had given the "Keep Pounding" speech four months prior to that lunch we had, and it remained fresh on his mind. He told me then that his speech—suggested by then-coach John Fox and given spontaneously in a hotel conference room in Charlotte the night before the playoff game—was the first time he ever told the players in any detail about his fight against cancer. He described it to me like this.

"I really would have told them whatever they wanted to know, because people do need to be educated," Mills said. "But most guys were so respectful of my privacy they really didn't ask much. So the speech before the Dallas game was the first time I really told them in much detail what was wrong with me."

Mills said he told the players to never give up on the field, no matter what happened. "When I found out I had cancer, there were two things I could do—quit or keep pounding," Mills told the team. "I'm a fighter. I kept pounding. You're fighters, too. Keep pounding!"

A Black-and-Blue Rallying Cry

Mills died in 2005 at the age of 45 of intestinal cancer. After doctors gave him three to 12 months to live in August 2003, when he was first diagnosed, he lived for 20 months. His son, Sam Mills III, is an assistant coach for the Panthers today and one of Sam and Melanie Mills' four children. Sam III has remained with the team ever since his father's death—a living link between the Panthers' past and their present.

His father's most famous two words have become a shorthand for the Panthers, symbolizing them vividly. If you are to understand the Panthers' history at all, the first player to start with must be Mills.

Since 2012, the words "Keep Pounding" have been sewn into the collar of every Carolina jersey. The "Keep Pounding" drum gets banged by a special guest just before kickoff at every Carolina home game. (NBA MVP Stephen Curry, Olympic gold medalists, Boston Marathon bombing survivors, former quarterback Jake Delhomme, and team owner Jerry Richardson have all done the honors.)

The team has marketed the slogan, handing out "Keep Pounding" towels before big games. The players invoke the phrase in fiery pregame speeches. It has become the Panthers' own version of Jim Valvano's "Never Give Up" speech, a black-and-blue rallying cry for the ages. Fans in the stadium now do a "Keep Pounding" cheer, in which one side of the stadium screams, "Keep!" and the other, "Pounding!"

Cam Newton calls "Keep Pounding" and its meaning "a way of life" for the Panthers. "It's not necessarily [just] two words that hang inside our jerseys, that you often see walking around this organization," Newton said. "It's a resilient attitude that we'll refuse to settle."

Panthers wide receiver Steve Smith heard the speech firsthand and told me in 2012 about Mills' words that night: "His speech was so impactful to me. Even nine years later, I remember it. You had a guy who had every opportunity to take pity on himself, to be like, 'I don't feel like dealing with this.' And he opened up. And he made it about something else. Something bigger."

Leader of the "Grumpy Old Men"

Mills' underdog story sounds like it should be a movie, and maybe it should. At 5'9", he was an undersized linebacker who got passed over, again and again.

Most NFL players enter the league at about age 21 or 22. Mills didn't debut in the NFL until he was 27. The first of his parents' 11 children to earn a college degree, Mills was a very good college player at Division III Montclair State in New Jersey—but his size meant that no one seriously considered drafting him. He had to get a regular job out of college, and made $13,600 a year as a wood-working and photography teacher at a New Jersey high school.

But he wasn't ready to give up on football. Mills won a roster spot in the short-lived USFL at an open tryout in 1982. He then became a standout in that league for the Philadelphia Stars. When Stars coach Jim Mora took over the NFL's New Orleans Saints, he brought Mills with him. The Saints weren't very good, but Mills was.

Mills played for New Orleans for nine years by the time Carolina's franchise was about to play its first games in 1995. Panthers coach Dom Capers and general manager Bill Polian wanted Mills even though he would be 36 by the time he played a game for the Panthers—the oldest starter on a defense that at one point had six starters over 30 and would consequently be nick-named the "Grumpy Old Men."

When Mills got to Charlotte he immediately became one of my favorite players to talk to in the locker room. He was insightful and self-deprecating, making himself the butt of most of his jokes.

To hire Mills, the Panthers offered him a two-year, $2.8 million contract. New Orleans belatedly matched the offer, but Mills—who had made the Pro Bowl four times for New Orleans—didn't like the Saints' initial reticence.

He told me once, "After all that I'd done playing in New Orleans, it kind of bothered me that they were only going to pay me the money because they had to pay it and not because they wanted to pay it. To me, it's almost like inviting somebody to your party or to some special event because your mom says you've got to invite them. If I found out I was invited to an event because somebody forced you to invite me, I'd rather not be invited at all."

The Shovel Pass

Mills' most well-known play for the Panthers came in 1995, when the team started 0–5. With Carolina trailing the New York Jets 12–6 in the second quarter, a blitzing Mills came through the line untouched. Jets quarterback Bubby Brister was supposed to throw a shovel pass on the play and couldn't make himself not do it when the play got gummed up—so he threw it directly to Mills.

The surprised linebacker caught the ball and slowly—s-l-o-w-l-y—headed toward the end zone. Somehow, he got there, from 36 yards out, and that was the key moment in Carolina's first-ever win.

Then-Panthers quarterback Frank Reich later teased Mills about his run: "I thought he was trying to do two things—score a TD and run out the clock."

"Hey, I got there," Mills responded.

Mills made the Pro Bowl for Carolina's team that got to the NFC Championship Game in 1996—the playoff win over Dallas was the first time he had ever won a playoff game—then retired after the 1997 season. He had been cut by the first two teams he tried out for in the pros—the NFL's Cleveland Browns and the Canadian Football League's Toronto Argonauts—but ended up with a sterling 12-year career.

When first told of his impending induction into the Panthers Hall of Honor in 1998, he said, "You're talking about a guy who was kicked out one stadium in Cleveland, kicked out of another in Toronto, and now is going to be a permanent part of one right here in Charlotte. That's very special to me."

The Diagnosis

No one on the current Carolina Panthers roster played with Sam Mills or was coached by him. No player inside the current locker room even met him. He is a legendary figure in many senses, and that is one of them—the stories about Mills now must be passed down. It is an oral tradition that longtime Panthers like assistant coach Ricky Proehl, trainer Ryan Vermillion, and equipment manager Jackie Miles all gladly take on, telling the younger players each year the stories about No. 51 to inform them about the team's history.

In 1999 Mills joined the Panthers as their linebackers coach, guiding players like Dan Morgan and Will Witherspoon. But in August 2003, almost out of the blue, came the cancer diagnosis. Doctors privately told Mills they weren't sure he would live into 2004.

Mills' family also kept a house in New Jersey, and that's where they were when Mills was first diagnosed in Charlotte. Richardson, who had become a close friend and mentor to Mills, had Mills stay with him and his wife Rosalind for the next several days. "When I go to the hospital for more tests a day or two later, he's right there," Mills said of Richardson at the time. "He's carrying my bag in. I wake up from the anesthesia, he's sitting over there in the corner. He's answering my telephone. Folding my clothes up. Telling me to rest. He wanted to make sure I got the best care."

Mills kept pounding during what would turn out to be one of the Panthers' two Super Bowl seasons. During a regular week, he would get seven hours of chemotherapy on Monday, seven more on Tuesday, and then three more on Wednesday. When he came home, his fingers would tingle and he would be exhausted and need to go into sensory deprivation mode. During the treatment, his black skin became several shades lighter due to the harshness of the chemicals being pumped into his body.

"When those treatment days are over, your body and your mind are both tired," Mills told me once. "I don't want to hear the radio. I don't want to see a TV. I don't even want to see the light. I turn the lights off in the house. It's like all of your senses are tired—your eyes, your ears, everything."

But Mills kept going. He would go back to work Thursday, coach through the game on Sunday and then start chemotherapy again on Monday. He impacted many of the people in the infusion center during those days, and he knew that was part of his calling. He especially liked going in to the center—as much as you can like going in to get chemotherapy—on fall Mondays after the Panthers won during their starry 2003 season. "You should see the smiles, the joy on those people's faces when we win," Mills said. "Here's an older person with a bag of chemicals, they're just smiling away because we won that game. Those things....Man, they make you feel so good."

Sam's Favorite Games

In that 2004 interview we did a year before he died, I also asked Mills in an interview to name his three favorite games ever. These were the three he picked:

1) **Playoff win vs. Dallas, 1996 postseason.** Carolina decisively beat Dallas 26–17, a team with four future hall of famers—Troy Aikman, Emmitt Smith, Michael Irvin, and Deion Sanders. "The first Dallas playoff game had to be one," Mills said. "That was a real big moment. We knocked off the big kids on the block at that time."

2) **Regular-season win vs. Tampa Bay, 2003.** Kris Jenkins blocked an extra point to send the game into overtime, and Carolina won 12–9. "That game I felt like brought our team to light as far as perseverance, hanging in there, never giving up," Mills said. "I mean, to block an extra point against, at that time, the world champions and to beat them on their home field? It said a lot about what we had to do and where we wanted to go."

3) **Playoff win vs Philadelphia, 2003 postseason.** "The third one would have to be the Philadelphia game in the NFC Championship in Philly," Mills said, referring to Carolina's 14–3 win on January 18, 2004. "To see us finally do it. To know that when the game is over, our next stop is the Super Bowl. That was so special to me."

Good Days, Bad Days

Mills' "Keep Pounding" speech came just before the Dallas playoff game in January 2004, and the Panthers won two more playoff games after that at St. Louis and at Philadelphia. That placed Mills and the Panthers on a national stage for Super Bowl XXXVIII (which Carolina would lose 32–29 to New England).

There was another Panther fighting cancer at the time, too—linebacker Mark Fields, who missed that season with a far more treatable form of cancer and later would return to play in the NFL for one more season. Fields remains alive today. The two of them held a joint news conference at the Super Bowl, where Mills—obviously weakened by treatments and sweating before the microphones—detailed some of his struggles.

"You have your good days and your bad days," Mills said at that press conference. "I'm just glad I am having days, you know?"

But let's not leave this important chapter of Panthers history with the final image being cancerous. No. 51 was too good a player for that. His number was retired by the Panthers not because cancer took him at far too young an age, but because of the way he handled himself on and off the field.

Let's end this chapter talking about the way Mills hit people. It wasn't dirty, but man, was it amazing. In the way he nearly blew people up on the field, he was more like Thomas Davis than Kuechly. Davis is widely known on the current Panthers team for leading the team each season in the sheer number of "OMG" kind of hits.

Mills was a guided 225-pound missile. In the opening game of the Panthers' 1996 season, he once met 265-pound Atlanta running back Craig "Ironhead" Heyward in the hole on a third-and-1.

The collison sounded like a car wreck, and Heyward got the worst of it. Not only did Heyward lose a yard, but he also hurt his shoulder and left the game for good. Panthers cornerback Eric Davis would later say Mills' tackle on Heyward was his favorite play of the 1996 season. Heyward told reporters right after the game, "Sam Mills hit me right on the shoulder, and it hurt really bad. I could have gone back in and played, but only if somebody had died."

It was tackles like that one that made wild man Lawrence Taylor—perhaps the best linebacker in NFL history—pay Mills what LT would consider about the highest compliment he could pay a man. "Just once," Taylor once said of Mills, "I'd like to get a hit like he does. It has to be better than sex."

8

JERRY RICHARDSON

THE CAROLINA PANTHERS played their first real game in 1995, but they were a gleam in Jerry Richardson's eye long before then. Richardson nurtured the Panthers through a gestation period of six-and-a-half years, from the time he first got the idea for the team in April 1987 while listening to his car radio to the time the other NFL owners unanimously awarded Richardson and Charlotte a franchise on October 26, 1993.

Since then, Richardson has been the only owner the Panthers have ever had. Born on July 18, 1936, Richardson is a former NFL wide receiver himself and remains a larger-than-life figure when he draws himself up to his full 6′4″ height. He can be an imposing man and is called "Mr. Richardson"—or just "Mister" for short—by many people in the Panthers' offices. Panthers general manager Dave Gettleman is one who uses that term of endearment, saying things like, "Mister told me that was a good idea, and he was right."

Richardson has had some serious health problems over the years—the most notable being the heart transplant that he received in 2009. That was the same year that Richardson had a very public split with his sons, Mark and Jon. Both had been team presidents, and both abruptly resigned under mysterious circumstances.

The resignations meant that the Richardson family business was no longer a family business. It had been widely assumed that Mark would take over as the team's primary owner upon his father's death—he was involved with the team's expansion effort since the beginning. (Jon, who had a long and difficult battle with cancer, died at age 53 in 2013.) But, instead, Richardson has now publicly stated that once he dies, the team will be sold to somebody or some ownership group within a two-year period.

This has led to all sorts of speculation as to whether the team would relocate after Richardson's death. (He has also publicly stated it would never move while he was alive.) The Panthers have an agreement with the city of Charlotte to stay through at least 2023, but they can actually get out of that deal starting in the 2019 season if they pay buyout penalties on a sliding scale. There is no escape clause before that.

With the amount of money the Panthers have been pouring into Bank of America Stadium for renovations, however—$73 million combined in 2014 and 2015, which was far more than required under their agreement with the city—it seems unlikely that a move will occur. The Panthers' streak of more than 130 consecutive sell-outs in Charlotte also helps the "Stay in Charlotte Forever" cause. So does the fact that the biggest plum in the franchise relocation game was taken off the market in 2016 when the St. Louis Rams moved back to Los Angeles.

Still, at some point in the near future, the Panthers and the city of Charlotte will need to renegotiate their deal to extend their agreement. They have long had a mutually beneficial relationship, and each side needs the other.

The Beginning

Richardson was a standout wide receiver for Wofford College in Spartanburg, South Carolina, in the late 1950s. That's the primary reason why Wofford—about 75 miles from Charlotte—has been the Panthers' training camp home each summer since 1995.

The future Panthers owner earned a spot in the NFL against long odds. He was not a highly regarded rookie but made the Baltimore Colts roster as a backup. He formed a bond with Colts quarterback

Johnny Unitas, who picked Richardson up and took him to training-camp practice every day.

In the 1959 championship game—this was in pre–Super Bowl days—Richardson caught a TD pass from Unitas and scored standing up.

Richardson knew that he wasn't going to get rich playing football, however. After one more season, he was out of the NFL. But he used his playoff bonus check of $4,864 from that 1959 title season as part of the seed money to open the first Hardee's restaurant in 1961 in Spartanburg. Hardee's was a fast-food joint, selling inexpensive hamburgers and fries, and it prospered. Soon it had grown into a chain.

Richardson would ultimately make tens of millions of dollars in the food business, at one point running not only Hardee's restaurants, but also Denny's and Quincy's, as well. In 1995, however, once the Panthers started playing, he stepped away from those businesses to concentrate on football.

Richardson had not seriously considered Charlotte as a possible NFL market until he heard on his car radio in 1987 that another businessman named George Shinn had persuaded the NBA to place a team in Charlotte that would eventually be called the Charlotte Hornets. That team plays in Charlotte to this day, although the city lost the original Hornets to New Orleans after a dispute with Shinn and his partners mostly concerning whether public money should fund a new arena for the basketball team.

Richardson made two incredibly good hires early in his efforts to get an expansion team in Charlotte. One was to hire Mike McCormack—a former NFL player, coach, and front-office executive—as a consultant. McCormack gave the bid a kindly spirit as well as an insider's credibility. The other was to hire PR genius Max Muhleman, who was instrumental in getting an NBA team in Charlotte.

Importance of the PSLs

Unlike all the other NFL expansion finalists in the early 1990s—St. Louis, Baltimore, Jacksonville, and Memphis were the four chief competitors—Richardson wanted to build and own the stadium himself. The other cities all had the promise of a rent-free stadium that would be paid for mostly by public money.

Given the sure thing of the other cities' stadiums, this privately funded stadium concept seemed uncertain to a lot of people. Well-known oddsmaker Danny Sheridan put Charlotte's odds at 50–1 of obtaining an NFL team in 1989. Montreal was also at 50–1. San Antonio and Sacramento both were given a better chance to get a team. (None of those other three cities would actually make the finals.)

Could Richardson finance such a massive undertaking like the stadium himself, even with Charlotte mega-banker and close friend Hugh McColl Jr. deeply in his financial corner? It turned out he could, but only because Muhleman came up with the PSL concept.

The permanent-seat license (PSL) idea, later copied by scores of professional franchises, went like this: In order for fans to purchase season tickets at the Panthers' proposed new stadium, they had to first pay what amounted to a user fee—the right to buy the seat each year. That right cost anywhere from $600 to $5,400 per ticket, depending on how good the seat was. This would be a one-time fee, but then the rights holder would be obligated to buy their season tickets every year or he would lose both his ticket rights and his original investment. So fans have more skin in the game, in other words, and dropping your season tickets carries the punishment of waving good-bye to your original investment. In this way, the Panthers have a much easier time selling out their stadium year after year, since PSL holders are wedded to the team in good times and bad because no one wants to lose the rights to their tickets without recompense.

The PSL concept was a monstrous success. It contributed more than $100 million toward the final bill for a stadium that would eventually cost around $187 million (a bargain by today's standards, when building a new NFL-ready stadium can cost $1 billion).

With stadium funding secured, Richardson became only the second man to both play in the NFL and then own a team in the league. The late George Halas was the first. The city of Charlotte threw him a parade shortly after the team was awarded, and it was at that event that Richardson promised the Panthers would win a Super Bowl in 10 years.

They have made the big game now on two different occasions, but after 20-something years, the promise remains unfulfilled. There is some urgency inside Bank of America Stadium to win a Super Bowl while Richardson is still alive to enjoy it.

"I Intend to Own the Team as Long as I Live"

Richardson's first Panthers team played 140 miles away in Clemson, South Carolina, while his stadium in Charlotte was being built. It would open in 1996. Those Clemson days are still regarded fondly by the most veteran Panthers fans, who had to get up and get out the door by around 7:00 AM on most Sundays if they planned to get down to Clemson with any time to tailgate. That was the year that Sam Mills won the Panthers their first-ever game by intercepting that errant shovel pass, and that expansion team went a very respectable 7–9 after starting the season 0–5.

Richardson has always stayed involved with the Panthers, but he has shunned the spotlight for many years. Back in those early seasons, it was not uncommon for Richardson to submit to interviews, allowing fans who read the resulting stories to understand his thinking. He hasn't done that regularly for decades, though. When Richardson did hold a press conference after not renewing John Fox's contract in early 2011, it was the first time he had answered questions in a format open to all media members in nine years.

Among the facts Richardson unveiled that day in a rambling, informative, and occasionally defiant news conference: He said he and his family owned 48 percent of the team, with the other 52 percent being owned by a group of 14 minority partners. He also joked with a reporter about the heart transplant he had received in 2009. "First, I've probably got a younger heart than you do," the owner said. "And I'm probably going to be here longer than maybe you think I am. I intend to own the team as long as I live."

At the Forefront

Although that news conference was unusual—and, given the mixed reaction to it, may never be repeated again—that doesn't mean Richardson is a recluse. Certainly he is a constant presence at the stadium. He meets with coach Ron Rivera on a weekly basis and still comes into the office almost every day, focusing on everything from NFL business (he's been deeply involved with league committees for a long time) to answering his mail (he is a stickler about that and often enlists help from others at the stadium to track down complicated answers to a fan's specific question). Richardson also attends notable hirings and retirements for the Panthers, although generally he reads a statement and takes no questions when doing so. And he can be very generous. For both of the Panthers' Super Bowls, he paid for all of his employees and a guest to come to the Super Bowl city, stay in a hotel, and go to the game.

As for contact with fans, Richardson greatly prefers one-on-one time as opposed to giving speeches or interviews. If you write him a letter, it's quite possible you will get a handwritten note back. If you send an email to the "Feedback" section on Panthers.com, occasionally you will get a phone call back from the "Big Cat" himself. (That nickname was first bestowed on Richardson by some of his braver players, like Kevin Greene, back in the mid-1990s.) If not Richardson, the call frequently comes from Panthers president Danny Morrison, a thoughtful and diligent extrovert who was once

Wofford's athletic director before holding the same job at TCU and then becoming the public face of the Panthers' business operations shortly after the Richardson-and-sons split in 2009.

Richardson still has someone drive him around the stadium in a golf cart before many home games and occasionally commandeers the golf cart himself. Fans post pictures of these trips on social media, which can be quite humorous when you see Richardson—always in coat and tie, usually looking somber—holding a tiny baby wearing a No. 59 Panthers jersey.

Will the Panthers win a Super Bowl during Richardson's tenure as the team owner? Hard to answer. But it is difficult to imagine the Panthers without Richardson at the forefront, even though that day is coming. All Carolina fans owe him a great debt of gratitude for creating the team that they love (as do I, for creating the team and thus the job that I've had for the *Charlotte Observer* covering the team since the mid-1990s). The stadium he has built has now had more than two decades' worth of big moments, and few were bigger than the Panthers' first two home playoff wins—both of them coming against the Dallas Cowboys.

9

THE HOME PLAYOFF WINS
OVER DALLAS

FOR THE PANTHERS' first 19 seasons, they had exactly two home playoff wins. Two! That number has more than doubled since then. Carolina's 2014 team beat Arizona at home in the playoffs, and then the sterling 2015 squad edged Seattle and then destroyed Arizona to justify its No. 1 seed in the NFC. But for the first 19 years, it was seriously slim pickings when you started talking about postseason wins in Charlotte.

But the two games the Panthers did win—played almost exactly seven years apart and against the same opponent—are still remembered fondly by fans today. To understand Carolina's history, you need to have at least a passing knowledge of those two games and all their eerie similarities.

The first was played in January 1997 against Dallas. The second was played in January 2004 against Dallas. Carolina never trailed in either game, beating the Cowboys 26–17 in the first one and 29–10 in the second. There wasn't much player overlap—seven years is an awfully long time in the "Not For Long" NFL—but there were a whole lot of coincidences when you take a hard look at the two games. Here are eight of them to ponder:

1) Sam Mills had a huge role in both games. Mills had a key interception in the first one as a player and gave the famous "Keep Pounding" speech on the eve of the second game as

a coach. His favorite was the first—his first playoff win as a player. And Mills took pride in the fact that Carolina had beaten a Cowboys team that had won three of the previous four Super Bowls and had four future hall of famers playing.

2) A Carolina head coach in the second year of his reign would lead the team. For Dom Capers, the 1996 season was his best highlight—it was the only time the Panthers had a winning record and the only time they advanced to the playoffs. For John Fox, his second season was also his best in Charlotte, although he would get the Panthers to the playoffs two more times in a nine-season run.

3) Carolina ran the ball very well with its primary tailback in both games. In 1997 Anthony Johnson had 104 yards on 26 carries. In 2004 Stephen Davis had 104 yards on 26 carries.

4) Both games were played in unseasonably warm weather, with temperatures of at least 63 degrees. In both games, the Panthers handed out rally towels to everyone who attended (blue for the first, white for the second).

5) John Kasay was very busy in both contests. The longtime Panthers place-kicker had four field goals in the first Dallas game and five more in the second.

6) John Madden—who many years later became something of a mentor for Ron Rivera—was the color analyst for both games. His play-by-play partner was Pat Summerall for the first game and Al Michaels for the second.

7) The winning Carolina quarterbacks were both early in their careers as starters and both earned their first playoff wins on the day. Kerry Collins was a strong-armed, second-year QB for Carolina who had yet to do much of anything wrong yet. (His career would short-circuit in his fourth year in Charlotte but he would eventually resurrect it with the New York Giants.) Jake Delhomme was older than Collins when he beat Dallas, but he was only in his first season as a starter.

The Panthers had hired Delhomme away from New Orleans only a few months before the charmed 2003 season began.

8) Both games ended with an impromptu, high-fiving victory lap around the stadium by the players—a tradition that Ron Rivera's teams have now carried on after their own playoff wins.

The victory lap following the 1997 win began organically. It was the idea of veteran Panthers wide receivers Willie Green and Mark Carrier, who convinced their teammates to leave the locker room and return for an encore lap around the stadium in various stages of undress. Linebacker Lamar Lathon—who had knocked Irvin out of the game with a legal hit—didn't have a shirt on for it, and many players only wore T-shirts.

The one in 2004 was initiated by Fox, who had been told of the celebration of seven years ago. He sent the players back out to mingle with fans following the victory. Someone gave Delhomme, a Louisiana native whose Cajun accent was widely admired and imitated, a necklace of Mardi Gras–style beads that he slipped around his neck.

That Panthers team would advance to the franchise's first Super Bowl, although the next two wins would come the hard way, on the road. Still, both those games—and both those Cowboys-corralling years—are remembered fondly by Carolina fans.

Something happened between those two peaks of emotion, however, that pushed the Panthers organization into the deepest valley it had ever experienced. Only three months after the first Dallas victory, the Panthers drafted a fleet wide receiver out of Colorado in the first round of the 1997 NFL Draft. That receiver's name was Rae Carruth. Before the second playoff victory against the Cowboys, he would be in prison, serving a sentence of nearly 19 years for hiring the hit man who killed the mother of his unborn son.

10

CHANCELLOR LEE ADAMS: SURVIVING AND THRIVING

THE DARKEST CHAPTER in Carolina Panthers history was unwittingly set in motion on April 19, 1997, when the team drafted wide receiver Rae Carruth with the 27th pick of the first round. There were other players available—twin brothers Tiki and Ronde Barber, quarterback Jake Plummer, and defensive end Jason Taylor, to name a few. But Carolina's wide receivers were getting old, the team wanted more speed, and Carruth could run a 40-yard dash in the 4.3s.

Yes, Carruth was fast, all right. But the Panthers had no way of knowing just how far and fast Carruth would run when his life careened off the tracks. He had not been in serious trouble before he got to Charlotte, so it wasn't like the Panthers knew they were drafting the player that would cause them the most negative publicity in team history—and, far more importantly, cost a young woman her life.

In the locker room in his first two years with the Panthers, I was around Carruth a lot and interviewed him a little. He did not like the media, even back then, and generally refused interview requests. I considered Carruth something of a brooding loner—although I would not have told you he was dangerous.

In one of the few lengthy interviews we had, he opened up about, of all things, uniform numbers. He switched uniforms a lot—five times in three years, by my count, when you included training camps and practices. Although he was slim, he told me that he believed he looked fat unless his number contained a 1.

Uniform numbers were disposable objects to Carruth. Sometimes, he considered people to be disposable objects, too.

Horrific and Hopeful

You probably remember something about being 16 yourself, right? You may even remember your "Sweet 16" birthday party. Once I realized in 2015 that this milestone in Chancellor Lee Adams' life was coming up, I became consumed for a couple of months about writing this story about his life and how it revolved around his beloved grandmother Saundra Adams, who has raised him from birth.

It became one of the most memorable stories of my career. I say that not because of the way I wrote it, but because of the material it provided: horrific, heart-rending, and thanks to Chancellor Lee and Saundra Adams, hopeful.

In 30 years as a professional journalist, this was one of my most-read stories by any measure, as well as the one that readers still bring up to me most often. Rather than try to rewrite it here, I am going to excerpt most of the original story and tell you a little more about the background behind it. Every Panthers fan should know something about Chancellor Adams, the son of Rae Carruth and the mother Carruth conspired to murder, simply because you owe it to yourself to understand the dark side of professional sports so you can better appreciate the light.

Here is the way my story began on the front page of the November 17, 2015, editions of the *Charlotte Observer*:

Surviving and Thriving
Chancellor Lee Adams Turns 16

In 1999 they tried to kill Chancellor Lee Adams before he was born.

They conspired to commit murder—to shoot and kill his mother. That way his life would end, too, and his father wouldn't have to pay any child support. It was a horrific crime that altered Chancellor's life forever and exposed us all to the dark side of professional sports.

And yet here is the son of former Carolina Panthers first-round draft pick Rae Carruth—smiling, holding onto his grandmother's arm and walking slowly toward the horse "Raider" that he rides every week.

Chancellor will turn 16 on Monday. He already had his "Sweet 16" party. He got to have a magician and his favorite dessert—yellow cake, with strawberry mousse in the middle and whipped cream icing.

"Chancellor is not just surviving," says his grandmother, Saundra Adams. "He is thriving."

The boy they could not kill goes to high school in Charlotte now. Chancellor is 5'4", about seven inches shorter than his father. The two bear a stunning facial resemblance. But he has a dimple in his chin just like his mom, and he also inherited her peaceful nature, Saundra Adams says.

Carruth—still in prison for hiring the hit man who killed Chancellor's mother, Cherica Adams—is 41 years old. He works as a prison barber and makes one dollar a day.

As a fleet wide receiver for the Panthers from 1997 to 1999, he used to make almost $40,000 per game.

Carruth is scheduled to get out of jail on October 22, 2018. Saundra Adams hopes Rae will at least be a small part of his son's life after that, although Rae and Chancellor haven't seen each other in 15 years.

Chancellor has special needs. Owing to his traumatic birth, he has cerebral palsy. Loss of blood and oxygen caused him permanent brain damage. He looked blue when he was born.

But the boy who wasn't supposed to talk can communicate a little with people who don't know him and far more with people who do. The boy who wasn't supposed to walk mostly uses a walker to get around now instead of a wheelchair and navigates steps without help.

"He's able to feed himself some," Adams says. "He's able to dress himself with minimal assistance. And the biggest thing is he's able to walk."

Beside him, every step of the way, has been Adams. She has devoted the past 16 years mostly to taking care of her grandson, ever since she took him home from the hospital on New Year's Eve 1999—less than three weeks after Cherica Adams died in the hospital.

It is just the two of them now, living together in a home in Charlotte that is filled with pictures of Cherica, whom Chancellor calls "Mommy Angel."

"I've never treated Chancellor like he's disabled," says Saundra Adams. "I treat him like he's 'abled' differently."

Chancellor's Horse Class

Some background: I covered Carruth from the day the Panthers drafted him in the first round in 1997 up to and through his trial (which ended in January 2001). Like the rest of Charlotte, I watched the trial with horrified fascination. Carruth's trial was Charlotte's own version of the O.J. Simpson saga, and it had a terrible corresponding human cost. I was not in the courtroom every minute for the actual trial, as we had a battalion of news reporters and columnists covering it, as well. Because it was telecast every day on the network then known as Court TV, I watched the trial on TV on most of the days I didn't cover it in person.

The day of November 16, 1999, remains seared into my memory—that was the day Cherica Adams was shot and Chancellor Lee Adams was born. As a newspaper, we had done a few anniversary stories with Saundra and Chancellor Lee over the years, but none since 2009. There have been other occasional other stories and national TV interviews, too, that have featured the proud grandmother and her grandson—most notably a wonderful piece by Thomas Lake in 2012 in *Sports Illustrated* that I would urge you to Google and read.

But you know how it goes. People forget. I will admit I had mostly forgotten.

Saundra and Chancellor Lee have lived in Charlotte for Chancellor's entire life. They are quiet heroes living out their lives in a small house without cable. It took an offhand conversation with a talented broadcast journalist who called me in mid-2015— she wanted to interview me for a TV documentary she and her cohorts were making about Carruth that would be aired at an undetermined future date—to remind me that Chancellor's 16th birthday was coming up.

That call jogged my memory. After agreeing to the TV interview, I also got in touch with Saundra myself and began to remember and research the story's background myself for the first time in many years.

Originally, I had hoped to attend Chancellor's 16th birthday party myself. Politely but firmly, Saundra Adams said, "No." She is a warm and gracious person but she does not like journalists in her home during family moments like that, which I completely understood. So Saundra suggested we instead meet one afternoon to talk during Chancellor Lee's therapeutic horse-riding class at a nearby farm. For years, Chancellor Lee had ridden horses at a wonderful program run by a gregarious man named Harry Swimmer and his stable of gracious volunteers.

This suggestion was helpful in a number of ways. Watching the horse-riding class was instructive because I wanted to write about what Chancellor Lee could do, not what he couldn't. Because he has speech difficulties, you cannot really conduct a traditional interview with him—he rarely speaks more than a few words at a time. So it was important to observe him in a familiar setting.

Back to the story from November 2015:

The 911 Call

In January 2001, Rae Carruth was sentenced to at least 18 years and 11 months in prison for his role in conspiring to murder his pregnant girlfriend. The triggerman, Van Brett Watkins, was sentenced to at least 40 years in prison. In court, he implicated Carruth as the plot's mastermind. The two other men involved in the plot have served their jail time and been released.

Three of the four men sentenced for the crime have apologized publicly to Adams. Carruth never did.

The murder case remains one of the most notorious in Charlotte history and likely the most grotesque example ever of domestic violence by an NFL player.

The Panthers had already become very popular in Charlotte but were only playing their fifth season at the time when Cherica Adams was murdered. In 1997 they had drafted Carruth to become one of their future stars....

Cherica Adams was a pretty young woman whose mellifluous first name was made up by her mother. "Cherica" was a combination of the entertainer "Cher," whom Saundra admired, and a purposeful misspelling of the last two syllables of the name of Saundra's Eureka vacuum cleaner.

A West Charlotte High School graduate, Cherica worked at a mortgage company and enjoyed socializing. She had an off-and-on relationship with Carruth for months after meeting him at a pool party thrown by another pro athlete in Charlotte.

When Cherica got pregnant, Saundra Adams says, Carruth wanted her to have an abortion. She refused.

On November 16, 1999, Carruth and Cherica went on a date but drove in separate cars to see a movie about a serial killer called The Bone Collector.

After the movie, she was following his car on Rea Road in southeast Charlotte when Carruth suddenly came to a halt. She stopped behind him.

Another car pulled up alongside her. Watkins shot five times into the BMW that Cherica was driving. Four of the bullets hit Cherica in the drive-by shooting.

None of the bullets hit Chancellor, but her blood was his blood. As she began to lose blood rapidly, he began to suffocate.

Somehow, Cherica found her phone and found the strength to make a haunting, gasping call to 911. She described the shooting, instigated Chancellor's rescue, and implicated Carruth. The recording was later played in court.

Part of her conversation with the dispatcher went like this:

> **Cherica:** *I was following my baby's daddy, Rae Carruth, the football player.*
> **Dispatcher:** *So you think he did it?*
> **Cherica:** *He slowed down and a car pulled up beside me.*
> **Dispatcher:** *And then shot at you?*
> **Cherica:** *Yes.*
> **Dispatcher:** *...And then, where'd he go?*
> **Cherica:** *He just left. I think he did it. I don't know what to think.*

Choosing Happiness over Bitterness

To think of what Cherica was able to do in that 911 call—the information she was able to provide even as her body was shutting down due to loss of blood—makes goosebumps stand up on my arms even today. I have four children myself, and I would like to think I could be that heroic when trying to save one of them. But who knows?

Saundra Adams, as you will see as the story continues, has a power of forgiveness that must come directly from her deep faith in God. She has raised a special-needs child on her own for more than 16 years, and yet she is genuinely happy much of the time rather than bitter. She doesn't denigrate Carruth at every opportunity, even though certainly she would be justified in doing so.

The story continued:

The Power of Forgiveness

Chancellor was born later that night, 10 weeks early, by emergency Caesarean section. Carruth was arrested on Thanksgiving Day. He would later panic and try to jump bail after Cherica died. But the FBI found him 500 miles away, hiding in the trunk of another woman's car at a Best Western motel in Tennessee. The trunk also contained $3,900 in cash and two bottles full of Carruth's urine....

Carruth—whose true name is Rae Wiggins—is now imprisoned in Columbia, N.C., in the state's eastern corner. He appealed his sentence numerous times, but all of his appeals were denied.

Carruth has never publicly admitted any involvement in the crime. He did not testify at his trial. He declined to be interviewed for this story.

In his only interview since the shooting, in 2001 with CNN/SI, Carruth proclaimed total innocence and said Watkins acted on his own....

Even though Cherica was her only child, Saundra Adams long ago forgave Rae Carruth. She says she had to, for Chancellor's sake.

"The main reason I want Rae and Chancellor to one day have a relationship is because it is his son," Adams says. "And that's why I chose early on that I would forgive Rae. Because I don't feel like I can offer unconditional love to Chancellor if I don't forgive Rae. That's his father. It's a part of him. Chancellor wouldn't be who he is without Rae. I want them to bond, or at least to meet again.

"Right now," she continues, "Rae is still in denial about his part in Cherica's murder. Not that Chancellor would change that. But if anybody were to ever touch his heart, to make him want to be truthful, I think it would be Chancellor."

A Panthers Fan

Chancellor once performed in a group dance on the field at Bank of America Stadium just before a Panthers game. No one in the media knew at the time that the son of Rae Carruth was out there on the same field where his father once played, but it is just one of several connections he has to the team.

Chancellor wears a Panthers cap to our interview at Misty Meadows Farm, where he does his therapeutic riding. They tell me to call him "Lee," his middle name, because that's what everyone calls him except his grandmother. It is easier for him to both say and spell "Lee."

"Hi," he says, reaching out to shake my hand.

"Hi, Lee," I say. "Nice hat. Are you a Panthers fan?"

"Yeah!" he says.

"Oh, he watches the Panthers," Saundra Adams says. "He knows they are having a very good season."

Saundra Adams and Chancellor got a private tour of Bank of America Stadium a few years ago. They saw the Panthers' locker room, including the space Carruth used to occupy. They met star wide receiver Steve Smith while he was still *with the team. ("He was so kind and patient with us," Saundra Adams says.) Chancellor loved it all.*

Chancellor loves many things. He loves baked chicken, green beans, and animated movies. He has a collection of DVDs. He loves to take all the movies out of their cases, mix them up in his room and then match them all up again. He loves jazz and once attended a Kenny G concert with his grandmother.

"He had to be the youngest person there," Adams says, "and he hummed along with everything."

Dr. Docia Hickey, a neonatologist, cared for Chancellor at the hospital when he was a baby and has stayed close to the family ever since.

"Chancellor has done remarkably well," Hickey says. "He's a happy young man. And he loves his grandmother as much as his grandmother loves him."

The "Smile Ministry"

The smile is what first strikes most people about Chancellor Lee Adams. It is a full-out, thousand-watt grin.

"He wakes up smiling and he goes to bed smiling," Adams says. "He's had that same happy spirit his whole life. I tell him he's in the smile ministry. I've had numerous people in stores come up and tell me: 'You know, I was in a really funky mood, and this boy just keeps smiling. And I just cannot be mad when he's smiling like that.'"

Chancellor has never known his mother, except through pictures. He has never known his father, although Saundra Adams keeps a few pictures of Rae Carruth around their house, too. His life mostly revolves around "G-mom," as he calls his grandmother, and all the places she takes him— school, physical therapy, horseback riding, and dance.

He doesn't ask about either of his parents much, Adams says, and he doesn't understand too much about her death.

G-mom uses pictures to tell him stories about his mother, though—including this one.

After his birth, Chancellor was immediately whisked away by doctors because of all his health issues. Cherica knew he was alive. But on the day after his birth, she lapsed into a coma from which she never awoke. So Chancellor and Cherica only spent a few minutes together, and only once—a few days before she died, in December 1999.

Cherica had gotten worse and worse, Adams says, and she was being kept alive only by machines. The family knew she was close to dying. They asked if Chancellor—who had gradually been getting better in the neonatal unit, one floor away—could come see her.

Dr. Hickey and a favorite nurse brought Chancellor to Cherica. They wrapped him in a blanket. They laid Chancellor on his unconscious mother's chest for five minutes.

"I will never forget that," Hickey says. "I will never forget the sadness, and the respectfulness, of everyone in that room."

Says Adams: "All of Cherica's monitors were stable. They were doing the work of keeping her alive. But when they placed Chancellor on her chest, the monitors shot up. Her heart rate was just going crazy. You knew she felt his presence there. I know that she knew he was well."

"He Just Did a Bad Thing"

Many people in Saundra Adams' position would show bitterness at the hand life has dealt them. She had been looking forward to being a grandmother. Instead, she became a single mother, taking care of a special-needs child, with her only child murdered. There is no end in sight to the work she does. She believes Chancellor will always live in her home, needing care, and will stay there even after she is gone.

But she has chosen to fill Chancellor's heart with love, not vengefulness.

"I just can't say how great she is," Hickey says. "That woman has devoted her life to her grandson, and she's done a wonderful job. She is happy. So many people could be bitter. But she isn't. She's a remarkable woman. Saundra Adams is one of my heroes."

Says Adams: "I choose to cherish what I have left more than mourn what I have lost. Cherica is not gone. I look at him and I see her. Every day.

"I tell Chancellor that his mom was shot, and his Daddy is in jail because of that, because Daddy did a bad thing. He is not a bad person, he just did a bad thing. And so that's why he has no parents here with him.

"But I don't want Chancellor ever thinking that any part of him is bad. Because there is nothing that is bad about Chancellor."

"Are You Happy?"

It is twilight now at the horse farm. An earlier drizzle has let up, and there are a few streaks of pink and purple in the sky. The 83 acres of Misty Meadows look like a landscape painting come to life. Harry Swimmer, who founded Misty Meadows with his wife, looks up fondly at the boy on the horse.

"Are you happy, Lee?" says Swimmer.

"Yeah!" Lee says, smiling even more broadly.

Lee sits up straighter in the saddle and looks forward. He clucks softly at the horse. Raider starts moving again.

And then Chancellor Lee Adams—the boy who was supposed to die 16 years ago—rides off into the sunset.

*　　*　　*　　*

A Postscript

After the "Surviving and Thriving" story was published, it was retweeted more than 3,700 times on Twitter. The original story was read by hundreds of thousands of people and reprinted in many places. Peter King of *Sports Illustrated* also asked me to write something for his excellent Monday Morning Quarterback website—mmqb.si.com—about how I wrote it.

Most significantly, though, the story made a number of readers want to help Saundra Adams, whose financial needs are considerable given Chancellor Lee's special situation. If you are among those readers, email me at ScottFowlerBooks@aol.com, and I will send you the address Saundra Adams uses to accept donations.

Because it is what Saundra Adams hopes for, I also do hope that former Panther Rae Carruth and his son have at least some relationship once he gets out of prison. I am not sure how she has managed to find that sort of forgiveness in her heart, but I am glad she did. Bitterness has a way of eating you alive from the inside.

And I will tell you after being around Saundra and Chancellor a number of times: They aren't bitter. They are genuinely happy.

11

THE FIRST PANTHERS SUPER BOWL

A DOZEN YEARS before Cam, Luke, and Ron there was Jake, Moose, and the two Johns.

The Panthers' first trip to the Super Bowl was paced by players like quarterback Jake Delhomme, wide receiver Muhsin Muhammad, and place-kicker John Kasay, with coach John Fox directing the team. That 2003 Carolina team would not have a lot of sustained success—it did not make the playoffs either the year before or the year after its Super Bowl season. But it did earn a cool nickname—the "Cardiac Cats"—and it also played a more exciting Super Bowl than the Panthers did a dozen years later. The Cardiac Cats scored three fourth-quarter touchdowns but still lost in the final seconds to New England, 32–29, on February 1, 2004.

That the 2003 team even made it that far was a dazzling surprise. Carolina had a six-year playoff drought from 1997 to 2002—dark times that were remembered more for quarterback Kerry Collins' alcohol-fueled flameout, Rae Carruth's arrest and trial and the 1–15 Panthers season of 2001. There was the occasional bright spot—quarterback Steve Beuerlein's game-winning draw play at Green Bay being the brightest one in a 1999 shootout at Lambeau Field. But mostly the Panthers had been overwhelmed by a tide of mediocrity after that first burst of success in their first two seasons.

Unlike the Panthers of 2015, who went 15–1 and by the end of the regular season were a No. 1 seed favored to make the Super Bowl, the Panthers of 2003 were never supposed to get to the biggest game. They were a No. 3 seed and had to win three playoff games—beating Dallas at home and then both St. Louis and Philadelphia on the road—to make it to Houston to face New England and quarterback Tom Brady in his prime.

But Carolina did all of that. Delhomme, virtually unknown before training camp began, became one of the most popular players in Panthers history that season. He emerged in the very first game, against Jacksonville, when Fox put him in to start the third quarter for an ineffective Rodney Peete. Delhomme threw a fourth-down, 12-yard touchdown pass to Ricky Proehl to lead the first of the Panthers' comeback victories that season. Delhomme's high-risk, high-reward style came to light in that first game—he was a Nevada gambler of a quarterback, and the play he threw the winning TD pass to Proehl on was fittingly called "Reno." He threw three TD passes in his first game as a Panther, but he also had two interceptions.

"When I play, I like to sling it around," Delhomme would say.

Suddenly, Carolina had a quarterback. It already had a couple of the best receivers in franchise history on the roster—second-year player Steve Smith (his career is covered more thoroughly in the next chapter) and veteran Muhsin Muhammad.

Muhammad was a fearless, tough receiver who was good at everything. He was especially admired by the coaching staff for the way that, even after he had become a perennial 1,000-yard receiver, he would sell out his body on blocks to buy his running back two extra yards.

As Delhomme said when Muhammad retired in 2009, "When I think of what a picture of a pro football player would look like, I think of Muhsin Muhammad."

Kasay remains the team's all-time leading scorer with 1,482 points—more than three times the point total of anyone else—and it will take many years and maybe decades before anyone comes close to that record. He was one of the team's very first free-agent signings, in 1995, and then kicked for Carolina for the next 15 years. Kasay was referred to as "the Last Original Panther" for the last several years of his time with Carolina and, like Muhammad and Delhomme, became a beloved member of the Charlotte community during his time with the Panthers.

Like Muhammad, who has interests in several Charlotte-area businesses, Kasay would make his permanent home in Charlotte after retirement and settle into the job as a high school athletic director at Charlotte Christian. Delhomme would ultimately return to his own hometown of Breaux Bridge, Louisiana, to raise and race thoroughbreds with his father and brother.

But in 2003, the Panthers' ninth season, all of that was in the future. The Panthers' first Super Bowl appearance was a bolt out of the black-and-blue—the team had gone only 7–9 the year before, in Fox's first year. Fox had quickly assembled a good defense, but his offense had left something to be desired in 2002.

He found a triggerman in Delhomme, however—a player who would take the chances that the Panthers needed to take. The Panthers started the season 5–0, finished it 11–5, and then advanced to the Super Bowl with a defense-driven, 14–3 win at Philadelphia in the NFC Championship Game. That win was paved by Carolina's devastating defense—the Panthers had five sacks, grabbed four interceptions, and allowed only three points. Muhammad grabbed a jump-ball pass between two Philly defenders for the game's first touchdown, then dropped to one knee and made a "Shhh" motion by putting his finger to his lips. That landed him on the cover of *Sports Illustrated* the following week and turned out to be all the points the Panthers needed to land in the Super Bowl.

A Bizarre Super Bowl

The Panthers' first Super Bowl was a captivating thriller. It is also still known for the conspiracy theory that the Patriots somehow taped some of Carolina's practices and knew the Panthers' plays. The theory has never been proven and no real evidence has ever been shown to verify it, but staunch Carolina supporters will also tell you it has never been *disproven*, either.

What is undeniable is the bizarre nature of the game itself, to say nothing of its infamous halftime show. Here are five strange but true facts about Super Bowl XXXVIII, which was ultimately decided when Adam Vinatieri made a 41-yard field goal for New England with four seconds left to prevent what would have been the first overtime Super Bowl in the game's history:

1) The game's first 11 possessions ended with zero points. With four minutes left in the second quarter, it was 0–0—the slowest start in terms of points for any Super Bowl.

2) The two teams combined to score on six of their final seven possessions. The Panthers actually scored TDs the last three times they had the ball—all on Delhomme touchdown passes, and all on drives of 80 or more yards—and they still lost. Delhomme threw for 211 yards in the fourth quarter alone.

3) Janet Jackson bared part of her breast during the halftime show—with an assist from Justin Timberlake—in what later became commonly known as a "wardrobe malfunction." That phrase quickly became part of the nation's vernacular.

4) Kasay, who had only kicked one kickoff out of bounds the entire season, badly hooked the Panthers' final kickoff out of bounds, giving New England possession on its 40. I have always maintained that New England would have scored on that drive even if it had started at its own 5. The Patriots had 68 seconds, three timeouts, and Brady. The Panthers had a very tired defense. But the kickoff, which Kasay told me he "agonized" about for years afterward, remains a sore spot for all Carolina fans and in some ways has unfairly overshadowed Kasay's stalwart career in Charlotte.

5) The second-half kickoff got delayed because a streaker who had dressed up as a referee climbed onto the field, undressed down to a G-string and started lewdly dancing in front of Kasay. The security men weren't very fast out of the gate and onto the field to tackle him, either. "It was like nobody would go get him," Fox would say later. "But this big, fat, naked guy dancing around? Hey, I wasn't about to go get him either."

A Frantic Fourth Quarter

Of the game's 61 points, 37 were scored in a nutty, nerve-jangling fourth quarter. Brady was the game's MVP, completing 32 of 48 passes for 354 yards without any sacks. In fact, he wasn't sacked the entire postseason behind an underrated Patriots line.

If Carolina had won, though, the MVP would have been Delhomme after that 211-yard fourth quarter. The game's longest play was an 85-yard pass from Delhomme to Muhammad.

Delhomme actually held the ball for 6.2 seconds—an eternity on any pass play—behind excellent protection as "Moose" sneaked behind New England's defense. Delhomme then threw it as far as he could. "I saw Jake heave it up, and I was just smiling when it came down," Muhammad said.

Said Delhomme, "What was great about Moose is that he didn't quit. He just kept going. They lost him back there, but I saw him. I threw it as far as I could, and he just made a great play after that."

Muhammad caught the ball 51 yards downfield and then stiff-armed Patriots safety Eugene Wilson so hard that Wilson suffered a torn groin on the play. When Muhammad ended up in the end zone, Carolina had taken a 22–21 lead. The Panthers went for two and missed.

New England scored a TD and made its own two-point conversion to make it 29–22. Carolina tied the game on a 12-yard Delhomme TD pass to Proehl—a play that mimicked in terms of both yardage and significance the Delhomme-Proehl connection at the end of the Week 1 Jacksonville game.

But New England wouldn't be denied. After Kasay knocked the kickoff out of bounds, the Patriots methodically moved 37 yards on six plays to set up Vinatieri's game-winner. The Panthers walked off the field, forlorn, knowing how close they had come. And although they vowed to remember that feeling and to get back to the Super Bowl ASAP, in reality it would not happen for a dozen years.

Super Bowl Postscript

All of the key players from the Super Bowl team would turn over before the Panthers would make it back again. Muhammad retired in 2010. Fox's contract wasn't renewed after the 2010 season, although he would later become head coach for both Denver and Chicago. Kasay was unceremoniously fired by the Panthers before the 2011 season began—they tried to replace him with Olindo Mare, which worked out poorly. Kasay could have been bitter about the end, but instead he chose to write a warm thank-you letter to Panthers fans that he entrusted to me to publish in the *Charlotte Observer*. I was honored to do so, and I will let an excerpt from that gracious note end this chapter. From Kasay's thank-you note to Panthers fans in 2011:

"Thank you for your encouragement when I failed. Thank you for the celebrations when we won. And most of all, thank you for letting me leave with a treasure trove of memories that time cannot erase."

12

STEVE SMITH & DᴇANGELO WILLIAMS— INCREDIBLE & UNPREDICTABLE

FOR MORE THAN a decade, the Carolina Panthers' leader in jaw-dropping plays was Steve Smith. The *"Oh, no, he didn't! Oh, yes, he did??!!"* kind of play—that was a specialty of No. 89.

Cam Newton has now become the Panthers' leader in athletic jaw-droppers. But any book about the Panthers would be incomplete without a chapter devoted primarily to the complicated, mesmerizing, angry, and intelligent talent that was Steve Smith. He was a force of nature for the Panthers for more than half their team history—a human tornado with furious and unpredictable power.

Smith played 13 years for Carolina and scored 75 touchdowns (including the postseason), which makes him far and away the leader in finding the end zone for the Panthers. He also scored what I still believe is the most famous and extraordinary touchdown in Carolina history, winning the double-overtime St. Louis playoff game in 2003 on a 69-yard TD strike from Jake Delhomme.

Stevonne Smith had a ridiculously good work ethic, great hands, and a chip on his shoulder the size of Mt. Everest. He came into the league thriving on disrespect—he didn't have to look far to find it then—and stayed with that theme even after he made the Pro Bowl five times. A doting father and humanitarian off the field, he played angrily on it. He spun the ball onto the ground after every big catch, its laces twirling like a miniature merry-go-round for so long that Smith sometimes got back into the huddle before the ball started to wobble on its axis.

He also had a bad temper that manifested itself a number of times in his 13 years with the Panthers. He and the Panthers had a messy parting—I thought Carolina cut Smith a year too early, because he could still play—and Smith ripped Carolina general manager Dave Gettleman in a radio interview in 2014 for firing him before the season began. He told Charlotte radio station WFNZ–610 AM that his release was a "personal" thing between him and Gettleman and that the Panthers GM didn't have the *"cojones"* to tell him or his agent he was being released before he heard the news on the radio. He also made one obvious reference in the interview to then-Panthers defensive end Greg Hardy, who was on a voluntary paid leave of absence due to a domestic violence charge. Hardy had several years previously shown up to a Panthers training camp with all sorts of scrapes due to a motorcycle accident.

"I've always been a distraction?!" Smith said on the radio interview. "But I didn't hit my wife. Yeah, I hit some teammates six or seven years ago, but I didn't beat my wife. I didn't get arrested for DUIs. I didn't fall off no motorcycles."

As Smith referenced in that 2014 interview, he did hit two different teammates in anger during his time with Carolina and was suspended by the team for it twice. The second one came in public view at training camp, when he broke the nose of starting Panthers cornerback Ken Lucas at a practice. He was remorseful after those incidents, and Lucas would accept his apology. Smith's rage was part of what fueled him, but he couldn't always keep it inside—it would leak around the corners and do some damage that required some cleanup.

As Smith said in 2011 about his time with the Panthers, "You have to admit that pretty much I made an ass out of myself for a long time here by letting my emotions get the best of me."

On a much more minor scale, I had several run-ins with Smith over his 13 years with Carolina. Although I always admired his on-field play and wrote dozens of positive columns about him over the years, I would also criticize him for sometimes petulant behavior. That is a sports columnist's job. We are not supposed to be cheerleaders. We are supposed to be truth-tellers, or at least the version of the truth that we see. Smith would get angry at me at times and not speak with me for a few weeks. Once, we had a long, clear-the-air phone conversation after Smith had said something nasty about me to a small group of other people I liked. Smith was truly apologetic, and I quickly accepted his apology. But there were still flare-ups. Smith occasionally thought it funny to blow a very loud air horn in the Panthers locker room shortly before reporters' time to interview players was up. It was humorous the first time. By the fifth time, it wasn't.

"The Best Player You're Ever Going to Get"

In many ways, though, Smith was a reporter's dream. Not only did he supply a seemingly endless number of big plays to write about with his dazzling skill on the field, he also issued a series of quotes that were by turn incendiary and insightful. He once told opposing cornerback Aqib Talib to "ice up, son"—that one got made into a T-shirt. After a Panthers win in which he caught only one pass for four yards, he proclaimed: "I'm no longer an asset to this team."

Smith told me this story a long time ago, but it is symbolic of his career. When he was first signed by the Panthers, he was a third-round draft pick for Carolina out of Utah. He wasn't going to get a great deal of money at that draft position. But before he ever played a single down for Carolina, he sat in the office of future Panthers general manager Marty Hurney in mid-2001 (although Hurney didn't have that title yet, he was already negotiating contracts).

Smith thought he was being undervalued—disrespected, in other words—by the Panthers' initial contract offer. He wanted Hurney to understand that.

"Marty," Smith said, "I'm going to be the best player you're ever going to get here."

Smith was 22 years old then. And until Cam Newton came along, he was exactly right. By then, Smith had already pulled himself up out of a difficult situation, and he brimmed with confidence. Raised by a single mother in one of Los Angeles's toughest neighborhoods, he took a job at Taco Bell in high school and paid for his prom that way. His grades weren't good, and he was hardly recruited at all. He ended up at Santa Monica Junior College, where he teamed with Chad Johnson (another future NFL wide receiver) and won a scholarship to Utah.

Like all great NFL wide receivers, Smith always believed he was open. As Cam Newton—who teamed with Smith for three years—related how Smith described the way he was being covered: "One man on him, 'I'm open.' Two men, 'Give me a chance.' Three men…'Throw it up and see what happens.'"

In the final season that the miscast George Seifert coached for Carolina in 2001, he used Smith only as a kick returner. (This despite the fact the Panthers went 1–15 that season and desperately could have used some offensive help from a player who may well make the Pro Football Hall of Fame.)

On the first real NFL play in which he ever touched the ball—the opening kickoff of the 2001 season—Smith ran the kick back 93 yards against Minnesota for a touchdown. Carolina won that game and then lost 15 straight. John Fox and his staff quickly saw what he had with Smith and made him an integral part of the offense starting in 2002. By 2003, he was ready to make what will always be the signature play of his Carolina career.

St. Louis and "X Clown"

There are now many candidates in the category of "Most Thrilling Game the Panthers Have Ever Played," but it's still hard to beat Smith's TD against St. Louis that won a playoff game on the first play of the *sixth* quarter. That game remains a favorite among all Panthers fans. St. Louis still had its "Greatest Show on Turf" offense in 2003, with running back Marshall Faulk and wide receivers Torry Holt and Isaac Bruce. All of them were very fast and seemed even faster on the artificial turf in St. Louis—St. Louis had won 14 games in a row at home, averaged 33.6 points per game there in 2003, and was favored by a touchdown.

Smith could run with any of them, though, and he was the man who made the ultimate play of the game. In a back-and-forth game that dripped with drama, Carolina led 23–12 at one point but gave up 11 straight points. The game headed to overtime, and on every possession it seemed like it would be over. Carolina had the ball twice. St. Louis had it twice. On all four of those OT possessions, the ball was advanced inside the other team's 40. And yet no one could score. (On one of those possessions, John Kasay made a 40-yard field goal that would have been the game-winner, only to have it called back due to penalty. He then missed from 45 yards.)

So the tension mounted and the game dragged on. Gradually, St. Louis's defense seemed to be wearing down Carolina's offensive line. As the first overtime period ended, Jake Delhomme had been sacked on three of his last five dropbacks. At the start of the second OT, the Panthers were facing third-and-14 from their own 31.

Carolina called the play "X Clown," and Smith had messed it up in practice several times the week before. But it had worked once already in the game for a 36-yard gain to Smith, and the Panthers decided to pull it out to try and convert the long third down. Against a cover-2 defense designed to prevent exactly what happened, Smith faked outside and cut toward the middle. Delhomme, with max protection and seven blockers, had time to throw a dart that Smith took in stride at the 50.

Jason Sehorn, St. Louis's safety, was supposed to make the tackle there. But Sehorn was already stumbling as Smith faked one way and then sprinted directly toward the end zone, untouched. He raised both his hands wide as he crossed the goal line. "I braced myself for the big hit, but it never came," Smith said later of the play. "And when I took off, I knew I was gone."

That play pushed the Panthers to the NFC Championship Game and all the way to the Super Bowl, and it also elevated Smith to the next level of greatness. Two years later, in 2005, he would win the rare receiving triple crown—leading the NFL in receptions, yardage, and touchdown catches. It was that season that Smith also had his best individual game ever, in the 2005 playoffs at Chicago. Smith caught 218 yards worth of passes in that game, burning future Carolina cornerback Charles Tillman several times. Smith had catches of 39, 46, and 58 yards in that game and said afterward he was just doing his job.

"If you lined up my momma out there, I've got to catch it over her, too," he said.

Smith isn't the only mercurial player among Carolina's all-time leaders. The career of running back DeAngelo Williams also had a few similarities that are worth noting.

DeAngelo's Time

The No. 1 draft pick of the Panthers in 2006, DeAngelo Williams remains the Panthers' leading rusher with 6,846 yards during his nine-year career with the team. His best season came in 2008, when he should have made the Pro Bowl but did not. Williams rushed for 1,515 yards that season and had 20 total touchdowns. He was one of the key cogs in a Panthers machine that went 12–4 in the regular season but then abruptly broke down in a 20-point playoff loss to Arizona in the divisional round.

That 2008 season was an outlier for Williams in retrospect— Williams never scored more than seven times in his other eight seasons with the Panthers and would have only one other 1,000-yard campaign (1,117 in 2009).

Williams was a gregarious running back and by far the more vocal half of the "Double Trouble" duo that also included Jonathan

Stewart. Williams was the speedier one of the two, able to break a run outside for 20 yards with relative ease if the blocking was right. He was one of the leaders of the movement that brings awareness to breast cancer each October in the NFL, when players accessorize with pink to urge women to get tested. Williams' mother died of breast cancer in 2014, and he has had several other family members who have been struck by the disease as well. After the NFL told him he couldn't wear pink accessories all season like he wanted to, he instead dyed the tips of his hair pink and has played that way ever since.

Like Smith, Williams was naturally an alpha male. He was always one of the loudest voices in the locker room. And while he didn't have nearly as many controversies in his Panthers career as Smith did, releasing Williams in 2014 (after releasing Smith the year before) did allow Cam Newton to become the undisputed alpha male of the offensive huddle.

Throughout his career, Williams always had to share the ball with someone—first DeShaun Foster, then Stewart, and then Cam Newton and Mike Tolbert, too. Sometimes, you could tell the running back didn't like it. When he ripped off a franchise-record 210 yards on 21 carries versus New Orleans in 2012, he was asked what was different about that day compared to others. Williams said it was due to the fact that for that game the Panthers "actually called runs."

After an injury-plagued 2014 in which he played in only six games and didn't score a single TD for the first time in his career, the Panthers fired him. Williams broke the news himself in an interview with Charlotte TV station WBTV. Like Smith with his unkind words for Gettleman, Williams went out with a bang. He said he was okay with being released in part because team owner Jerry Richardson had not reached out to him nor gone to the funeral when Williams' mother died in May 2014. This made Williams' exit somewhat awkward, of course, and short-circuited any idea of a wave of good feelings from Panthers fans washing over Williams as he exited stage left.

Said Williams in the TV interview: "It stung to know that a place of business that you've worked for, you've bled, you've played through injuries, you've done everything you possibly can for this organization to be successful, and then upon your darkest hour, they let you handle it by yourself."

And, like Smith, Williams had some football left in him after the Panthers dumped him. Smith signed with Baltimore in 2014 and quickly had another 1,000-yard season, including a game in which he burned Carolina for two TDs. Williams signed with Pittsburgh in 2015 to be a backup, then got to play a lot due to other Steelers injuries and ended up making a lot of fantasy football players happy when he scored 11 rushing TDs —the second-highest total of his career.

Williams likes to use social media a lot and is more honest than many athletes on it, both for better and for worse. He posted his release letter from Carolina in 2016—the one where he officially got fired—saying he had kept it so that it motivated him every day. Like Smith, Williams also is prone to saying something controversial every now and again. It happened again in 2016, shortly after Peyton Manning won a Super Bowl in his last game by beating Carolina 24–10. Williams said on Twitter that Manning was so bad in 2015 that he "couldn't play dead in a Western," then doubled down on that criticism by saying in an interview on ESPN that Manning played like "garbage" in his final season. All this came right when Manning was retiring, leaving some to criticize Williams more for his tone-deaf timing than for the veracity of his statements. (Statistically, Manning's final season was his worst and at one point got him benched.)

In one of the most public Twitter scoldings ever by a coach to a player, Pittsburgh's Mike Tomlin decided to weigh in after Williams kept defending his negativity toward Manning in more than 100 subsequent tweets. "DWill (@DeAngeloRB) quit while you are behind! #Really" read Tomlin's tweet.

That didn't stop Williams from tweeting, but he did lay low on Manning for a while. The Panthers' No. 1 wide receiver and No. 1 running back of all time don't believe in censoring their opinions on life, and they are very confident men who have made a great living in the NFL for a long time. But it is also true that the Panthers' most sustained success—coincidentally or not—has been achieved without them.

13

KEVIN GREENE & JULIUS PEPPERS

FOR ALL THE well-deserved hullabaloo about the current crop of Carolina Panthers, none of them have made the Pro Football Hall of Fame.

Kevin Greene has already gotten there. Julius Peppers quite likely will join Greene in Canton, Ohio, one day. So before we explore the Panthers' surge from 2013 onward, it's worth looking back at two of the greatest pass rushers in Carolina history.

Greene and Peppers could hardly have more different personalities. Greene was the loud extrovert, his motor constantly revving. Peppers was the quiet introvert who had the reputation of occasionally taking the rest of the play off if he was well-blocked initially. Greene's athletic talent was not as apparent on first glance; he was a walk-on at Auburn and then a fifth-round NFL Draft pick. Peppers was such an athletic freak that the Panthers made him the No. 2 overall draft pick of the 2002 draft. He has played in both a Final Four and a Super Bowl—a basketball lover from childhood, Peppers told me once that he considered the Final Four to be a bigger deal.

But the two men had one key similarity—they both were experts at getting to the quarterback. Greene was elected into the Pro Football Hall of Fame in 2016, his 12th year of eligibility, in large part because he had 160 career sacks over 15 seasons and ranked third in the NFL in that category when he retired (sacks have only been an official NFL statistic since 1982).

Like Greene, Peppers has produced sacks at an elite level well into his thirties. He played for Carolina far longer than Greene did—eight years for Peppers, three for Greene. That's why Peppers remains No. 1 on Carolina's all-time sack list with 81.

Greene's "Childish Exuberance"

Sporting shoulder-length blond hair for much of his NFL career, Greene was a larger-than-life character who actually played only 20 percent of his career—three of 15 seasons—for Carolina. But he made an outsized impact in those three years of 1996, 1998, and 1999.

"People called me crazy," said Greene, who also dabbled in professional wrestling and once shared a wrestling ring with Ric Flair. "But I loved playing football. When you're passionate about something, that love is going to show."

A prototype edge rusher out of a 3-4 defensive scheme, Greene collected 41.5 sacks in his three Panthers seasons, averaging nearly one sack per game played. He celebrated every sack as if it were the first one he had ever made. But unlike Cam Newton, Greene's celebrations were hardly ever criticized. As his former Panthers teammate and current NFL Network analyst Eric Davis told me in 2016, "Kevin celebrated, and nobody had a problem with it. Kevin Greene did a dance every single sack. Cam does a dance every touchdown, and there's a problem. We decide one is cocky and one is just exhibiting childish exuberance."

Greene was one of the best pure pass rushers ever—he led the league in sacks twice, with Pittsburgh in 1994 and then in his first year with Carolina in 1996. But he was an underrated run-stopper as well and, for most of his career, also covered receivers out of the backfield adequately. Although his huge sack numbers might suggest otherwise—he trailed only Reggie White and Bruce Smith in that category when he retired—Greene wasn't a one-trick pony.

Of Greene's 15 NFL seasons, eight were spent with the L.A. Rams, three with Pittsburgh, one with San Francisco, and three with Carolina. He was a big part of Carolina's 1996 team that advanced all the way to the NFC Championship Game, teaming with Lamar Lathon. Greene christened the two "Salt and Pepper," and they combined for 28 sacks that year.

Greene's Two Mistakes

Greene had two major mishaps in the eyes of Panthers fans, however. In 1997 he was under contract for Carolina but held out for more money after leading the NFL in sacks the year before. This resulted in a bitter dispute with future Hall of Fame general manager Bill Polian. Greene ultimately played for Carolina's biggest rival at the time—San Francisco—that season.

He would return to the Panthers in 1998. But a few months after his return, Greene angrily grabbed assistant coach Kevin Steele by the collar in a sideline argument. Coach Dom Capers allowed Greene to keep playing in that game after that happened. This was a source of discontent in the Carolina locker room—a number of players felt they would not have been granted the same latitude, and they were undoubtedly correct. After experiencing some backlash for going soft on Greene during the heat of battle, the Panthers ended up suspending Greene for the next game.

"I lost my composure," Greene said in the locker room after the incident. "What I did was wrong."

But Steele quickly forgave Greene, and so did Panthers fans. With his 2016 Hall of Fame election, Greene became the first player in the hall who had played multiple seasons in Charlotte to make it. The late Reggie White, the only other player in the Hall who played at all for the Panthers, had only a single mediocre season in Charlotte at the tail end of his career. White did almost all of his sack damage in Green Bay and Philadelphia.

Greene became an assistant coach in the NFL after retiring. He won the Super Bowl ring with Green Bay that he had never picked up as a player while coaching his alter ego, Clay Matthews—another exuberant linebacker with long blond hair. But he stepped away from that coaching job in 2014, concerned he wasn't spending enough time with his family. He then helped coach his son Gavin's high school football team in Destin, Florida, in 2015. But with his son now headed to college, Greene hopes to get back into coaching.

A visit Greene took to Charlotte late in the 2015 NFL season reminded him of how many people still remember him. You still see some No. 91 Panthers jerseys dotting the stands at every game in Bank of America Stadium, and Greene sought out one of the fans wearing one before the Panthers–Tampa Bay game. Greene said the conversation went like this:

> *Greene:* (approaching fan) I just want to thank you for wearing my jersey all these years later.
> *Fan:* No way! It's not you. Kevin?! No!
> *Greene:* Yes, yes, it is me.
> *Fan:* No freakin' way! No freakin' way! (Pause) Can I get a picture?

Never camera-shy, Greene posed for the picture. He told me later: "It's just nice that people remember what I was after all these years."

Peppers' Multi-Sport Prowess

Fans remember Peppers, too, and as the years pass less of those memories are sour ones and more are tinged with nostalgia. Peppers' departure from Carolina after the 2009 season rankled many, as Peppers made no secret of wanting to get out of Charlotte and turned down a Carolina contract offer that would have made him the highest-paid defensive player in the game. Panthers fans couldn't understand why a home-grown product like Peppers—he went to both high school and college in North Carolina before the Panthers drafted him—would want to leave his home state.

But for most of the 2000s, Peppers was a dominating force on the Panthers' best teams of that decade. He was one of the best players on Carolina's playoff teams in 2003, 2005, and 2008. His athletic ability was so awe-inspiring that Steve Smith, no athletic slouch himself, once said he was just happy to be in every team picture right beside Peppers. (Since Smith wore No. 89 and Peppers wore No. 90, they always were next to each other.)

Julius Frazier Peppers was raised by his mother, Bessie Brinkley, in the small town of Bailey, North Carolina. Peppers' father supplied his name—Julius Frazier Peppers, with the first name a tribute to Julius Erving and the middle name a nod to boxer Joe Frazier—but not much else. As befitted a young man with namesakes in different sports, Peppers starred in both football and basketball as a teenager for Southern Nash. He was so good that the school eventually retired his jersey in both sports. UNC recruited him to play both sports, and he did, although his scholarship was officially in football. One of the perhaps apocryphal legends surrounding Peppers in high school is that once, after a three-hour football practice, he started back-flipping down the football field in full pads.

Peppers grew up only 55 miles from Chapel Hill, and his favorite sport as a kid was basketball. But he only played two years of it at Chapel Hill, with one of those as a sixth man for UNC's Final Four team in 2000.

"The Final Four was kind of like my first *big* game," Peppers once told me. "I had played in big games before, but not like that. That was fun. I was looking up in the stands and seeing Muhammad Ali and John Wooden. That was great."

Peppers was valued much more highly as a football player, however, and reluctantly he gave up hoops for football in college for his redshirt junior year (his last at Chapel Hill).

Less Havoc Than "LT"

In his eight seasons with the Panthers from 2002 to 2009, Peppers made the Pro Bowl five times and averaged 10 sacks per season. He was never the NFL's Defensive Player of the Year like Luke Kuechly was in 2013, but he did have an occasional penchant for the spectacular. He once had a 97-yard interception return as a Panther and in another game plucked a Michael Vick fumble out of the air and ran 60 yards for a touchdown. The Panthers actually lined him up as a wide receiver several times near the goal line early in his career. He never caught an NFL pass, but was given so much respect by defenses that a couple of times opponents actually double-teamed him.

Peppers grew to dislike his celebrity status in North Carolina, however. He wouldn't sign a long-term deal with Carolina after his rookie contract ran out, and the Panthers had to "rent" him in 2009 with a franchise tag that meant they paid him slightly more than $1 million per game. They decided not to do that for a second straight year in 2010, and Peppers basically caught the first plane out of town to Chicago, where the Bears gave him a huge deal. After the 2013 season, he would switch teams again, this time playing for Green Bay. He would call his ending to his Panthers career "a little sour," and he was routinely booed in Bank of America Stadium when he returned with another team.

Although naturally shy, Peppers could be gracious. When UNC accidentally posted his academic transcript online and it was discovered in 2012, everyone concerned was embarrassed. The transcript showed that Peppers had barely stayed eligible throughout college and had accumulated numerous low grades. (Although, Peppers would point out, it did not indicate academic fraud.) Peppers said he was "upset" about the mistake, but only a few days later, he gave UNC $250,000 for a scholarship fund that supports African American students.

Always compared to former UNC great Lawrence Taylor, in general Peppers wreaked less havoc on and off the field compared to "LT." While a steady sacker, a great athlete, and a nine-time Pro Bowler, he never led the NFL in sacks like Greene did. It is possible Peppers will need a Super Bowl ring late in his career to validate his eventual membership into the Hall of Fame. But he will remain one of the greatest athletes the Panthers ever employed.

By the time the Panthers made their breakthrough in 2013, though, Peppers was long gone. In his place was a mixture of young players on the cusp of greatness and older ones trying to hang on for one more shot at the title. And the man who was assembling all of that talent was a grinder who liked nothing better than to watch film of NFL games in a darkened room. His name was Dave Gettleman.

PART III

THE BREAKTHROUGH

2013

14

DAVE GETTLEMAN'S
ONE LAST CHANCE

BY THE BEGINNING of the 2012 season, Dave Gettleman thought his shot at becoming an NFL general manager had come and gone. "Very honestly, I had given up the ghost," Gettleman said in our interview for this book.

Before the 2012 season had begun, four GM jobs had opened around the league. Gettleman was then the director of the New York Giants' pro personnel department, and the Giants had been one of the most successful franchises in the NFL over the past decade. But he was also 61 years old, and he knew that his age was working against him, whether anyone would say so or not. He couldn't get a sniff at any one of those four jobs.

"You've got all these younger owners, and they want to win with peers," Gettleman said. "I'm an old man, okay? Then you've got these owners who want to win the press conference. You're not winning the press conference with Dave Gettleman."

And although Gettleman had won two Super Bowls by then as a critical part of the Giants personnel department, he didn't think that was helping him much. "Let's be honest," he said. "Eight years ago [in 2008], we elected a president with no résumé. So résumés mean nothing. That's a national referendum. So if you think about that...that's a microcosm of society. Everybody wants fresh. New. Young. And sometimes it is the way to go. But I knew the only way it was going to happen was for an older owner to seriously take a look at me. I knew that. And I thought time had passed me by."

"I Had Become a Crazy Workaholic"

Gettleman was a self-described "grinder," most comfortable in a darkened room with what he calls a "clicker" in his hands. He liked to run game film back and forth, over and over, to spot subtleties in players. He knew his stuff. Somewhere, deep inside him, was the man who would eventually be named the NFL's Executive of the Year by the *Sporting News* in March 2016 for his work on a 2015 Panthers squad that won 17 games.

But in 2012, Gettleman was a long way from that honor. He had been a college scout for NFL teams for 11 years and then a pro personnel guy for 15. He had sat in 26 different draft rooms. He could discuss every NFL team's fourth offensive guard or fifth cornerback in detail without notes. But that just didn't seem to be enough to get one of the 32 jobs he longed for as an NFL GM.

In fact, Gettleman had gotten to the point where he had decided to give up some responsibility with the Giants. He was working too much, he said, and letting his job define him. He knew that. Of his own volition before the 2012 season, he approached the Giants' ownership and said he wanted to reduce his role, no longer running his pro personnel department on a day-to-day basis as he had done for the previous 13 years. Instead, he became the Giants' senior pro personnel analyst. He would still work for New York, but the role wouldn't be nearly as time-consuming.

"From July 25 to February 8 the previous season," Gettleman said, "I had three days off. And I worked 85–100 hours a week. I had become a crazy workaholic. And that was a big reason I had to take a step back."

So in 2012 Gettleman cut those hours in half. He worked only Monday through Thursday. His primary responsibility for months was practice squads—both the Giants and those of other teams. Certainly there are players to be found on practice squads— Gettleman would later find starting offensive tackle Mike Remmers on one for Carolina. But it's not exactly the same as holding a bushel of draft picks in your hand or deciding how many years to extend Cam Newton's and Luke Kuechly's contracts.

"It gave me a chance to evaluate everything," Gettleman said. "You know that old song—'What's it all about, Alfie?' It was like that."

The end of the road wasn't the very next exit for Gettleman's career, but you could certainly see the signs on the map. Gettleman— so well-liked in the Giants' offices that he was nicknamed "the Mayor"—was slowly phasing himself out.

The Accorsi Connection

Then, out of the blue, came Gettleman's one last chance at a GM job. Panthers owner Jerry Richardson fired general manager Marty Hurney after Carolina's 1–5 start in 2012 and did not promote someone else immediately from within. Instead, Richardson had former Giants GM Ernie Accorsi consult heavily with him on who Carolina's next GM would be starting with the 2013 season.

Accorsi had worked with Gettleman for years, thought he would be a great GM, and had recommended him for the Giants' GM job after the 2006 season, which Accorsi had decided would be his last as the Giants' full-time general manager. But Accorsi had also pushed Jerry Reese, another internal candidate, for that position, and Reese had gotten the job over Gettleman.

Accorsi thought both men really deserved to be GMs. (Certainly Reese was no slouch, as the Giants won the Super Bowl following the 2007 and 2011 seasons.) After retiring as a full-time GM, Accorsi found a second career as an NFL consultant and recommended Gettleman for several jobs, none of which Gettleman had gotten.

But then came Carolina, and suddenly Gettleman's window of opportunity had opened after more than 25 years in the NFL. Richardson hired Accorsi to consult, and the former Giants man provided Richardson a list of several names but made it clear Gettleman was his top pick. Richardson, who was 76 years old by then and a heart transplant survivor, didn't think it was a problem to hire a 61-year-old. He and Gettleman hit it off in Gettleman's initial interview. Richardson was from the South and Gettleman from Boston, but to use one of Gettleman's favorite words the way he says it, it wasn't "hahd" at all for the two men to find common ground.

On January 9, 2013, Richardson named Gettleman the Carolina Panthers' new GM—only the third man to officially hold that title in team history after Bill Polian and Hurney. Gettleman said it felt like winning the lottery.

"One of the things a GM has to do is he has to be able to fix things," Richardson said in introducing Gettleman. As a reminder to everyone there that he had fixed a few things in New York, Gettleman wore to the press conference one of the Super Bowl rings he earned with the Giants. It was the first big press conference he had ever had, and he handled it well. He may not have won it nationally, but he won it locally.

"I'm pretty simple, my wife will vouch for that," said Gettleman, who was accompanied to the press conference by his wife Joanne and their three children. "I believe in faith, family, and football. Those are my priorities. I'm called a grinder and I think that's a compliment."

It got emotional, too—Gettleman choked up talking about his late mother-in-law. Yes, his mother-in-law. He also talked honestly about finally getting his dream job at age 61. "I just needed someone who was looking for an older, more mature guy," Gettleman said at that opening press conference. "That's really what it came down to. Our culture is the next whiz-bang is the next great thing....It was one of those deals where, 'Oh, he's an old dinosaur. He's probably cranky.'"

"Not for the Faint of Heart"

Gettleman turned out not to be at all cranky. He was charming, gruff, and opinionated. He wore shorts and flip-flops on hot days at practice. Perhaps most importantly, he wasn't overly loyal to the players Carolina already had. It wasn't Gettleman who had pushed the Panthers down into the well of salary-cap hell. That was Hurney, who had made some excellent draft picks (Newton, Kuechly) but also had a tendency to reward his own draft selections with monumental salaries (Charles Johnson, DeAngelo Williams) if they had a modest amount of NFL success.

Gettleman would instead become known as the man who didn't mind trading or releasing popular players—including Steve Smith, linebacker Jon Beason, Williams, and cornerback Josh Norman in April 2016—if he thought they had lost a step or didn't fit his vision or simply (in Norman's case) were very good players who had become too expensive. He knew the old adage from baseball man Branch Rickey that it is better to trade a player a year too early than a year too late and sometimes applied it.

"My chair is not for the faint of heart, okay?" he said. "You have to have confidence in what you're doing and your evaluation skills. There are times I knew I was going to make unpopular decisions and I couldn't let that concern me. It's all about the greater good."

Rivera said that Gettleman's approach was refreshing but also noted that he now tells Gettleman all the time it may be more difficult to let go of his own draft picks when that time comes. "One of the hardest things to do as a coach or GM is when it's time to move on from players," said Rivera, adding that Mike Ditka once told the coach that he held onto some of the 1985 Bears team too long out of loyalty. "Dave was able to do that, and there was no real connection for him [with the players who predated Gettleman]. Now what will be interesting is three to five years from now, will he be able to move on from some of these guys that he signed?"

Gettleman acknowledges this will be difficult. "I spend a lot of time with our players," he said. "I get to know them. To me, they're not just widgets. So for me, it's going to make it tougher and tougher [to release players he signed with the Panthers for many years]. But at the end of the day, I've got to make the best business decision for the Panthers. I have to. That's my job. I have to look at the greater good."

Hog Molly Heaven

In any event, Gettleman looked at the Panthers in early 2013 with fresh eyes and saw them lacking in a number of places. Said Gettleman when I asked about his general philosophy for building a team, "You've gotta have a Q [quarterback], it goes without saying. You have to have pass rushers. You have to have touchdown scorers. And it's also, 'Big men allow you to compete.' [Former New York Giants coach] Tom Coughlin said it. And when he said it to me that day, you know sometimes how just the light bulb goes on? The more concisely you can say something, the more powerful it is. You don't want to hear me going all *War and Peace* when I can say it in one sentence."

Gettleman also borrows an old baseball adage when deciding where to spend time and money. "I firmly believe in strength up the middle," he said. "We're very similar to a baseball team, where you need the catcher, the pitcher, the shortstop, the second baseman, the center fielder. For us: offensive linemen, quarterback, defensive tackles, the middle linebacker. And safeties are critical, too, because they run the back end."

Gettleman knew the Panthers had the quarterback already. Although Newton needed to improve in several phases entering the 2013 season, Gettleman realized quickly he was set at the NFL's most important position. But the Panthers just weren't big or strong enough inside on defense. "Guys that are heavy-bodied, line-of-scrimmage changers are big for the team," Gettleman said. Often, it's the difference between making and missing a fourth-and-1 conversion. So Gettleman used his first Panthers draft to try and change that while also inserting the phrase "hog mollies" into the vernacular of Panthers fans.

By definition, a hog molly is a North American freshwater fish. To Gettleman, though, the phrase stood for an enormous offensive or defensive lineman. He particularly thought Carolina needed help up the middle on defense, where a couple of steamroller types would free middle linebacker Luke Kuechly to roam and also aid a group of defensive backs who were fairly mediocre entering the 2013 season.

Ever since George Seifert had drafted future Pro Bowl defensive tackle Kris Jenkins in 2001, Carolina had not used a top-50 pick on a DT. Hurney never did so in all his years at GM. Hurney had some great hits among his first-round draft choices, but his later picks were often iffy, and the Panthers had been average on the interior of their defensive line for a long time.

"You've Got to Raise Your Own"

By the time Gettleman got to his first draft as the king of the room instead of one of the soldiers, he had already done some solid work in free agency and settled nerves around the building with the phrase, "I'm not going to clean house." On the field, he had re-signed cornerback Captain Munnerlyn, found safety Mike Mitchell, and grabbed wide receiver Ted Ginn Jr. All three signed one-year deals, would play significant roles on the 2013 team, and would eventually leave for more money (Gettleman would say in 2016 he wished in retrospect that he had signed Mitchell and Ginn to two-year contracts at the time to keep them around longer). The GM believed strongly in those sorts of under-the-radar signings that improved the middle third of the roster; he did not generally like the idea of purchasing high-dollar free agents.

"You've got to raise your own," Gettleman said, referring to the NFL practice of trying to draft your way to a championship rather than buying one. "You fill in with unrestricted free agents. Getting in the unrestricted free agent market with big-ticket guys is very dicey."

Gettleman and Rivera got to know each other quickly and liked what they saw. The two had what Gettleman called "a blind date" shortly after he got the job. "Ron picks me up on a Thursday for breakfast," Gettleman said. "When we sat down, I told him, 'This is the way I want it to go. This is what I'm interested in: Collaboration. Brutal honesty. Constant communication. And being able to make the tough decisions.' And I said to him, 'I will make you only one promise: I promise I will do everything in my power to make this work. Because all I give a shit about is winning. That's all I care about, Ron. And you need to make that same promise.'"

Rivera did, of course. He needed to win even worse than Gettleman. Two losing seasons to open his head-coaching career meant he was on a short leash. That was the first of hundreds of meetings for the coach and the general manager, whose friendship quickly blossomed.

"I think sometimes we look at each other and we're brothers from different mothers," Gettleman said. "He's from an immigrant family, I'm second-generation. We have the same values. No bullshit. Honest. Direct. Morality. So it's not like we're the odd couple."

While Gettleman didn't try to come in and hire his own coach, he also didn't fire anyone else. He accepted the rest of the Panthers front office for what it was and was taken in by the team in turn. He had some philosophical ideas about pro personnel scouting he wanted to implement and did. He had never seen a draft board put together the way the Panthers did it, but thought it so "fantastic" that he adopted it. "They accepted me and my Yankee craziness," Gettleman said. "We learned to work together."

It took Gettleman three weeks to get a clicker back in his hands, but after that he never stopped evaluating, even though a lot of people below him were paid to do so as well. He disdained anyone he called an "I.E."—an instant evaluator who would watch perhaps one game's worth of film on a player and decide he couldn't live without him.

"I love watching film, and I can't lose my touch," Gettleman said. "I can't lose those evaluating skills, because then you can be easily swayed. People can bullshit you. Everybody in the building knows that you can't bullshit Dave about players. You can't sell him a guy who can't play, so don't waste your time. At the end of the day, I'm going to do my homework."

Gettleman's First Draft

So they wanted to raise their own great players? That sounds good but only works if you draft the right guys. So Gettleman's first draft in 2013 would be a tone-setter, allowing Panthers fans to see how the new guy from the North really drove when it came time to put the pedal to the metal. And Gettleman pressed the pedal, all right—directly into a pile of hog mollies.

Gettleman's first-ever pick as the Panthers' GM was Star Lotulelei, a 320-pound defensive tackle out of Utah. Lotulelei had once been considered a possible top-three pick, but he had a heart scare in the lead-up to the draft. Though doctors would clear him, the issue dropped his draft stock. When Lotulelei dropped all the way to the Panthers, Gettleman exulted and would later say it took the Panthers only "23 seconds" to turn in their draft card.

"What Star does is he impacts the game on every snap," Gettleman bubbled the night he drafted Lotulelei. "The other huge thing he does is he's going to occupy two [blockers] quite often, which is going to keep Luke [Kuechly] free. So it gives Luke more protection, which makes our defense better."

Then came Gettleman's second-round pick, and it would turn out to be an even bigger hit. Defensive tackle Kawann Short of Purdue, thought to be a better pass rusher than Lotulelei but not as good against the run, lasted until the No. 44 overall pick. Two picks, two hog mollies. At the time, Gettleman said he thought Short was also a first-round pick who had dropped, as well as the best pass-rushing defensive tackle in the draft.

Short would have a breakout season in 2015, becoming a first-time Pro Bowler and leading Carolina with 11 sacks—a team record for a defensive tackle. Lotulelei's contributions have been quieter but very steady. Both immediately played a lot for a team that had been mediocre in the middle but already had two very good defensive ends—Charles Johnson was still close to his prime in 2013, and Greg Hardy's domestic violence issue had yet to surface. The Panthers would end up No. 2 in the NFL in total defense and points allowed in 2013 while leading the league in sacks.

"You look historically at the Super Bowl champions, and you show me one that's had a bad defensive front," Gettleman said just after he drafted the players who would commonly become known as "Star" and "KK" in the locker room. "Doesn't happen—I'm telling you."

That was one of many Super Bowl references Gettleman peppered his comments with from the very first day he first got to Charlotte. He had been involved with six Super Bowl teams in his career as a scout and personnel man (going 3–3 in the biggest game) and had no doubt he and the Panthers could get there again. As he told Rivera at that same breakfast meeting, "If we do this right, you and I are holding up the trophy with Mr. Richardson."

It was a nice sentiment. But, as Gettleman might say, now came the "hahd" part—the Panthers needed to actually start winning more games than they lost. And for that, their head coach was going to have to make a shift in philosophy that ran counter to his every instinct.

15

THE BIRTH OF RIVERBOAT RON

THE SITUATION WAS familiar. The Carolina Panthers were in another close game in the fourth quarter. A win or loss hung in the balance, ready to be tipped one way or the other by one play or one decision.

This time it was in Buffalo, in Week 2 of the 2013 regular season. Carolina had lost its opening game 12–7, but had played pretty well against a Seattle team that would eventually win the Super Bowl that year. A late DeAngelo Williams fumble inside Seattle's 10 had short-circuited what could have been a huge Panthers win. Now the Panthers were up 20–17 on the road versus Buffalo but in a tricky situation—with two minutes left in the game, they had the ball and a first down at the Buffalo 30. But the Bills had all three of their timeouts.

The bugaboo for coach Ron Rivera in his first two seasons had been Carolina's inability to win close games. Entering the Buffalo contest, Rivera's teams were 2–13 in games decided by a touchdown or less. He had thought about this during the off-season and had quietly made a decision—he needed to be more aggressive as a coach.

Here, then, was his chance. The Panthers could bleed the clock, kick a field goal, and try to force Buffalo to go the length of the field for a touchdown. Or they could be more aggressive in their play-calling, knowing that a TD would give Carolina a 10-point margin and put the game out of reach.

Rivera and the Panthers started conservatively. They ran on first, second, and third downs—twice with DeAngelo Williams and once out wide with Mike Tolbert. Those three plays forced Buffalo to use all of its timeouts and gained nine yards. Now came the big decision: Carolina faced a fourth-and-1 on Buffalo's 21 with 1:42 to go. A first down would end the game, because the Panthers could run out the clock after that.

The Panthers had all sorts of options to make that one yard, even though Williams had never been particularly reliable in short-yardage situations and Jonathan Stewart was out with an injured ankle. Newton had by that time become arguably the most effective short-yardage runner in the history of NFL quarterbacks. Tolbert, a human bowling ball, was also very good when you needed a single yard. A play-action pass to Greg Olsen might go for a touchdown because the Bills would certainly sell out to stop the run.

The downside: if the Panthers went for it and missed, the Bills could drive down the field and force overtime with a field goal. Carolina's secondary was very banged up and playing a lot of reserves, and a Bills drive of any type was certainly possible even though Buffalo had a rookie quarterback in EJ Manuel.

A field goal would be the most conservative choice. Assuming Graham Gano made the 39-yard attempt, Buffalo would then have to go about 80 yards with no timeouts in roughly 90 seconds to score and win. Rivera thought about it during Buffalo's third timeout, knowing he had told himself in the off-season that these were the types of decisions he had to make a more aggressive call on if he was going to take Carolina to the next level.

And then, ultimately, he couldn't pull the trigger. Caution won the day but lost the game. Rivera pulled Carolina's offense off the field and sent in Gano. Gano made the 39-yarder, giving Carolina a 23–17 lead, but it was short-lived. Manuel directed the Bills offense down the field with ease against the Panthers' banged-up secondary. He was also helped tremendously by a 20-yard pass-interference penalty on Luke Kuechly, which negated a Panthers interception on third-and-6 at the Carolina 31 and instead gave Buffalo a first down at the 11. After that came a nine-yard scramble by Manuel and then his two-yard touchdown pass to a wide-open Stevie Johnson. The Buffalo receiver beat Josh Norman on the play after Norman (then a reserve, and playing hurt) didn't pick up on a call from nickel back D.J. Moore to switch assignments and cover Johnson. Buffalo's winning TD came with two seconds left.

The Panthers trudged off after the disheartening loss—this one by the score of 24–23. Wide receiver Steve Smith compared the loss to "going to the dentist and getting several teeth pulled without any anesthesia, laughing gas, nothing." Rivera said, "That's about as bad as it gets." His team was now 2–14 in one-score games. And he knew he had to do something about it while he still had the chance.

Turning Anguish into Answers

It wasn't the first time Rivera had been beaten after coaching conservatively. In a critical game at Atlanta the year before in 2012, Rivera faced another fourth-and-short situation but decided to punt to the Falcons. The punt couldn't have worked out better— it was downed at the 1—but Panthers safety Haruki Nakamura immediately allowed a 59-yard pass over the top of his head. The Falcons soon kicked the game-winning field goal and won 30–28.

But the Buffalo loss really stung. Rivera thought about what he should have done differently on the trip home to Charlotte that night and during his drives home from Bank of America Stadium over the next few evenings. He was heartsick, knowing he had never been a timid player in his NFL career but had turned too often into a timid coach. Through the first 34 games of his NFL head-coaching career, Rivera had gone for a first down on fourth down fewer times than every NFL head coach except one.

That one was John Fox, the coach Rivera had replaced with the Panthers. Fox was known for a number of sayings in Charlotte, and one of the most famous was, "A punt is not a bad play." Rivera was coaching the same way.

On one of those drives, Rivera was thinking so hard about the Buffalo game that he made an error. "I wasn't paying attention, was thinking about that game, and I ran a red light," Rivera said. "Then I almost got T-boned by another car."

That moment brought some clarity to Rivera. "I think the turning point for me really came after that Buffalo loss," he said. "There is still a lot of anguish over it for me. But I needed to make that transition. I needed to realize that playing conservative, playing close to the vest...sometimes you've just got to throw all that away."

In the meantime, Panthers fans were sharpening their pitchforks, ready to run Rivera out of town. The *Charlotte Observer* took an unscientific online poll after the Buffalo loss, asking whether Panthers owner Jerry Richardson should fire Rivera immediately. There were more than 8,800 responses in 24 hours, and 83 percent of the respondents said, "Yes."

Rivera knew something the general public did not, though—Richardson had promised him he would never be fired in the middle of a season. "He told me the one thing I didn't want you to do is look over your shoulder," Rivera said of Richardson. "I wanted you to coach. But what happened was, in the Buffalo game, that was probably the game that really, really told me, 'You know what? To hell with the book.'"

The change to "Riverboat Ron" wasn't immediate, nor was it immediately successful. After a 38–0 shutout of the New York Giants got some of the critics off his back but didn't provide much opportunity for gambling, Rivera went for it on a key fourth-and-1 the next week against Arizona with the score tied 3–3 in the second quarter and Carolina at the Cardinals 15. The play call was perfect, as was the throw from Newton to Brandon LaFell. But LaFell dropped it, and the play went largely unnoticed in a 22–6 Arizona win. The debut of "Riverboat Ron" would be postponed for one more week. The Panthers, in the meantime, were 1–3—and Rivera knew a third straight season without making the playoffs would likely spell the end for him and his coaching staff.

"We were at the crossroads," Steve Smith said at the time. "It was going to go one of two ways. We were either going to fight our tails off and see how it shook out, or this ship was going down and it was going down fast. And heads were going to roll. It was make or break for the players—and for the coaches."

Fourth-Down Fever

The official birth of "Riverboat Ron" came on October 13, 2013, in a road game at the Metrodome against Minnesota. It was a relatively fast birth, too. First quarter. First Panthers drive. Fourth-and-1 from the Vikings 32.

Instead of sending Gano out for another field goal, Rivera had Carolina go for it, and Tolbert bulled for two yards. Emboldened by that success, Rivera would try it again only a few plays later. This time, Carolina faced a fourth-and-1 from the Minnesota 2. The Panthers ran a play-action pass, with Newton hitting Smith for a touchdown. It was 7–0 instead of 3–0, and the mood change on the sideline was palpable.

Although it was only a difference of four points and only a midseason game, players quickly realized the significance of what Rivera had done. Offensive players, who had long lobbied for more risk-taking, were particularly effusive. "I think he is kind of breaking his mold to a degree," Newton said of his coach, "and giving the whole team confidence with him."

It wasn't just that, of course. The Panthers had already assembled a fine nucleus of players by 2013. They just needed a spark. Suddenly, Rivera could do no wrong, and neither could the Panthers. They blasted Minnesota 35–10. Then they beat St. Louis, Tampa Bay, and Atlanta—all by at least 15 points. A 10–9 win at San Francisco got Carolina to 6–3.

The Miracle at Miami

Rivera's gambles were paying off, and nowhere could you find a more audacious one than the risk he took at Miami on November 24, 2013. Carolina's offense had played badly most of the day and trailed 16–6 entering the fourth quarter. Newton cut it to 16–13 with a five-yard TD run, and soon afterward the Panthers got the ball back. But they couldn't move, and they faced fourth-and-10 from their own 20. There was 2:33 left on the clock. Carolina had one timeout. Most NFL coaches would punt in that situation, figuring a defensive stop would allow for time for a field-goal drive. A missed fourth-and-10, on the other hand, would just about end the game.

Rivera went for it.

Newton fired a dart to Smith, who bounced off two Dolphins for 19 yards. In a poll I later took of 16 Panthers players, that fourth-and-10 conversion was judged the best play of the entire season.

Carolina quickly got into field-goal range, and Miami started using timeouts to save time. But instead of playing for a field goal and overtime, Carolina took some more risks, having Newton throw once to Ted Ginn Jr. and run the ball himself. It all paid off when Newton found Olsen for a one-yard TD with 43 seconds to go. Carolina would win 20–16.

The Panthers were starting to arrive, aided by a coach who was acting more like he believed in them. "I think that really helped me, and I think it also helped the team," Rivera said of his fourth-down gambles in 2013. "I think the guys began to realize, 'Hey, Coach does trust us. Coach does want us to put it all out there.' And I think that was the one thing that was kind of missing from this team, that 'put it all out there' thing. Because if I'm not going to put it all out there, why should they?"

By the time the Panthers pulled off their miracle in Miami, people in the Carolinas believed. But that wasn't the case nationally.

The Panthers would need to show America that they were a team to be reckoned with. They would do that with two of the most thrilling home wins in team history, played a single month apart—against Tom Brady and New England in late November and then against Drew Brees and New Orleans in late December.

16

COMEBACK AGAINST NEW ENGLAND

EVERY TEAM IN any sport that has a breakthrough can point to a few games and a few plays that made a difference. A win over a rival. A clutch play from an obscure player. A realization that, "Hey, we can do this!"

For the Carolina Panthers, the 2013 season was full of those sorts of moments. That was the year the Panthers went from NFL purgatory—they had missed the playoffs every year since the 2008 season—to NFL relevance. Riverboat Ron Rivera emerged. The team's best players got better. General manager Dave Gettleman improved the roster all over the place.

But in terms of actual games, two were more significant than any other. Both occurred at home, in Bank of America Stadium, allowing Panthers fans to see up close that the team that had been lost for so long had now been found. The first one came on a Monday night against New England, the measuring stick of NFL excellence for a decade. The second came 34 days later, on a stormy Sunday afternoon against New Orleans and is featured in chapter 18. Both featured last-minute drives, thrilling finishes and enough "Did you see that?" moments to occupy weeks' worth of sports conversation. They are worth exploring in detail, because without those two games the Panthers would never have climbed as far as they have.

Gruden Sounds Off

One of the most informed announcers in the NFL is Jon Gruden, who won a Super Bowl at Tampa Bay as a head coach and later found a new home at ESPN as the prime-time analyst for *Monday Night Football*. Gruden and I had gotten to know each other a bit over the years, and I respected his opinion as much or more than any other analyst in football. (I consider Gruden and NBC's Cris Collinsworth to be tied for No. 1 in terms of NFL insight.) Rivera, for his part, admitted he also liked to watch Gruden call a game because the former coach sometimes pointed out something on TV that Rivera had missed.

I usually tried to talk to Gruden just before he was about to broadcast a Panthers game, because I knew he would study film closely and see the team from an insightful outsider's perspective. The week before Carolina's November 18, 2013, game against New England was no exception.

The Panthers were 6–3 at that point and New England was 7–2. The game was undeniably bigger for Carolina than for the Patriots. Panthers fans had never forgotten the Super Bowl loss to the Patriots nearly 10 years before, while New England had had a bushel of big games both before and after that one. It would be the most important Panthers home game since the 2008 season.

By the time I talked to Gruden the Friday before the game, he had studied both teams at length and decided he would be watching two playoff teams on Monday night. "I think Carolina will end up winning 10 or 11 games this year," said Gruden, whose estimate was actually too low—the Panthers would ultimately win 12. "I just can't tell you how impressed I am with that defense. I haven't seen anybody hold San Francisco to 151 yards total offense. Have you? Especially on the road. Gosh, Carolina could have easily beaten Buffalo....This Panthers team could easily be undefeated. There's a lot of upside. Provided they stay healthy and take care of the football, this is a team that can do some damage."

Gruden was referring to the Panthers' 10–9 win at San Francisco the week before, in which Carolina had sacked Colin Kaepernick six times and managed to hold the 49ers to only three field goals.

Of Cam Newton, Gruden said, "He's relying on his teammates more than he has in the past instead of trying to do it all himself. The most amazing thing about Newton to me is I don't think people realize all the different fundamentals he has to execute in the course of the game....It's an unbelievable array of plays this guy runs. It really is amazing. I've seen him develop and take care of the ball better. And still, when he breaks loose, man, he's a load to bring down."

Gruden saved his highest praise for Kuechly, though. "I think he's the best linebacker, hands down, in football," Gruden said. "This kid is very unique. He can knock you down easily. He can find the ball. He can cover. I mean, he makes a play against [Atlanta tight end] Tony Gonzalez, I had to go outside and shake my head and get some air. This double move that Tony Gonzalez runs against everybody, Kuechly just wheeled and intercepted it. There's nothing the kid can't do."

Despite all of those glowing compliments, however, Gruden said he wasn't at all sure Carolina would win because of the Tom Brady–Bill Belichick combination that had won so many games together. "This is a New England team that gets into a lot of tight football games," Gruden said, "and it's still got [Coach Bill] Belichick and Brady, and it still usually finds a way to win those in the fourth quarter."

As for the game's atmosphere, Gruden said, "I'm sure there is genuine excitement for Panthers football, because this is the biggest game they've had in some time. I think the thing that's most enticing is that this might be the last time you get to go see Tom Brady play if you live in Charlotte. That's a surefire Hall of Famer right there. If I had a chance to come watch Luke Kuechly and this top-ranked defense against Tom Brady, I wouldn't miss it."

Almost everything Gruden said proved to be prescient, especially the part about Brady and Kuechly. They would lock horns on what was ultimately the game's biggest—and final—play.

Cam Newton (in red) and Josh Norman fight during the Panthers' 2015 training camp in Spartanburg after Norman intercepted a Newton pass and tried to run it back for a touchdown in a practice. Both men would later point to the incident as one that brought the team closer together.
Photo by David T. Foster III

Panthers coach Ron Rivera (left) and general manager Dave Gettleman constantly talk about improving the team. Since Gettleman arrived before the 2013 season, the Panthers have made the playoffs every year. Rivera was named the NFL's Coach of the Year in both 2013 and 2015. Photo by David T. Foster III

Saundra Adams (left) and her grandson Chancellor Lee Adams, the son of former Carolina No. 1 draft choice Rae Carruth, who was convicted of conspiring to murder Chancellor and his mother when he was an unborn baby.
Photo by Jeff Siner

Thomas Davis (left) and Luke Kuechly combine to form the NFL's best linebacker tandem. Both are very fast, but Kuechly says there's no doubt who's faster: "It's Thomas." Photo by Jeff Siner

Tight end Greg Olsen (88) caught the game-winning touchdown pass in a regular-season game against Seattle in 2015 as the Panthers finally beat the Seahawks. Olsen has become one of the most productive tight ends in the NFL and also serves as a team captain. Photo by David T. Foster III

Left tackle Michael Oher (73) solidified Carolina's offensive line when he arrived in 2015 and was rewarded with a three-year contract extension after the season concluded. Photo by Jeff Siner

Cam Newton strikes his familiar Superman pose against Green Bay and then again with a group of children (below) who had all received a "touchdown ball" from Newton over the years. In 2011, as a rookie, Newton began the tradition of first striking the Superman pose and then handing off the ball the Panthers just scored with to a lucky child in the stands. Photos by Jeff Siner

Bulldozing fullback Mike Tolbert (35) is widely acknowledged as the team's best dancer. He celebrates a touchdown (above) as Cam Newton looks on. Newton (right) popularized the "dab" after big plays in 2015 and had teammates do it in team pictures, too. That trend caught on so widely that, by 2016, Newton said he was going to retire the "dab" from his celebrations and move on to something else. Photos by Jeff Siner

Luke Kuechly (59) had interceptions on back-to-back plays against Dallas QB Tony Romo on Thanksgiving Day 2015, one of which he returned for a touchdown. Kuechly and Cam Newton shake hands (below) during the convincing win after another big play. Photos by David T. Foster III

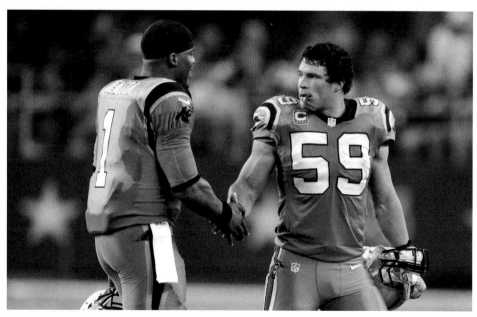

*Kawann Short (99)
brings down Atlanta
quarterback Matt Ryan
for one of his 11 sacks
in 2015. The player
teammates call "KK"
has become one of the
NFL's best pass-rushing
defensive tackles.*
Photo by David T. Foster III

*After Kelvin Benjamin
went down with a
season-ending knee
injury in training camp,
Ted Ginn Jr. (19) emerged
as Carolina's No. 1
receiver by necessity.
Ginn had 10 receiving
TDs in 2015, the most by
a Panthers receiver since
Steve Smith in 2005.*
Photo by Jeff Siner

The New York Giants' Odell Beckham Jr. (left) and Josh Norman spent most of one afternoon in a personal war in December 2015. Photo by Jeff Siner

Cam Newton rocks the football like a baby in late December 2015 in a game at Atlanta, sending a private signal to those who knew that his own baby had been born three days earlier.
Photo by David T. Foster III

"I've Seen This Story Before"

Night games are different in the NFL. The uniforms look better. The fans have a longer time at their tailgate parties to get rowdier. The feeling outside Bank of America Stadium 90 minutes before the Carolina–New England kickoff was incredibly amped—scalpers tried and succeeded at selling tickets way above face value. Fans dressed in black were everywhere. The Panthers were going to wear black jerseys and silver pants, and so they had requested that their supporters also wear black for a "blackout" effect. Spotlights illuminated the dark sky.

Carolina began the game well, taking the ball 90 yards in nine plays on their second drive. Newton's nine-yard TD pass to Brandon LaFell gave Carolina a 7–0 lead and was the only TD through the first half, which Carolina led 10–3.

The pace picked up in the third quarter. New England found the end zone first, as Brady hit tight end Rob Gronkowski for a nine-yard TD to tie the game at 10. Carolina's next drive then featured one of Newton's signature plays of the season.

On third-and-7 from the Carolina 37, the quarterback found himself in deep trouble. With no one open, he had to scramble to avoid a sack. And scramble. And scramble.

As the crowd "oohed" and "aahed" over each near-miss, Newton ultimately avoided six tackles on the play. He gained 14 yards officially, but ESPN quickly put up a graphic showing that he had run 75.8 yards to pick up those 14. It was an amazing play, and Newton made it count for even more by moving Carolina the rest of the way down the field and then throwing a 15-yard touchdown pass to Olsen. Carolina led 17–10 as the fourth quarter began.

Brady was not going to go quietly, though. He engineered back-to-back scoring drives—one a TD, one a field goal. With 6:32 left in the game, Carolina had the ball but trailed 20–17. What followed was the kind of signature drive a young quarterback like Newton really needed to start establishing himself among the game's elite.

Immediately, the drive got in trouble, as Newton faced a third-and-6. But he scrambled again, running for 15 yards. Soon thereafter, a third-and-2. Newton ran for three. Another third-and-7—this time Newton threw, and New England was called for defensive holding.

The Panthers were running the clock down. The two-minute warning came and went. It was obvious this would be their last real chance to take the lead. A field goal would possibly send the game into overtime if Brady didn't direct another scoring drive himself. A touchdown would put Carolina ahead by four.

On second-and-15 from the New England 25, Newton looked for Ted Ginn. It was a curious choice in one way—Ginn didn't have a single catch all night. But in another way, it wasn't. Ginn showed up time and again during the biggest moments of the Panthers' 2013 and 2015 seasons. (He skipped town to Arizona, admittedly chasing a bigger paycheck, in 2014.) And this play Ginn made, using his speed to grab a 25-yard TD pass. The stadium exploded with noise. Carolina led 24–20.

That left Brady with 59 seconds, however, and all three of his timeouts. Even after that dream drive, Panthers fans everywhere were having nightmarish visions of Brady and the Super Bowl following the 2003 season. There was no way this was going to be easy. Brady threw three straight incompletions, setting up fourth-and-10 at his own 20, but not many people were surprised when he fired a 23-yarder to Gronkowski on fourth down. This game was too good not to be decided on the last play.

The Patriots kept moving. The clock kept running. Finally, Brady had a first-and-10 at Carolina's 25 with only six seconds remaining. Was it the game's last play? No. Brady fooled Carolina by throwing short instead of in the end zone, gaining seven more yards on the dump pass in just three seconds.

Newton, on the sideline, could barely watch. He knew of Brady's dozens of fourth-quarter comebacks. Remembered Newton later,

"I said jokingly in the locker room, 'I've seen this story before. I've read this book before.'"

The Final Play

Now it was time for the final play. Three seconds left. Ball at the Carolina 18. Everyone in the stadium expecting it to go to Gronkowski, who had already scored once. Brady dropped back, waited a split second and then fired the ball down the middle at his big tight end. Kuechly, in coverage, bear-hugged Gronkowski in the back of the end zone just before the ball arrived. Brady's pass was badly underthrown, though, and Carolina safety Robert Lester cut underneath the play and intercepted it cleanly.

A flag was immediately thrown and announced—pass interference on Kuechly. The clock was on 0:00. But since the game can't end on a defensive penalty, the result would be New England getting one untimed down on Carolina's 1. NFL teams score about 50 percent of the time on plays from the other team's 1, so Carolina's odds of winning had just decreased dramatically. The stadium murmured in anticipation.

But wait...the officials were huddling. The flag had been picked up. And suddenly they were waving off the flag, with the head referee explaining that the ball had been "uncatchable" because it had been so underthrown. This angered Brady, who tried to argue his way back into getting the flag—but to no avail. Pandemonium ensued at the stadium. Carolina had been both lucky and good, and had beaten the mighty Patriots. The fans who were so loud all night drew praise from Rivera. "It was phenomenal," Rivera said. "This city wants it, and we're going to give it to them."

Patriots Postscript

On Twitter the next day, I told Panthers fans that a game that good and that controversial deserved its own nickname. I asked for suggestions. Here were some of my favorites:

Sweet Hug Carolina
Cuddle-kowski
Man Hug
LUUUUUUU-cky
Karma
Gronkitis
Need a Hug
Cool Hands Luke
Immaculate Perception
Immaculate Interception
Immaculate Exception
The (Un)Catch(Able)
Hanky Panky
And, my favorite of all:
Robbed Gronkowski

17

GREG OLSEN, SECURITY BLANKET

DURING HIS VERY first press conference as a Carolina Panther in the team's 2011 training camp, new tight end Greg Olsen was asked what the role of a tight end should be. "You're kind of a security blanket," Olsen said of the tight end's role. "That's something we hope we can build—that relationship and trust—so the quarterback can lean on us."

By 2013, Olsen was firmly established in that role for Cam Newton. The quarterback had learned to rely on No. 88 for the tough catches, the third-down catches, the goal-line catches and just about everything else, too. Olsen had become for Newton what Rob Gronkowski was to Tom Brady and Jimmy Graham was to Drew Brees. He was not just a threat to pick up 10 yards; he was a threat to bust the game wide open.

Pro Bowl picks are notoriously slow to catch up with the way the game is going. There's an old adage in the NFL that you often don't make the Pro Bowl until at least one year after you should have, but then you often do make the Pro Bowl toward the end of your career at least one year longer than you should.

I don't know if Olsen will get the payoff at the end of his career, but by 2013 he was a Pro Bowl tight end for the Panthers. In fact, although he wouldn't officially make the league's all-star game until 2014, he should have made it for the first time in 2012. That was the year Olsen began what would turn into a four-year streak with at least 69 catches, 800 yards, and five TDs per season for Carolina.

The problem, perhaps, was that Olsen wasn't showy enough. Gronkowski tried to drill a hole in the ground on every spike. Graham, a former college basketball player, would sometimes leap to dunk the ball over the goalpost crossbar (until the NFL outlawed the move before the 2014 season after Graham had knocked two different goalposts ajar).

When Olsen scored, he would either hand the ball to a referee or else give it to Newton, who would in turn hand it to some delighted kid in the end zone as part of the Panthers' "Sunday Giveaway" celebration (chronicled in chapter 6). It just wasn't Olsen's way to call attention to himself.

"Maybe I should start celebrating a little bit more, dunking and doing all that stuff," he said once. "Because I think sometimes that's what draws a lot of attention. But that's just not who I am."

But Olsen—the smart, detail-oriented, old-school middle son of a New Jersey high school football coach—has become such a big part of Carolina's offense over the years that eventually the attention came. He posted back-to-back 1,000-yard receiving seasons in 2014 and 2015, impressing even one of the greatest tight ends ever in Tony Gonzalez.

"I didn't think you could go to the Super Bowl with a tight end as your No. 1 receiver," said Gonzalez, now a CBS Sports analyst but formerly a 17-year NFL veteran and standout tight end. "The Panthers proved me wrong."

Finally a "Fun Tight End"

I've seen every pass-catcher the Panthers have ever employed, and I can tell you with surety that none of them had better hands than Olsen. Watching him work with a JUGS machine—the automatic pass-thrower that is standard on all NFL practice fields—is like watching Steph Curry's three-point warmup routine. Olsen makes one-handed catches. High catches. Low catches. His hand-eye coordination is way above average, even in the rarefied air of the elite athletes who populate the NFL.

As offensive tackle Jordan Gross said shortly after Olsen was signed: "I've heard a lot for eight years from fans about how we've never had a fun tight end to watch. Well, we've gotten our wish now."

Catching the ball is one thing. Blocking is quite another. While Graham's career suffered when he was traded to Seattle in 2015—the Seahawks actually asked him to block, which New Orleans rarely did—Olsen prides himself on being an every-down tight end who can handle any assignment. At 6'5" and 253 pounds, he and Newton are almost exactly the same size. While the knock on him early in his NFL career was that he didn't block well, he has improved enough in that skill that the Panthers never take him off the field.

The Panthers were lucky to get Olsen. It's rare that an uninjured, productive tight end who was a former first-round draft choice comes on the market. But one of Marty Hurney's best moves in his tenure as general manager came when he heard that Olsen was available.

Chicago had selected Olsen late in the first round in the 2007 draft out of the tight end factory that is the University of Miami. But the Bears had switched offensive coordinators since then to Mike Martz. Like John Fox at Carolina during his tenure—who thought of tight ends mostly as additional offensive linemen and completely wasted a good one named Gary Barnidge who would later have a 1,000-yard season in Cleveland—Martz deemphasized the tight end in his system. Olsen was deemed expendable. The Bears would later regret the trade many times—Martz didn't last long in that role—but by then it was too late.

Looking for Another Antonio Gates

Olsen reported to the Bears training camp as usual in the summer of 2011, only to find that the team was planning to trade him. He ended up in Carolina, where the Panthers gave a third-round pick to Chicago and simultaneously signed Olsen to a contract extension to ensure he would be Newton's security blanket for years to come. I watched Olsen that first week in Spartanburg and quickly wrote a column comparing him to Wesley Walls—the only other really exciting tight end the Panthers have ever had. Walls was a five-time Pro Bowler for Carolina who had his own TD celebration. From Mississippi, Walls liked to hunt. When Walls scored, he would sometimes drop the ball and pretend to shoot a clay pigeon out of the sky.

Rivera had advocated a more dynamic tight end for the Panthers from his very first press conference—he had seen Antonio Gates up close for years in San Diego and knew what he could do. "I practiced against those guys for four years, trying to figure out how to stop Antonio," Rivera said of his time as a Chargers assistant. "That made me understand just how important that sort of guy really is."

From the beginning, Olsen was a great help to Newton—and not just catching the ball. With a fast football mind honed by years of study under his father, Olsen often made play or assignment corrections in the huddle in the early days when Newton needed them. Like a good NFL quarterback, Olsen knew where everyone should be on every play.

"I don't think Greg gets a lot of credit for his football awareness," Newton said. "He's extremely good at that. A lot of times on the field, he does a great job with just finding ways to get open....I scramble and I step up, and when he senses that I have trouble, he finds a way to get open. I think that's a credit to him having the lineage of football expertise in his past being coached by his father."

Olsen shared pass-catching tight end duties in 2011 with veteran Jeremy Shockey, so his numbers weren't memorable. But the Panthers decided not to re-sign Shockey in 2012, and Olsen became the team's primary tight end.

It was in that same year that Olsen went public with what could have stayed a very private issue—his son's health. Because of the Olsen family's decision to go public, numerous other families were able to benefit from the Olsens' generosity with their time and money.

Jerry Richardson's Gesture

When Olsen was with the Panthers in 2012, he decided to talk openly about an ongoing family crisis and the team's response to it. Olsen and his wife, Kara, had met at the University of Miami, gotten married, and already had one young son named Tate. Now Kara was expecting twins—a boy and girl. And during what should have been a time of joy, an ultrasound turned up a possible abnormality in the boy's heart.

Further testing confirmed that the boy was going to be born with a congenital heart defect known as hypoplastic left heart syndrome (HLHS), a rare disease marked by an underdeveloped left ventricle and aorta. More prevalent in males, HLHS affects between one and four babies in every 10,000 live births. It prevents the left side of the heart from pumping enough blood to the body, forcing the right side to overcompensate. Left untreated, the extra workload will eventually cause the right side of the heart to fail.

In their research, the Olsens heard about an experimental in utero surgery that was being performed at a Boston hospital on some babies that had been diagnosed with HLHS before they were born. They booked a flight to Boston for the next day. Both sets of grandparents would accompany them.

But before they left, Panthers team owner Jerry Richardson called Olsen and said he hoped the Olsen family wouldn't mind, but he would rather they go on a plane that Richardson had chartered. And if you don't mind, the owner said, I'd like to go with you.

So Richardson went, accompanying the Olsens for two days' worth of doctors and tests. Although it turned out their unborn son was not deemed to be a good candidate for the surgery, they never forgot this remarkable gesture.

In October 2012, the Olsens returned the favor. When the twins were born, they named the girl Talbot and the boy T.J.—with the *J* standing for Jerry in honor of the Panthers' owner. T.J. then underwent the first of his three scheduled open-heart surgeries before he was a week old. He spent most of his first month of life in a Charlotte hospital but was healthy enough to be released from the hospital before Thanksgiving.

Olsen never missed a game during T.J.'s various surgeries and hospital stays, but he often spent the night in the hospital and then went straight to the stadium during the worst times.

"Greg is a professional in every sense of the word," Panthers coach Ron Rivera said. "Football is what he enjoys doing, it's what he loves to do as his distraction in life. If you look at all the things he and his family have gone through, the one haven he has had is to come here to the stadium."

Paying It Forward—with Nurses

That wasn't the end of the story, though. The Olsens—with a newborn baby and another young son at home as well as T.J. and his health issues—felt overwhelmed. They thought they needed full-time home health care for the next six months, until T.J. had his second surgery. Even though their insurance didn't cover it, the Olsens hired a young woman to perform essential nursing services for them.

"We had a nurse who lived with us for about six months," Olsen said. "She was part of our family. She ate with us, stayed with us, helped take care of the kids—it was incredible. But obviously, it's not cheap."

After T.J. had his second surgery and was doing well, the Olsens thought that they needed to "pay it forward" and help other families who have a child diagnosed with HLHS and must face the grueling, multi-surgery process. Olsen already had established a charitable foundation called "Receptions for Research" in honor of his mom, Susan, who had developed breast cancer while Greg was in high school and eventually had beaten it. That foundation raised money for breast cancer research, and Olsen had brought it with him from Chicago when he was traded.

Now he added a program called "The HEARTest Yard" at Levine Children's Hospital in Charlotte. It has one express purpose—to provide families, for free, the same in-home nursing care that Olsen's family benefited from in the critical six months between the affected child's first and second surgeries. It also comes with a large helping of the Olsen family, who get personally involved with the more than two dozen families the program has helped.

Take the Registers, for instance. Luann and her husband, Brian, had thought until the day of his birth that their son, Brantley, would be a normal baby. Nothing unusual had shown up on her ultrasounds. But Brantley was born with HLHS and in emergency surgery less than 24 hours after he was born.

The Registers met the Olsens at the hospital four days later. "He talked to us as Greg Olsen the dad, not as Greg Olsen the football player," Luann Register said. "And he has a son who has HLHS, just like our son, and he and Kara told us everything we could expect to happen. They said we were strong, and that we were going to be okay."

The Olsens since kept in touch through social media, birthday parties, and hospital visits. The Registers took advantage of the in-home nursing care once Brantley came home from the hospital. "If not for the HEARTest Yard and that program, I would have had to quit my job, or my husband would have," Register said. "And then we probably would have had to sell our house, because we wouldn't have been able to afford it. And then on top of that, we would have lost a good insurance provider. So, as we've told Greg and Kara numerous times, 'You guys saved our lives.'"

Olsen was the Panthers' Walter Payton Man of the Year nominee in 2015 for his charitable work, which also includes several other programs. Said Kim Ortmayer, a registered nurse at Levine who has often treated Olsen's son T.J. during his hospital stays, "Greg is really just a normal person when he's here. He's a dad. I've seen him belting out songs from *Frozen*. I've seen him upset when something is happening with T.J. I've seen him sleep on these uncomfortable recliners we have, night after night. I've seen him sit on the floor with a parent who has just lost their kid—just talking to that dad and hugging him. He just wants everyone to do well."

Unlike linebacker Thomas Davis in 2014—whose charitable outreach is similarly awesome and wide-ranging—Olsen didn't win the Walter Payton Award. As you can imagine, Olsen didn't care about that. He was going to be there for the families in similar situations whether or not he won an award for it. He and his wife just wanted to be those families' security blanket, much like Olsen is on the field with Newton.

18

THE NEW ORLEANS STORM

WHEN A FRANCHISE isn't doing well, you get a game like the New England game maybe once in five years. (Case in point: hardly anyone remembers any Panthers game between 1997 and 2002 except for the Steve Beuerlein draw play against Green Bay in 1999.) When a team is breaking through, however, you might get a game like the New England game only five weeks later—and that's exactly what happened to the Panthers on December 22, 2013.

This time the game was on a Sunday afternoon instead of a Monday night, and this time it poured rain for part of the time. But the final result was remarkably similar—a four-point Panthers win keyed by an extraordinary drive and a Newton touchdown pass in the final 60 seconds. These were the games the Panthers wouldn't and couldn't win before in the first two years of the Rivera-Newton era. But after going 2–14 in games decided by a touchdown or less through Week 2 of the 2013 season, they had turned that statistic completely around. Carolina went 5–0 in November and December in one-score games, finally getting over its biggest hurdle.

The Panthers–New Orleans game in Charlotte in 2013 had unseasonable weather for late December—72 degrees at kickoff, and eventually some of the hardest rain any Panthers fan had ever experienced during a game. Both teams entered with identical 10–4 records, and the winner seemed nearly certain to win the NFC South.

The Saints had drummed Carolina 31–13 in New Orleans only two weeks before. In that victory, New Orleans had scored 31 consecutive points after Carolina took an early 6–0 lead, and the Superdome had been rocking and provided a distinct home-field advantage. Newton, however, thought that Bank of America Stadium could do the same thing for Carolina two weeks later. The quarterback noted on the Wednesday before the game that there's been "a lot of talk...about how loud the Superdome can get. And no one's mentioning how loud Bank of America can get. From the past couple of weeks it's been extraordinary. We're going to need that and then some come Sunday. I think it's an opportunity for everyone to see something that has not been here for a while...I believe and I know and stand by this firmly, that we have the best fans in the NFL because we have a fan base from two states.... People come from South Carolina and North Carolina to show their support. Even from Georgia or Virginia. It's an opportunity for us to do something big."

With the game occurring three days before Christmas, the six black panther statues outside the stadium had their Christmas wreath collars on as usual. A festive mood pervaded. And the game started off very well for the home team, with Newton hitting Smith deep down the middle for 44 yards on Carolina's very first series. But then Newton made his worst mistake of the game. On second-and-15 from the Saints 16, Newton threw high and behind Ginn and had the ball intercepted as the crowd groaned.

It didn't get any better for a while for Carolina. The first quarter was scoreless. Then quarterback Drew Brees—a pain in the Panthers' side for many years—got his team in range for two field goals. The Saints led 6–0 just after the two-minute warning when, on a third-down play, Panthers linebacker Thomas Davis made an acrobatic interception at the New Orleans 43.

One play later, DeAngelo Williams burst through the Saints for a 43-yard TD run. Despite getting outplayed for much of the first half, Carolina would take a 7–6 lead into halftime.

In the third quarter, the monsoon came. There had been some light rain before, but now everyone in the sellout crowd was taking a shower. It was hard to see the field, and almost impossible to throw the ball with any accuracy. The water was pouring so hard off the upper deck of the stadium into the lower deck that there were several places that literally looked like waterfalls, and the fans under those areas all had to vacate their seats. In the meantime, Kuechly was making every tackle. By the official press box count, he would finish with 24 for the game, which tied an NFL record. (Panthers' coaches later reviewed the game film as they always do and credited Kuechly with two more tackles, for 26.)

Kuechly also made a critical third-quarter interception of Brees during the rainstorm, somehow hanging onto the ball. The Panthers increased their lead the same quarter, with Graham Gano hitting a 40-yard field goal into the teeth of the rain to make it 10–6. But in the fourth quarter, the rain stopped and Brees found his rhythm. The Saints embarked on a 97-yard drive that featured tight end Jimmy Graham, who caught a 46-yard pass to get it started and a five-yard TD pass to finish it. New Orleans led 13–10 midway through the quarter.

Rolling the Dice with Defense

Carolina's offense, meanwhile, just kept having trouble. The Panthers went three-and-out once, got a defensive stop, and then failed to make a first down again. Riverboat Ron faced another big decision on fourth-and-7 from the Carolina 36 with 2:04 left. He could either go for it or count on his defense, which had played well almost the whole game, to not allow the Saints a first down and get the ball back. One first down would seal it.

This time, Rivera rolled the dice with the defense. He skipped going for the fourth-down conversion and punted. The Panthers only had two timeouts left. But New Orleans then doubled down on Rivera's conservatism, running the ball on three straight plays instead of letting Brees throw it just once to try and finish the game.

The three runs gained only two yards as the defense came through once again and rewarded Rivera's faith.

After a Saints punt, Carolina got the ball back at its own 35 with 55 seconds to go and no timeouts left. Its fans—rain-soaked and raucous—knew that the next minute would either give them a memorable story to tell their children or simply send them home looking like half-drowned cats.

Domenik Who?

Newton entered the huddle with a stern face and without his favorite receiver, Smith, who had suffered a knee injury early in the game and was in the locker room watching. The quarterback also could not run as well as he usually could, owing to an ankle injury. If the Panthers were going to win, it had to be with Newton's arm.

"He just said, 'Let's get it done,'" Panthers offensive tackle Jordan Gross said of Newton's first words in the huddle. "He went into his focus mode. He wasn't the jovial self that he can sometimes be."

That the Panthers could get it done was very questionable. Carolina had punted eight times. The team was 0-for-9 on third-down conversions. Newton had thrown that costly early interception in the red zone. On the first play, Newton dropped back and was under pressure. Olsen ran a clear-out decoy route, trying to attract defenders and open the middle of the field for a deep crossing pattern by Ginn.

Newton held the ball just long enough, even though it meant he would take a huge hit. Then he threw a laser to Ginn, who made the catch, sped through half the Saints secondary, and stepped out of bounds after a 37-yard gain. It was a monstrous play. "Just great timing," Ginn said. I asked Olsen later what he thought he would most remember about the drive in 10 years.

"Running down the field on that first play and just seeing Cam throw a missile, and just hoping it winds up in Teddy's arms," Olsen said.

"They were playing very soft coverage, especially with the [rainy] conditions," Newton explained later. "Just keeping us honest and trying to get us to check the ball down [for a short gain]. But with great protection I had time to sit in there and let the routes come open."

With the ball at the New Orleans 28 and 0:46 still left, the Panthers' focus changed. Instead of hoping to scrape up enough yardage to get a tying field goal, now Carolina could go for the touchdown and the jugular. "The first play just changed the dynamics of not having any timeouts completely," Olsen said.

On first-and-10 from the New Orleans 28, Newton tried a short pass to Ginn. It was incomplete. On second down, he made eye contact with Olsen just before the snap. "Greg really called an audible," Newton said. "He felt as if he could get [open] with tight coverage by [New Orleans safety] Roman Harper."

Harper would eventually join the Panthers the next season and have trouble guarding Olsen in practice, too. It was no sin—nearly every safety in the league had trouble with Olsen. This time Olsen made a 14-yard catch to the Saints 14. Now 0:28 remained, so the Panthers spiked the ball on first down to stop the clock.

New Orleans gambled on second down, bringing a blitz. Newton looked to his left—where Steve Smith would line up on the play Carolina had called—and instead saw Domenik Hixon. Hixon was the Panthers' No. 4 receiver and had barely played all season. He had never made a big play before for Carolina, and he would never make one again. But this time he was running what most NFL teams label a 7 route, which is named that because the receiver draws an imaginary 7 with his pattern, starting at the bottom of the numeral.

The Panthers offensive line held up. Hixon broke off his pattern toward the front corner of the end zone, and Newton threw it low and hard. "It was one of those deals where, if I didn't catch it, no one would have caught it," Hixon said. Hixon lowered his hands in the left corner of the end zone. He dove. And he caught it.

There was bedlam in the stands. But it was somewhat restrained by the officials reviewing the play, just like every scoring play. They took a close look. On the sideline, Hixon kept assuring his teammates he had gotten his hands under the ball. "People ask me if I caught it," Hixon said. "I was about 99 percent sure—but you'd like to get confirmation."

And after a few more seconds, he had it. The official signaled TD. The Panthers had gone 65 yards in 32 seconds with no timeouts. "Catch of the year!" Olsen later said of Hixon's grab. It was also the only touchdown Hixon would ever score for Carolina. After Brees threw four desperation passes that fell short, Carolina had won the game 17–13.

The victory—coupled with Carolina's 21–20 squeaker of a win the next week over Atlanta—allowed the Panthers to finish the season with a 12–4 record and hold the No. 2 playoff seed in the NFC. That assured a first-round bye. But Carolina's first playoff opponent had already given the Panthers a tough time in November and now were coming to Charlotte ready to finish the deal: it was the San Francisco 49ers. Their appearance would begin an 11-month streak of mostly bad news for a Panthers team that thought it had turned the corner, only to find out there was still much more to do.

PART IV

THE STUMBLE

January to Early December 2014

19

THE SAN FRANCISCO LETDOWN

ONE OF THE Carolina Panthers' signature wins of their break-through 2013 regular season had been a 10–9 squeaker on the road against San Francisco. Because the 49ers were widely considered one of the NFC's two best teams—the other being Seattle—the November 10, 2013, victory had shown the Panthers and their fans that they were for real. In one of Carolina's best defensive performances of the season, the Panthers had held San Francisco's powerful offense to 151 total yards and three field goals and had sacked Colin Kaepernick six times.

The Panthers had not had much offensive success in that game, either, but had scored barely enough against the reigning NFC champions to overcome an early 9–0 deficit. DeAngelo Williams had broken two tackles on a 27-yard TD run, and Graham Gano had kicked a 53-yard field goal in the fourth quarter that held up as the Panthers defense completely shut down Kaepernick on two fourth-quarter drives that followed.

Afterward, Newton called the game a "maturity jump" for the team. "We've been somewhat uncertain of how we will turn out in these types of games," Newton said. "We needed that type of game, just to be in a dog fight, in somewhat of a barn-burner, to show what type of team this really is."

That was then. This was now. It was two months later, and the Panthers were facing the 49ers again. This time the game would be in Charlotte. This time Carolina would have had a week off, while San Francisco had to play on wild-card weekend (and won 23–20 at Green Bay on a last-play field goal). But this time the 49ers were healthier and out for revenge against a Panthers team they were convinced had stolen a victory from them earlier in the season.

It would be the first playoff game of any type for the Panthers since Jake Delhomme had committed an ungodly six turnovers (five interceptions, one fumble) in a 20-point home loss to Arizona following the 2008 season. That this playoff game would come at home—just like the last one had five years before—provided the opportunity to exorcise some demons for a Carolina fan base that had had a hard time forgetting Delhomme's gaffes and the ensuing four no-playoffs years.

What happened, though, did little to exorcise those demons. In fact the Panthers started stumbling on the date of this playoff game—January 12, 2014—and didn't really stop themselves and stand fully upright again for 11 months.

"Guys Lost Their Cool"

The weather wasn't the problem—sunny and 54 degrees, which for a Charlotte day in mid-January isn't bad at all. The talent wasn't really the problem—many of the key players in the Panthers' run to the Super Bowl two years later were already in place.

What was ultimately the problem was that the Panthers didn't act like they had been there before—and, in reality, many of them hadn't. Ron Rivera had played in a Super Bowl and coached in one as an assistant, but this would be his first playoff game as a head coach. It was Cam Newton's first playoff game. And Luke Kuechly's. And Josh Norman's. And many others.

It started going badly early. On third-and-6 on San Francisco's first drive, the Panthers were about to get off the field on an incomplete pass when aggressive safety Mike Mitchell came flying in and hit a 49ers receiver late. Instead of zero points, the 49ers ended up with a field goal. Mitchell would call the flag a "terrible call" five times in his postgame interview, but his "until the echo of the whistle" playing style meant that he flirted with those sorts of calls all the time. Mitchell was the one who added some "pepper" into Carolina's secondary, as Jon Gruden had once said. This time, it came back to bite him.

"I can't wait to play them with a new set of refs in a new game," Mitchell would say afterward. That moment would never come, however—Mitchell took a big deal to go to Pittsburgh in the off-season.

On the 49ers' very next possession, nearly the same thing happened. Cornerback Captain Munnerlyn head-butted Anquan Boldin, causing another 15-yard penalty on the Panthers. Again, the 49ers ended up with a field goal out of a drive that likely would have been nothing. It was 6–0 San Francisco, and by this time the stadium was incensed. Rivera, normally calm and in control under all circumstances, was screaming at the officials. This later would become his biggest regret about the game—he thought that the team had followed his lead, losing its composure.

Said Rivera the next day in the aftermath, "Guys lost their cool, lost their temper, lost their composure—and that's on me. I'm the head coach and I've got to make sure these guys understand the situation and circumstances, and we can't get caught up in that. It was unfortunate it happened that way, and it was one-sided, but that's what happens."

It was one-sided in some respects, and that's what Panthers fans sometimes remember from this game. Boldin got involved in all sorts of extracurricular activity and also head-butted a Panthers player, which the officials totally missed. San Francisco had 12 men in the huddle on a play it scored on—first-and-goal from the Panthers 1—and the refs missed that, too.

But to concentrate on the missed flags obscures the larger point in this game—Carolina was outplayed. And much of that stemmed from the offense's breakdowns in critical situations.

The first one came after those two Phil Dawson field goals had given the 49ers a 6–0 lead. Carolina drove to the San Francisco 3, where it faced second-and-goal. A run by Newton netted two yards. It was third-and-goal at the 1. The Panthers put in a sixth offensive lineman and gave the ball to battering ram fullback Mike Tolbert over right guard. No dice.

It was fourth-and-goal from the 1 and time for one of the game's signature plays. If Carolina had made it, perhaps the whole season would have turned out differently. Fans were unsurprised when Rivera decided to go for it—the riverboat gambler was coming out again. And the play call wasn't surprising, either—Carolina let Newton, its best player, try a quarterback sneak.

The result? No gain. Newton was stuffed. And suddenly, the Panthers looked very vulnerable.

"Silly Penalties, Silly Mistakes"

Still, the Panthers would take the lead in the second quarter. After forcing a San Francisco punt, Newton hit Steve Smith with one of the best throws of his career, dropping the ball into a well-covered Smith's hands for a 31-yard TD. Smith, who came into the game with an injured knee, made a beautiful catch and then pointed to the knee as if to say, "Does it look okay now?"

Carolina got the ball back and quickly drove to the shadow of the San Francisco goal line once again on the strength of a 35-yard pass from Newton to Olsen. It was second-and-goal from the 1, and Newton was tackled for no gain again. Then, on third-and-goal from the 1, the 49ers were whistled for encroachment. The ball was placed at about the one-foot line. Surely Carolina could knock it in this time.

Well, no. The Panthers couldn't. Again, Tolbert's number was called. Again, Carolina's offensive line was overrun and Tolbert could make no headway. This time he lost a yard. With fourth-and-goal from the 2, this time Rivera took the field goal. Altogether, Carolina ran four plays in two different series of plays from San

Francisco's 1—two Newton runs and two Tolbert runs—and didn't score on any of them.

"Two third-and-a-foots and we get a total of three points," Olsen said disgustedly afterward.

"It's hard to think of all the points we left out there," offensive tackle Jordan Gross echoed.

Graham Gano's short field goal would give Carolina a 10–6 lead, but the Panthers would never score again. San Francisco put up the game's final 17 points, with the most devastating blow being a third-quarter, four-yard run for a TD by Kaepernick, who then mocked Newton's "Superman" TD pose. Kaepernick would later laugh and call the disparaging move a "shout-out." Newton said later, "That's not the first nor will it be the last time somebody does that." By this point in his career, the quarterback was used to it and knew his public displays set him up for mockery when things went poorly.

Ultimately, Newton was also outplayed by Kaepernick. Their careers would take very different arcs in the following years—with Newton's arrow pointing up and Kaepernick's down. But on this day Newton threw two interceptions and Kaepernick had no turnovers of any type.

"Silly penalties, silly mistakes, and not seizing the moment," was how Newton would describe it later.

"It came down to two pretty obvious things," Olsen said. "Goal-line offense and penalties. You do the math on those, and the score looks a lot different."

On offense, the Panthers scored only 10 points—the exact same number they had scored in the 10–9 win two months before. That game notwithstanding, 10 points is hardly ever enough to win a playoff game. (Carolina would find that out again, two postseasons later, in the Super Bowl.)

And on defense, the Panthers secondary had all sorts of problems. Besides the two early penalties, cornerback Josh Norman committed the most blatant foul of all, taking a swing at a 49ers player on the ground to give San Francisco a fourth-quarter first down. Robert Lester gave up a 45-yard pass when he didn't come over to help on a deep route and also missed a tackle that allowed Frank Gore to go on a 39-yard gallop. Drayton Florence committed a pass-interference penalty in the end zone. In the meantime, the offense didn't score a point in the second half.

"To go out here and have a home game that we really didn't show up for in the second half and play football, it's tough," Panthers wide receiver Brandon LaFell said.

It was a bitter end to a sweet season for the Panthers. But it was only the beginning of the Panthers' stumble.

20

GREG HARDY: RELEASING THE KRAKEN

THE FIRST 12 games of the 2014 regular season went wrong for a lot of reasons for the Carolina Panthers. None of those reasons was bigger, though, than the dark cloud caused by the Greg Hardy saga. It followed the Panthers around for more than a year, starting from the very day that their playoff loss to San Francisco concluded.

At 25, Hardy was the Panthers' quirkiest, most enigmatic player—and one of their most talented, too. After an 11-sack season in 2012 in which he showed great promise, Hardy had an even better season in 2013. The defensive end's 15 sacks tied a single-season record for the Panthers. He played in the Pro Bowl following the season. Among his guests in Hawaii for that game was his girlfriend at the time, a Charlotte woman named Nicole Holder.

The tempestuous relationship between Hardy and Holder was not yet public knowledge then. What was public was the fact that Hardy was an unrestricted free agent and an extremely valuable man in the NFL. As a defensive end who could regularly get to the quarterback, he played one of football's most important positions. The Panthers had a salary-cap quandary on their hands. If they simply let Hardy go, he would undoubtedly get another job in the league with an eight-figure annual salary and perhaps chase after and sack Cam Newton in a key game down the road.

The Panthers also could choose to use their franchise tag on Hardy, which would guarantee him $13.1 million for the 2014 season—no matter how much he played—and then give them the option of signing Hardy to a long-term contract. Or they could stake even more of their future on him by signing Hardy to a long-term deal that might cost them $50 million or more, depending on the number of years.

It was a *Let's Make a Deal* sort of moment for Carolina: Door No. 1 (let Hardy walk); Door No. 2 (one year, $13.1 million); or Door No. 3 (more years and many more millions).

Those are the sorts of decisions general manager Dave Gettleman gets paid to make, and he makes them all the time at various levels on the pay scale. What made Hardy's situation unique was his talent coupled with his personality. That personality had mostly been viewed as harmlessly "out there," as his teammates often said—at least at that point.

On game days, Hardy would tell anyone who asked that he turned into the "Kraken"—a mythological sea monster. And he took this role play very seriously. He painted his face. He stuck in either black- or white-colored contacts. He would write the word "KRAKEN" on a strip of tape and stick it over the name on the back of his jersey for warmups. (NFL rules didn't allow him to keep it there for the game.) His personality was embraced by the media (including myself), who found him entertaining and willing to try just about anything. Hardy posed for the *Charlotte Observer* several times for portraits, including once as Santa Claus along with fellow defensive end Charles Johnson.

But Hardy's real alter ego was the Kraken.

"The Kraken is a giant monster that just demolishes everything that moves," Hardy told me once. "On Wednesday or Thursday, I go down in my subconscious. I find him, and I unlock the cage. About Saturday he usually comes out. Then he's always out on Sunday. I don't control him then. What he does when I'm not there, I don't know."

That sort of thing seemed fine to most people—certainly, NFL athletes fire themselves up for games in all sorts of strange ways. But Hardy's unusual personality (and some effort-level concerns) had been part of the reason he had lasted all the way until the sixth round of the 2010 draft. He also had an outsized sense of what he could accomplish—it was far more than just your garden-variety confidence. Hardy, who had played a little basketball in college at Ole Miss without great results, once boasted to our newspaper that he could beat LeBron James in a game of one-on-one basketball. He also predicted at one point that he could lead the NFL with 50 sacks (the single-season record is 22.5).

In 2011 Hardy showed up to Spartanburg for training camp heavily bandaged due to a motorcycle wreck that he would say could have killed him. In 2012 he posted a picture on Twitter that appeared to show him driving a car at more than 100 mph. Coach Ron Rivera and other staff members had to occasionally pull Hardy aside and tell him he had to be more careful with what he did off the field.

"There were a couple of times I disciplined him, and nobody else knew about it but him, me, and the general manager," Rivera said of Hardy.

After four years with Carolina, though, Hardy had improved tremendously as a player. He and Johnson had formed a fearsome defensive-end tandem with the Panthers in 2013, although Hardy had not been a factor in the playoff loss to the 49ers. Carolina wanted Hardy, though. When it came time to make a decision as to what door to choose, I thought the Panthers made the right one at the time based on the information that they had.

"Stories in the Dark of Night"

The San Francisco game was the last one Hardy had to play under his modest original deal. In the locker room after the Panthers' season-ending loss to San Francisco, Hardy was asked if he wanted to "get something done" with the Panthers.

"I'm not going to 'get anything done,'" Hardy said. "I'm going to get what I want. Once I get what I want, we're good with whoever. Hopefully it's this place."

Gettleman said in his press conference right after the season ended that it wasn't implausible that the Panthers would let Hardy walk out the door, as some teams had done in other similar situations with big-name players over the years (and the way Gettleman himself would let Josh Norman, another star defensive player, leave in April 2016).

"Everybody lets players go," Gettleman said. "There isn't a team in this league that hasn't let a big dog walk out the door. And don't print that I'm saying that he's going to go. I'm just making a statement....Everybody's on the outside looking in. So when a team makes a decision to let a big guy, to let a quality player—and not a myth, but a legitimate quality player—walk out the door, the first thing you do is you sit back and say, 'What are they doing?' Well, the fact of the matter is there's stuff going on behind closed doors that we don't know about. I don't care what team it is. I don't care about what sport it is. You don't know all the facts....There's a million reasons why things like that happen. There's a lot of stories in the dark of night that never get told."

How prescient this statement proved to be from Gettleman—although at the time he was obviously speaking more in generalities because he would end up employing Hardy once again. The stories "in the dark of night that never get told," or at least never told fully—that sounded an awful lot like a night in the life of Hardy that would be coming up four months later.

As Cam Newton has said a number of times, however, "Hindsight is 50-50." The Panthers couldn't know what hadn't happened yet, and they made a decision in February —a few weeks after the playoffs—to do what I thought was the correct move at the time. The Panthers chose "Door No. 2" as their option with Hardy—guaranteeing him $13.1 million for the 2014 season and leaving themselves a chance to sign him to a longer-term deal. They didn't mortgage their future for him, but they also didn't let him leave and sign with another team. Hardy signed this one-year deal shortly afterward (it isn't official until it gets signed).

Then came May 13, 2014.

A Bizarre One-Day Trial

There are a few facts not in dispute about the evening of May 12, which verged into the early morning hours of May 13 and resulted in Hardy being charged with misdemeanor domestic violence. Hardy and Holder had broken up at the Pro Bowl in February. That much seemed to be clear. But they had then occasionally gotten back together and had sex. And on that night they were going out again in Charlotte with a few other friends.

That much is certain. It is also certain that Hardy and Holder had a volatile relationship. Every witness who would testify in an unusual one-day trial held in Charlotte in July 2015 would agree to that—when Hardy and Holder were getting along well, it was great. When it was bad, they fought verbally. A lot.

Beyond that, it's hard to tell exactly what happened on May 13 between the two of them. Hardy and Holder both testified in court, and their stories were area codes apart. They couldn't even agree if they had ever lived together—she said they did, he said they didn't.

In their testimony, they spoke of $2,000 bar tabs (Hardy paid, of course) and VIP tables. Holder had once had a affair with the rapper Nelly, who owns a small slice of the Charlotte Hornets, and said Hardy had been jealous of that brief tryst. The mood during the night in question changed for the worse, Holder said, when "to top everything off, a Nelly song came on" during one of their nightclub stops.

For his part, Hardy said he was not a violent person off the field and that anyone trying to portray him as such was misguided. "I'm not one to fight," he said on the stand. "I don't even fight dudes."

Eventually, after a night of partying and drinking, Holder and Hardy ended up back at his luxury uptown apartment. At that point, Holder said, Hardy assaulted her. Hardy said it wasn't true. Specifically, Holder testified, he flung her from a bed and threw her first into a bathtub and then onto a futon covered with rifles (Hardy's guns were later displayed in court). Hardy also tore off a necklace he had given her, Holder said, threw it into a toilet, and then slammed the lid on her arm when she tried to dig it out. He later put his hands around her throat.

"He looked me in my eyes and he told me he was going to kill me," Holder said. "I was so scared I wanted to die. When he loosened his grip slightly, I said, 'Just do it. Kill me!'" Hardy would instead call 911 and fabricate a number of statements, prosecutors said, so that he looked like the victim instead of Holder.

The defense's story was very different. Hardy's attorney described Holder as an erratic young woman who wanted to be back at Hardy's side so she could return to the limelight. Hardy said any wounds Holder had were self-inflicted. The defense attorney also got Holder to admit she had used cocaine earlier in the evening.

The 10-hour, one-day trial was presided over by district judge Becky Thorne Tin. I sat through it all, and it has to be one of the 10 strangest days I've ever had on the job. One small revelation after another came out during the trial—for a while, it was unclear whether Holder would even show up. Ultimately, the judge believed Holder about the most salient part of the trial. The judge thought Holder had indeed feared for her life and that Hardy had assaulted her and threatened to kill her. She found the defensive end guilty of two misdemeanors—assaulting a female and communicating threats.

But that wasn't the end of it. Not close. Hardy's attorneys immediately appealed the verdict, which had the effect of setting the district judge's verdict aside entirely. Instead, Hardy was scheduled for a jury trial in February 2015—after the Panthers 2014 season had concluded.

The Most Expensive Sack in NFL History

This all put the Panthers in an unenviable bind. Hardy was technically free and clear—because of the way the court system worked, his appeal meant that the original conviction was no longer applicable. The Panthers could have him practice and play.

In the court of public opinion, however, Hardy's name had certainly been stained (as had the Panthers, who saw the name "Rae Carruth" pop up in the background paragraphs of Hardy-related stories far too often for their liking). Meanwhile, another case that had absolutely nothing to do with Hardy—the Ray Rice case, which had been badly mishandled by the NFL—was also changing forever the league's approach when its men hit women.

Rice had punched a woman named Janay Palmer—who was then his fiancée and three months later would become his wife—in the elevator of an Atlantic City casino in February 2014. A video of this punch—and of Rice dragging his unconscious fiancée out of the elevator—would surface publicly seven months later. The NFL originally gave Rice an embarrassingly short two-game suspension for his behavior but later, responding to criticism, beefed up its off-field conduct policies and suspended Rice indefinitely.

After the full elevator video surfaced via TMZ in September 2014, the Baltimore Ravens immediately terminated Rice's contract. Although his indefinite NFL suspension was ultimately overturned, Rice couldn't find NFL work after that.

That was the backdrop of the Hardy case. There was no video evidence in Hardy's situation, however. And the Panthers, who knew they were going to have to pay Hardy $770,000 for every game whether they played him or not, decided to play him in Week 1 against Tampa Bay.

Hardy contributed a single sack in Carolina's 20–14 win. I believe this was the most expensive sack in NFL history, for it cost $13.1 million. Hardy would never play another snap for Carolina, although no one knew that at the time.

After the Rice video surfaced, the Panthers came under much greater scrutiny for allowing Hardy to play in the season opener. Rivera was asked if that was a mistake at the time. "I don't know," the coach said. "What is right? We do the best we can, though. Hey, nobody's infallible. We all make mistakes. We all correct those mistakes and we try to go forward....We have to get this issue correct. We've got to do the right things and we're trying to do the right things."

Said Gettleman, "At that time we felt it was the right thing to do. It's constantly changing. There's no rulebook for this."

It took a while for it all to play out. At first, following the outcry over the Rice elevator video (which came out one day after Carolina's Week 1 win), the Panthers deactivated Hardy for one week only—Week 2 of the season. They were being besieged by Hardy questions. Rivera—a husband and a father of a college-aged daughter—made the call. Said Rivera, "Part of the reason why I made the decision [was that], if you play him and you win, then it's, 'You don't have a conscience.' If you play him and you lose, then he's a distraction."

Rivera said in our interview for this book that he botched the explanation to the other players as to why he wasn't playing Hardy against Detroit and that DeAngelo Williams let him know. Williams was one of the players Rivera occasionally went to when he wanted to know how things he said were playing in the locker room.

"DeAngelo was what I call unfiltered," Rivera said. "So when I made the decision not to play Greg Hardy in the Detroit game, and the way I presented it and talked about it to the team, I didn't realize it at the time, but it was vague, and it wasn't enough for the players. Later on I asked DeAngelo, 'How did that go?' And he said, 'Coach, you f—— that up. You need to go back and make that right.'"

By Week 3 of the 2014 NFL season, though, as Rivera would say, "The climate changed." Major NFL sponsors were making noise about the league being too soft on domestic violence cases. The Minnesota Vikings suddenly put Adrian Peterson—who was involved in a child-abuse case—on an "exempt list" that few people had even heard of until that day. The Panthers then stashed Hardy on the same list, which would allow him to be paid but not allow him to play.

When Hardy's court date was later postponed until February, it meant he would not play all season for Carolina. His absence hung over the Panthers all year from an on-the-field standpoint. He was a ghost—officially on the team and certainly on the payroll, but never in the locker room anymore. Charles Johnson was not as effective without Hardy on the other side, and the Panthers' overall sack total fell from 60 in 2013 (No. 1 in the NFL) to a modest 40 in 2014 (tied for 13th). The team's overall defensive rank went from No. 2 to No. 10.

Hardy Signs with Dallas

There were more twists to come. In February 2015, when Hardy was supposed to go on trial again but this time with a jury, the district attorney abruptly dropped the case. The DA did that after Holder disappeared. Prosecutors said at the time and would later tell the NFL they had reliable information that Holder had received a financial settlement from Hardy to ensure that she wouldn't sue him in civil court. "The DA's office has also been made aware that the victim has reached a civil settlement with Mr. Hardy," read the official statement. And the DA's office also said of Holder, "Without her testimony, in this particular instance, the State could not proceed." Photos of Holder's injuries would surface online months later, causing more outrage but not much else.

So Hardy was free—never officially convicted of anything, still healthy, and only 26. He was a free agent again, this time with no franchise tag upon him. The Panthers decided they were done with Hardy and did not get involved in bidding for him. The Dallas

Cowboys instead signed him to a one-year deal that was worth $11.3 million if he met various incentives.

Hardy then became the Cowboys' problem. The NFL did its own investigation and, despite the dropped charges, suspended Hardy for 10 games. The league determined that it was never going to get accused of going soft on a domestic violence issue again. An arbitrator later reduced that suspension to four games.

Hardy served that suspension, played the other 12 games in 2015 and had six sacks. He also had one sideline blowup where he pushed a Cowboys assistant coach and one awkward interview where he praised the looks of Tom Brady's wife. He didn't affect the Panthers-Cowboys game in 2015 (Carolina won easily), and he didn't affect the Cowboys' bottom line (Dallas went 4–12).

What he did affect dramatically, however, was the 2014 season of the Panthers. Carolina had planned for Hardy to play and hijacked a large part of its salary cap to ensure that he would. When it all went south, the Panthers' image suffered. So did their pass rush. So did their team.

But Hardy wasn't the only notable absence in 2014. The Panthers found themselves rebuilding left and right after a slew of retirements and free-agent moves. Many of those made the team's stumble for the first three quarters of the 2014 season a bit more understandable—though no less painful—in retrospect.

21

THE EXODUS AND 3–8–1

WHEN YOU WIN in the NFL, you become a target.

Other teams try harder to beat you. They also look more closely at your roster. You are becoming "relevant," to use one of coach Ron Rivera's favorite adjectives. But when you get noticed and have nearly two dozen free agents about to go on the market—as the Panthers did following the 2013 season—you also get raided.

The Panthers had a bad 2014 off-season. There's no other way to put it. The Greg Hardy situation dug its claws into the team from May onward, and that was the biggest blow. Any time you lose a player who was a Pro Bowl defensive end with 15 sacks the year before, that's hard to make up for on the field. Plus, dealing with the fallout from Hardy's infamous night on May 13 took a lot of mental energy.

But there were many other jabs that went along with that upper-cut. Some were guys who were grabbing hold of bigger contracts, and given the short shelf life of an NFL player, it was hard to blame them. Some were guys deciding they had had enough of the game— roughly half the offensive line retired. And some were self-inflicted. General manager Dave Gettleman released the Panthers' best all-time wide receiver Steve Smith following the 2013 season, even though Smith had had a decent season the year before (745 receiving yards, second to Greg Olsen) and had scored the team's only touchdown in the playoff loss to San Francisco. Smith would go on to have a 1,000-yard season in Baltimore in 2014.

Jordan Gross, a rock at offensive tackle for 11 years, was a very difficult loss. He had been a starter from day one as a rookie in 2003, and in eight of his 11 seasons he had started every single game. Gross had been around so long he had protected the blind side for everyone from Jake Delhomme to Vinny Testaverde to Jimmy Clausen to Cam Newton. Well-liked and respected by everyone in the organization, he had taken a pay cut to continue playing for Carolina in 2013 and then made the Pro Bowl for the third time. He sounded honestly unsure after the loss to San Francisco if he would return for a 12th season.

"You'd like to think you're irreplaceable and there's no way anybody could live without you," Gross said then. "But that's not the truth. Every year, players much more important than me leave teams for one reason or another. And those teams survive and somehow make it the next year. There's a saying I've heard for the NFL: 'Everybody's useful. Nobody's necessary.' And that's really the truth of it."

Gross and Smith were two of the most vocal and obvious leaders of the Panthers offense, and their departure set the stage for Cam Newton to have an even bigger role. But the loss of two offensive captains during the same off-season was difficult on a number of levels. Smith's departure was messy, as he didn't like being fired or the way Dave Gettleman handled it and went public with his displeasure. Smith said in a radio interview with Charlotte's WFNZ in late 2014 that he was "stabbed in the back." In a different interview with the same station, Smith also told Panthers fans before Carolina's game with his new Baltimore team that they should "put your goggles on, because there's going to be blood and guts everywhere."

Gross, on the other hand, would end up retiring in February 2014 at one of the best retirement ceremonies you will ever see. Instead of a standard speech, Gross chose a selection of pictures to represent his career and told funny stories about each one. A noted prankster himself and star of a Panthers-produced podcast called *This Is Gross,* the offensive tackle was surprised by center Ryan Kalil at the end of the press conference. During the period for question and answers, Kalil suddenly stood up and led a locally renowned barbershop quartet in singing "Happy Trails" to Gross with some altered lyrics. The best and truest one was this:

> *Happy trails to you,*
> *Until we meet again.*
> *Happy trails to you,*
> *You'll be missed on third-and-10.*

Gross's departure was only the beginning of the exodus. Ted Ginn's breakout year led to him "chasing the money," as Ginn would admit later, with a new deal in Arizona. Cornerback Captain Munnerlyn found more dollars in Minnesota. Safety Mike Mitchell, who despite a costly penalty in the San Francisco game had had a strong season in 2013, bolted for Pittsburgh. Wide receiver Brandon LaFell left for New England, where he would catch passes from Tom Brady instead of Newton. LaFell ruffled feathers on his way out, explaining his decision to Patriots reporters: "I had a chance to play with a Hall of Fame quarterback. One day Cam will be there probably, but he's not there now."

Add Smith and Gross to that mix, as well as Hardy, and there went seven key pieces from the 2013 Panthers team. Versatile reserve offensive lineman Geoff Hangartner, who also retired, made it eight. Offensive guard Travelle Wharton, who waited until just before training camp and then retired as well, made it nine.

Mitchell had choked back tears just after the playoff loss, saying, "I haven't played on a team with this type of coaches, these types of teammates, probably since I was a 17-year-old boy. I had a great group of guys and I want to finish this."

But there would be no going back to 2013. That team itself was finished, just like every NFL team every year. There is never such a thing as complete continuity when you have 53 players on the active roster. The Panthers' most important pieces remained in place—Newton and Kuechly—but the ground had shifted under the Panthers in many ways.

A Decent Start

The 2014 preseason was notable mostly for two things: rookie wide receiver Kelvin Benjamin looked like the real deal right away, and Newton got hurt. Already coming off a surgically repaired left ankle that had short-circuited some of his off-season work, he then suffered a hairline rib fracture in a preseason game against New England. That put his availability for the season opener in doubt. In the meantime, Carolina was trying its best to make the switch to a somewhat overmatched Byron Bell at left tackle. Rivera chose discretion over valor and made Newton miss his first NFL game in the opener versus Tampa Bay. Derek Anderson filled in ably, completing 24 of 34 passes, including touchdowns to Benjamin and Greg Olsen, and Carolina won 20–14.

Still, there were dismaying signs. The Panthers led 17–0 but then gave up two late touchdowns to a poor Tampa Bay team and barely held on. Carolina won again the next week, too, as Newton returned against Detroit.

From there, though, Carolina flopped. The Panthers defense, with its rebuilt secondary and without its best pass rusher, began to have all sorts of problems. Pittsburgh whipped the Panthers 37–19. Baltimore, with an angry Smith scoring twice and gaining 139 yards receiving against his old team, blood-and-gutted the Panthers 38–10. A Carolina victory over Chicago stemmed the bleeding for a while. Then came a 37–37 tie against Cincinnati—sealed only when kicker Mike Nugent missed from 36 yards on the final play of overtime. "I was sending a lot of bad voodoo that way," Panthers center Ryan Kalil said afterward of the last kick. "Just kind of calling the universe to say, 'Miss it. Miss it. Miss it.' And then the universe answered."

Carolina's record at that time stood at 3–2–1, which sounded like a countdown of some sort. And so it was—a countdown to what was about to become a horrible two months.

A Six-Game Losing Streak

Newton had a monster day against Cincinnati—with 107 yards rushing and 284 passing—but Carolina couldn't stop the Bengals offense. Cincinnati star wide receiver A.J. Green didn't play, but the Bengals still racked up 37 points and 513 yards. Bengals linebacker Vontaze Burfict illegally twisted the ankles of both Newton and Olsen that afternoon, although fortunately he didn't manage to hurt them worse.

What came later did hurt, though. The Panthers lost six games in a row—more than they had lost the entire 2013 season. And several of the losses were embarrassing. Green Bay led Carolina 21–0 before the first quarter ended in Lambeau Field in a game that should have had a mercy rule. Three weeks later, helped by Carolina turning the ball over on two of its first three offensive plays, the Philadelphia Eagles drilled the Panthers 45–21.

Everyone seemed to be throwing for 300 yards or more against Carolina—Andy Dalton, Joe Flacco, and Mark Sanchez all surpassed the mark. New Orleans beat the Panthers 28–10 in Charlotte. Even when Carolina played relatively well—as it did against Seattle—the Panthers lost 13–9. Nothing was working. Newton regressed. The loss to the defending Super Bowl champions occurred in part because on a third-and-7 from the Seattle 34, Newton scrambled left and then tried to fling the ball backhanded to Olsen. The resulting interception changed the game's momentum.

Against Atlanta, Riverboat Ron Rivera turned into "Reluctant Ron" when it mattered, playing for a field goal instead of going for a touchdown. Graham Gano promptly missed the 46-yard kick. The breakdowns came from everywhere, including special teams. On November 30, 2014, Carolina dropped to 3–8–1 with a 31–13 loss to Minnesota. The Vikings blocked two punts that day and returned them both for touchdowns—the first time in decades that an NFL team had done that. And the Panthers looked painfully slow, prompting Carolina to waive both cornerback Antoine Cason and backup linebacker Jason Williams two days later after both surrendered big plays. It was that Minnesota game that prompted Rivera to "go young" at several positions so that the team could get faster.

Entering the game at New Orleans on December 7, 2014, the Panthers hadn't won a game of any kind for two months. Six of their eight losses had been by 18 or more points. Somehow, they were still in the playoff race, because everybody else in the NFC South that season was below .500, too. But there was nothing to suggest that a huge turnaround was coming.

Something very good loomed around the bend, however. And something very bad, too. The Panthers were close to pulling themselves up by their own bootstraps. But Cam Newton was also a few days away from getting into a car wreck that could have killed him.

22

"SOMEBODY'S SUPPOSED TO BE DEAD"

ON DECEMBER 9, 2014, the Carolina Panthers finally had something to celebrate. After a no-win November had dropped them to 3-8-1, the Panthers went to New Orleans and did something completely unexpected. They blitzed the Saints 41-10. After nine minutes, New Orleans had run only three plays—turning the ball over on two of those—and Carolina was already up 17-0. Quarterback Cam Newton had been extraordinary, throwing for three TDs and running for a fourth as Carolina racked up 497 yards.

Two days later, Newton was headed toward Bank of America Stadium. Tuesdays are officially the players' day off during game weeks, but lots of NFL starting quarterbacks work on that day studying film. Newton has done so for years, and he was headed into the stadium about lunchtime to meet the teams' backup quarterbacks and watch some tape.

Only one block from the stadium, Newton was driving his 1998 Dodge Ram pickup at 35 mph, traveling south on South Church Street. On Newton's left, coming from West Hill Street at a 90-degree angle, was Nestor Pellot Jr. The 46-year-old man was driving a Buick sedan. Pellot was legally trying to drive across the street at the intersection of Church and West Hill—Charlotte's fourth-most dangerous intersection, according to traffic statistics.

Neither driver saw the other in time. Neither was ultimately judged at fault in the crash, either. Newton tried to swerve right to avoid the Buick when it appeared in front of him, but instead it "clipped the back of my truck," he would say later. Newton's truck skidded and overturned on the bridge over Interstate 277. If it had flipped onto the road below—which was definitely a possibility given the path the collision sent Newton's truck flying—things would have been far worse.

As it was, Newton's air bags deployed following the truck's flip. His windows shattered. Part of his roof caved in. Dazed, the quarterback climbed out of the truck's rear window. Pellot also was able to exit his own vehicle and was not seriously injured.

Bystanders, photographers, and reporters all arrived to the scene before paramedics. (The wreck occurred only about 50 yards from the main entrance to the *Charlotte Observer*.) *Observer* photographer Todd Sumlin snapped a picture that went viral, of Newton laying down in the street but smiling. This would be the photo Ron Rivera would later cite when he said, "When I saw that smile, when I saw those pearly whites, I knew it would be okay."

An ambulance took Newton to Carolinas Medical Center. Early reports were still sketchy, as social media went crazy trying to make sense of one of the most famous athletes in sports having a wreck on a sunny day at lunchtime. "I'm hearing that the car rolled four or five times and that he broke both his legs," fullback Mike Tolbert said, recalling the first reports on Twitter that he saw.

Rivera started getting messages about the crash, and at first thought they were a hoax. He quickly realized they were not. Cecil Newton, Cam's father, began receiving messages in Atlanta (where Cam grew up and where Cecil and his wife, Jackie, still live much of the time) that read, "Praying for Cam" or "Praying for your family." He had no idea what the messagers were about, but he knew it wasn't good.

Tests showed that Newton had two small fractures in his lower back. He wasn't cut. He wasn't bruised. He was extremely lucky. Pictures of his smashed truck sprinted from corner to corner of the

Internet, and Newton saw enough of them to know how fortunate he was.

Said Newton in a press conference two days after the accident, "I'm looking at this truck and I'm like, 'Somebody's supposed to be dead.'"

A Flashback to Phills

As soon as they heard the news about Newton's wreck, a number of longtime Charlotteans had a painful flashback to January 12, 2000. That was the day that Bobby Phills of the Charlotte Hornets accidentally killed himself driving a souped-up black Porsche after a team practice. Phills was going way too fast, speeding on his way to meet teammate and close friend David Wesley for a late breakfast at a local pancake house.

The Hornets would later retire Phills' number, and there were all sorts of tributes. But Phills didn't get to see his kids grow up, and his young wife became a widow, and there was a hole in the community that never quite got filled. It is difficult to even contemplate what would have happened to Charlotte if Newton had been killed in a wreck slightly less than 15 years later.

Newton's near-miss did have a few repercussions. At the hospital, some of the medication Newton received made him so dizzy that he had a hard time standing up straight. One of the most elusive and athletic quarterbacks in the NFL couldn't walk to the bathroom without help. Nurses gave him a yellow bracelet that read "Fall Risk" and placed it on his left wrist. More than a year later, Newton still wore that bracelet frequently as a reminder of the accident and how life should never be taken for granted.

"I don't wear it in a fashion sense," Newton said. "I wear it as a reminder that so many people worry about the things we talk about. The negatives, the, 'Oh my God, he's going to do this. Oh man, it's too hot outside. I'm going to get sunburnt.' Not just appreciating that the sun's out."

In the immediate aftermath of the wreck, Newton said he was smiling in the newspaper picture and for much of the time following the two-car collision because he couldn't believe he had dodged what could have been a season-ending—or even career-ending—injury.

"I'm on somebody's fantasy league, and I think it's the man upstairs," Newton said. "I really couldn't talk afterward because I was in such shock. I got myself out of the truck, and I couldn't stop smiling...because it's like God had his hands on me."

Newton's back injury wasn't serious enough to keep him away from the stadium, and three days after the accident he was back on the practice field wearing the customary, "can't hit the quarterback" red jersey. However, he wasn't throwing yet.

"As far as when I'm coming back, who cares?" Newton said. "That's not something that I'm worried about right now. I'm just thankful to have breath in my lungs."

Anderson Gets the Start

Rivera had made the decision shortly after Newton's wreck that backup quarterback Derek Anderson—who had already beaten Tampa Bay in the season opener when Newton's cracked ribs had kept him out—would start for the Panthers again versus the Buccaneers on Sunday.

Once teammates made certain Newton was okay, they started peppering him with good-natured insults about missing the Tampa Bay game for the second time in a row. "He was getting a lot of jabs that he was just really scared of Tampa," center Ryan Kalil said. "We said it was a little bit extreme to fake a car injury to get out of playing Tampa."

Anderson, though, was a solid backup. The quarterback teammates called D.A. wasn't nearly as athletic as Newton, but he threw the ball well and had once made the Pro Bowl himself as a Cleveland Brown. "Cam is a franchise, elite type of guy," Panthers tight end Greg Olsen said. "But D.A. could play in a lot of cities. A lot of teams would love to have him right now."

So Anderson readied the 4–8–1 Panthers for the Buccaneers. Carolina sat in third place in the NFC South, but Atlanta and New Orleans were only 5–8. If Anderson could get the Panthers a win versus Tampa Bay, it appeared likely Newton could come back in the following game—12 days after the wreck in Charlotte to face Cleveland. Tony Romo had once had the exact same injury in his back—two transverse process fractures—and had returned after missing one game.

As for the troublesome intersection, it got an upgrade—although not the stoplight Newton has campaigned for several times since. Engineers had the stop sign enlarged on West Hill. Reflective striping was added to the sign. Lines around the intersection were repainted. In 2015 there was only one angled crash at the intersection. It had been averaging 5.4 crashes per year. To Newton, who frequently drove and rode on the same road after the accident, the site provided a daily reminder of life's fragility.

"I'm just lucky to come out of there unscathed with just the little injury that I did have," Newton said. "Every time I see that flashback of looking at that truck, I'm surprised that nothing serious was done to me."

PART V

THE RECOVERY

Mid-December 2014 to January 2015

23

A DECEMBER TO REMEMBER

FOR 11 MONTHS, the Carolina Panthers had seemed to run over every nail on the road. They had lost a home playoff game to San Francisco. They had lost their star defensive end, Greg Hardy, to a domestic violence incident. They had nearly lost their quarterback permanently after a scary auto crash. They had lost every game they played in November. At one point, they had not won a game of any sort for 63 straight days.

Despite all of that, though, the Panthers had never fallen out of the playoff chase. They had picked a very good year to have a very mediocre year. The NFC South was going to be won by a team with a losing record—that was the thesis entering December, and it was the truth heading out of the month.

The NFC South had always been a curiously balanced division. Since its formation in 2002, its four members—Carolina, Atlanta, New Orleans, and Tampa Bay—had taken turns winning. Not a single team had repeated as NFC South champion. The Panthers wanted to change that. Amazingly, it was still possible.

Carolina had seemed almost dead before its dazzling 41–10 win at New Orleans on December 7, 2014. That total team effort was a precursor to a number of similar thumpings the Panthers would give opponents in 2015. At the time, though, it was an outlier—a shocker of a game in which Newton accounted for four TDs. With the offensive line finally solidified, running back Jonathan Stewart hit his stride again, rushing for 155 yards on 20 carries and taking one of them 69 yards for a TD.

Then Newton had his wreck, which meant Anderson would go against Tampa Bay for the second time that season. Anderson was just okay—the Panthers scored only one offensive TD and never had a gain of more than 21 yards—but it was enough. Anderson hadn't been able to go to sleep the night before the game, tossing and turning. Finally, watching a golf tournament in Australia did the trick.

Anderson got the Panthers into Tampa territory on all 11 possessions, and also tickled the home crowd by doing a Cam Newton salute after running for a first down in tribute to his buddy. Graham Gano sprinkled in four field goals. Greg Olsen (110 yards) and Kelvin Benjamin (104) both had 100-yard days. "People can make all the jokes they want," said Carolina wide receiver Jerricho Cotchery, who scored the Panthers' only touchdown. "We are playing meaningful football in December. Everyone's trying to make a mockery of our records in the division. But at the end of the day, we have an opportunity to make the playoffs. And we're excited about that."

Decimating "Johnny Football"

With Newton back in the saddle and Carolina 5–8–1, the Panthers next played Cleveland at home. The Browns have been in a quarterback quandary for most of the last 20 years, ever since Bernie Kosar finally hung up the cleats. Their latest attempt at finding one would prove to be one of their worst. After drafting Johnny "Football" Manziel out of Texas A&M in 2014 with the No. 22 overall pick, Manziel would be so unimpressive on the field and so unrepentantly problematic off of it that Cleveland would fire him outright after two seasons.

But at this point in his rookie year, Manziel was still considered a bit of a folk hero—albeit a somewhat tarnished one. His first NFL start had come the week before, and Cleveland had lost 30–0 to Cincinnati. The Browns decided to give Manziel another chance the next week in Charlotte, which meant there were a lot of Newton-Manziel headlines leading up to the game.

Manziel was a bust. By the second quarter, Manziel had completed only 3 of 8 passes for 32 yards when the Browns called a designed quarterback run of the sort the Panthers occasionally would let their own quarterback do. But Newton outweighed Manziel by close to 50 pounds, and on this play that was very apparent. The slightly built Manziel took big hits from Carolina safety Colin Jones and linebacker Luke Kuechly and fell down. He tried to get up, then fell again as his hamstring gave out. That was it for Manziel, who was replaced by Brian Hoyer.

This whole sequence drew some cheers from some fans in Panthers stadium—as well as some Browns fans who were totally cool with Manziel leaving the game for good. Newton would rip all the fans who cheered Manziel's injury the next day, calling the action "classless" and saying you should never "celebrate" a foe's injury.

"For the crowd to respond in that type of way—we're better than that," Newton said. "That's not who we are."

On a gray afternoon, Cleveland got better with Brian Hoyer at quarterback. The Panthers had major trouble generating points and only led 10–6 entering the fourth quarter. Still, Cleveland had generated little offense and the game seemed to be in hand with the Browns at their own 19—until Hoyer found tight end Jordan Cameron open by at least 10 yards. That 81-yard touchdown pass stunned the stadium and put Cleveland up 13–10 with 9:59 to go. Kuechly would later take responsibility for the blown coverage.

Newton then quickly directed the Panthers to the end zone, however, with the TD coming on a great adjustment and a nine-yard pass to Stewart (who also ran for 122 yards on the day). Carolina went up 17–13. There was one nervous moment left for Panthers fans, however, when Josh Norman made an acrobatic interception of a Hoyer pass, crisscrossed the field while running it back 33 yards and then got stripped of the ball while holding it carelessly. The Browns recovered, getting a fresh set of downs.

Said Norman afterward, "God and his angels allowed me to catch it, and the devils and the demons were allowed to steal my joy."

The Panthers never let the Browns inside the 40 again, however, even after Norman's rare two-turnover play. Carolina escaped with a 17–13 victory. That win, coupled with other results, meant the final game of the regular season—Carolina at Atlanta—would be for the NFC South title, the No. 4 NFC playoff seed and the home playoff game that went with that.

"Now it all comes down to one game," Rivera said. "That is all we can ask for—to be in that situation."

Defensive Domination in Georgia

On the final Sunday of the regular season, the Panthers and Falcons would battle inside the Georgia Dome. It would be the second straight season that the two teams had ended that way. In 2013 Carolina had barely escaped Atlanta, 21–20, to finish up 12–4 and win the NFC South.

Now the South was up for grabs again. At least 5,000 Panthers fans made the four-hour drive from the Charlotte area down Interstate 85 to give their team some support, but at the beginning they were drowned out by 66,000 Atlanta fans intent on yelling their team into the playoffs.

There are several Panthers players who are from Georgia and take every Atlanta game very personally. The three most prominent—Newton, defensive end Charles Johnson, and linebacker Thomas Davis—would all play a significant role in this game.

Carolina got the ball first, opening in the no-huddle attack that had become a favorite of Newton's because it allowed him more time to see the defense and go through his pre-snap adjustments. He zipped a pass on first down to Olsen for 18 yards, then threw another to his tight end on the very next play for nine more. Those would turn out to be Olsen's only two catches of the afternoon, but they were tone-setters. Carolina moved smartly down the field, stalled inside the 10 and got an early field goal.

After an Atlanta punt, Newton directed Carolina 87 yards on its next drive, this time ending it in a five-yard TD pass to backup tight end Ed Dickson. It was 10–0. Atlanta managed a field goal to make it 10–3, but then Carolina's defense took over the game completely.

Atlanta quarterback Matt Ryan—who has usually been a feast-or-famine player in his rivalry with Carolina—showed early that this would be one of his rocky days. On second-and-20 from his own 9 and under duress from Johnson, Ryan looked deep for Roddy White. He instead found Carolina safety Roman Harper, who grabbed the interception and returned it 31 yards for a TD. Not long after that, Davis had a 33-yard fumble return that set up Newton's four-yard run for a TD. By halftime, Carolina led 24–3. You could hear the roars of "L-u-u-u-uke" every time Kuechly made a tackle in the Georgia Dome, and chants of "Let's go, Panthers" were starting to be audible too.

"Join the Party!"

Any hopes of an Atlanta comeback would soon be thwarted. Ryan threw an apparent pick-six when Davis caught his pass in the third quarter and went 50 yards for a TD. That would have been the first TD for the player they call T.D. Alas, it was nullified by a penalty on Davis for illegal contact.

But on the very same drive, just five plays later, Carolina safety Tre Boston had the biggest moment of his young career. He latched onto his own interception at Carolina's 16 and weaved 84 yards for Carolina's second pick-six of the game. This time there was no flag. That TD made it 34–3 and sent a lot of Falcons fans streaming out of the Georgia Dome before the fourth quarter even began.

"The guys played out of their minds today," Panthers defensive end Charles Johnson said of his defensive teammates.

Norman proclaimed, "This defense is unbelievable. Did you see the way we were flying around? I'm on Cloud 25!"

So thorough was Carolina's defensive domination that Newton only had to throw 16 passes all afternoon, completing a modest 10 for 114 yards. There was no scoring in the fourth quarter, so it was still 34–3 with 2:41 to go. About the only fans remaining in the Georgia Dome were those same 5,000 Panthers supporters, all dressed in black or blue and yelling, "Let's go, Panthers!" Newton egged them on during a timeout, running around the field, repeatedly waving his arms up and down, asking for more noise.

In the locker room, the Panthers were in a joyous mood. They had had a December to remember, posting four straight wins to make the playoffs again. It was the first time in team history Carolina had earned its way to the postseason in back-to-back years. As media members entered the locker room to start interviewing players, Panthers fullback and unofficial team deejay Mike Tolbert turned up the music. Tolbert, also known unofficially as the team's best dancer, started swaying to the beat. "Come on in!" he yelled. "Join the party!"

Newton was late getting to that party. As the game ended, he was headed toward his teammates when cheers of "We want Cam! We want Cam!" pulled him back. The quarterback turned around and ran about half the length of the stadium, slapping hands with all the Panther supporters who had grabbed front-row seats that had been vacated by frustrated Atlanta fans. He even dismantled one barricade on his own so he could give a few more high-fives.

There were no "We want Jonathan!" chants at the end of the game, which was fine with Panthers tailback Stewart. He had never been much for the limelight. But Stewart's emergence as a true No. 1 running back in December had been an enormous part of Carolina's success. It would also impact both the team's decision-making in the 2015 off-season and its postseason.

24

JONATHAN STEWART— FINALLY FIRST

FOR ALMOST ALL of seven years, Jonathan Stewart played second fiddle to DeAngelo Williams. Stewart would understand this musical analogy. Besides being a brutally gifted running back, he is a gifted pianist who named one of his pianos "Beauty." Stewart doesn't much like the spotlight, but that doesn't stop him from tickling the ivories every summer at Wofford College in training camp at a piano set up in a common room. Rookies walk by every year, stunned at who is playing it so well.

As a running back, however, Stewart didn't escape the long shadow of Williams for years and really didn't want to. He was comfortable there. Williams had a two-year head start on Stewart—he was Carolina's first-round draft pick in 2006, while Stewart was the same thing in 2008. Williams was the gregarious one—the one who nicknamed the duo "Double Trouble," the one who treated Stewart like a little brother. The two bonded early in Stewart's career at a pro wrestling match—Williams was a big fan and suggested it—and stayed close after that.

In those first years, Stewart might have said one word for every 20 Williams uttered. Quarterback Jake Delhomme preferred a nickname of his own devising for the twosome, calling them "Penn and Teller." If you've never seen that act, the two are violently talented magicians with a rapid-fire patter. The patter is all generated by Penn, however. Part of the gag is that Teller never speaks.

An answer Stewart gave in a press conference once is instructive. When asked to describe his personality, he offered six words: "Consistent. I don't know. Just...chill."

Williams was the flashier player on the field, too. He was more prone to the occasional 40-yard burst than Stewart, whose yardage came mostly in punishing runs of under 10 yards. Williams always started the game, too, if both players were healthy. Stewart had briefly become the starter once, but seemed tentative in the role and more comfortable coming in the second or third series, off the bench.

At the end of 2014, however, the Panthers didn't have a choice. Although Stewart had developed an injury-prone reputation, this time it was Williams who was hurt. Stewart would need to be the team's bell cow, and he embraced the role. Stewart played the best he had since 2009—the glory year of the "Double Trouble" combo, when both running backs rushed for more than 1,100 yards.

Now Stewart started to pile up big runs and 100-yard games. He had 155 in the eye-opening win over New Orleans, followed by 75 against Tampa Bay, 122 versus Cleveland, and 49 against Atlanta as the Panthers made the playoffs. In the playoff games to come against Arizona and Seattle, his role would only increase.

Because Cam Newton also functioned as a very good running back, the Panthers had an overcrowded backfield that included Newton, Stewart, Williams, and fullback Mike Tolbert, as well as backup running back Fozzy Whittaker. In some years, like 2012, the Panthers devoted more money to the running back position than any other team in the NFL. Something had to give, and in early 2015 the team decided it would be okay to part ways with Williams. The Panthers wouldn't have done that if they weren't so confident in Stewart, who would make his first Pro Bowl after the 2015 season.

"He's very difficult to tackle," Seattle coach Pete Carroll said of Stewart. "He's very explosive in contact and he's got good speed to get away from you and make big plays."

All of Me

Stewart grew up on the other side of the country from Charlotte, raised by a single mother in Lacey, Washington, about an hour's drive from Seattle. He attributes his deep faith in God and his humble nature to his mother, Lora Faison, and older brother Cory, who served with the U.S. Army in Afghanistan.

The most highly touted running back in the country as a senior, Stewart stayed in the Pacific Northwest for college. He went to Oregon, had a fine career there, and was drafted by the Panthers in 2008. Coach John Fox already had Williams, but he had long advocated a two-back system because of the punishment endured by NFL backs.

Stewart was a bruising runner who, at 5'10" and 235 pounds, was about as much fun to tackle as a cactus. He made a quick impact, rushing for 836 yards his first season and 1,133 his second season, in 2009, despite starting only three of 32 games. But knee and ankle injuries began to creep up on him, and he didn't have a yardage total that big again until 2015.

In one stretch, from 2012 to 2014, Stewart missed 20 of a possible 48 games due to various leg problems. Like Cam Newton's press conference every Wednesday and hot dogs at halftime on home-game Sundays, media members who covered the Panthers could count on at least one trip per week to Stewart's locker to ask him how he was feeling and if his latest injury would allow him to play that week.

But the narrative changed for Stewart in late 2014, and that new storyline continued in 2015. In the off-season, Stewart learned to play the ballad "All of Me" by John Legend. If you are familiar at all with the song, Legend wrote it for the woman who would become his wife. It has a line about "perfect imperfections"—and, applied to Stewart, those would have to be his injuries. But, when he was healthy, as he was at the end of the 2014 season and for almost all of 2015, the Panthers always got all of Stewart.

25

THOMAS DAVIS— GOOD GUY, BAD INTENTIONS

EVERYONE IN THE Panthers locker room was looking forward to the team's home playoff game against Arizona on January 3, 2015. It was fair to say, though, that no one wanted to win it more than linebacker Thomas Davis.

Davis was the longest-tenured Panther and often referred to by teammates as Carolina's heartbeat. Beloved in the same sort of way that the late Sam Mills was when he was a Panther, Davis was the first NFL player to endure three anterior cruciate ligament tears on the same knee and returned to play. By the time of the Arizona playoff game, Davis had played for three full seasons on that thrice-repaired knee. Panthers quarterback Cam Newton said Davis had an "aura" surrounding him because of all he had been through and jokingly would nickname Davis "Charlotte's Sweetheart" because of his sterling reputation.

Just before the Arizona playoff game kicked off, it would be up to Davis to look around the locker room and figure out what his team needed. That was one of Davis's many roles on the team— the captain was always the last Panther to give a pregame speech. He never prepared them in advance, preferring to let them happen organically. The speeches got so popular that some teammates also called him "Pastor Davis" because of the eloquent, emotional way in which he spoke.

"There's always a message that needs to be delivered," Davis said, "and I try to deliver it. I don't plan ahead. It's more passionate if you don't. You wait for the feeling. You wait for the moment to arrive. And then you give the team what it needs."

Davis was the only remaining Panther who actually knew what winning a playoff game in a Carolina uniform felt like. He had been a quiet rookie out of the University of Georgia on the 2005 Panthers squad that had won two straight playoff games in early 2006 before losing in the NFC Championship Game at Seattle. Davis had mostly played safety back then, when his right knee was unscarred. Now it was nine years later, and Carolina had not won a playoff game since. Their last two home playoff games had ended poorly—a 20-point loss to Arizona following the 2008 season and a 13-point defeat at the hands of San Francisco the year before. Davis had no desire to retire, but a great desire to stem the tide of mediocrity that had swallowed the Panthers for much of his decade-long career.

"I've been here half the organization's existence—10 out of the Panthers' 20 years," Davis told me days before the Arizona game. "And we've never won a Super Bowl. I've never even won a playoff game after that rookie year. I need more time to do all the things I want to accomplish."

The NFL's "Baddest Special Teams Player"

The Panthers' first-round draft pick in 2005, Davis came into the NFL as a superior athlete who did not have a definite position. I remember his first-ever press conference as a Panther when he was asked about his tackling philosophy. He replied with seven words: "Get to the ball with bad intentions."

While the Panthers weren't sure whether Davis would ultimately be a linebacker or a safety, they knew he did have one job he was drafted to do.

"When he came in as a rookie we loved watching him," said Jake Delhomme, who was the Panthers' quarterback in 2005 and a teammate of Davis's for the linebacker's first five seasons. "He was so young and raw and fast. People forget he was drafted for one reason—to stop Michael Vick."

Vick was Cam Newton back then—a dual run-pass threat who could dominate a game on the right day. Davis was one of the few players fast enough to run alongside Vick before the quarterback's career short-circuited due to injuries and his infamous off-field troubles involving dog fights. With Davis serving as Vick's personal on-field "spy," Carolina started to close the gap on its closest NFC South rival.

This was all before Davis had any knee problems, and the Panthers looked for ways to exploit his speed. They would even place him outside in punt formation as a gunner, letting him run down the field to try and get to the other team's punt returner. "He was the baddest special teams player in the NFL his rookie year," Delhomme said. "He literally just beat up people physically like you wouldn't believe as our gunner."

Davis's rookie year was notable for another reason, too. It was then that he met his future wife, Kelly. The two of them now have a blended family that includes four children.

A superstitious sort, Davis won't step on the three giant Panthers logos that are embedded into Carolina's locker room carpet. "And he always wants me to take all four children to the game," Kelly Davis said, "because we usually seem to win when I do that."

The Walter Payton Award

In 2007 the Davises established what has become one of the most reputable charitable foundations attached to an athlete in the Carolinas. It was called the "Thomas Davis Defending Dreams Foundation," a nonprofit organization set up to serve underprivileged children with an emphasis on students in middle school. Since its inception, it has distributed more than $500,000 worth of aid—most of it in the Charlotte area but also some in Davis's homestate of Georgia.

Davis won the NFL's Walter Payton Man of the Year award in 2015. The award, one of the league's most prestigious, goes to a single NFL player every year and is based on community service as well as on-field excellence. When Davis was announced as the Panthers' nominee, owner Jerry Richardson issued a statement that read in part, "I have had the pleasure of watching Thomas Davis grow into the confident, mature, caring man he is today. No one takes his position of influence more seriously than Thomas on the field or in the community."

Raised by a single mother in Shellman, Georgia, Davis understands well the idea of poverty and the plight of the children his foundation helps.

"I had at least two Christmases where I didn't get a single gift," Davis told me once. "I didn't understand it. All you think as a kid is that I wasn't good enough this year, so Santa didn't bring me a gift. You try to figure out what you need to do better next year.... So we are trying to keep that from happening to other kids as much as we can."

The head of the foundation is Kelly Davis, who runs it as a volunteer. "Because of that, every single cent that goes into the fund goes back to the kids," Thomas Davis said. "We get such joy from doing it. It doesn't feel like work."

"Thomas Even Gets Me Excited"

The Panthers figured out pretty quickly that Davis was a little slow for a safety but extremely fast for a linebacker, and he settled into that position early in his career. He was a fine player for the Panthers in the late 2000s. His speaking ability? It needed some work.

"I used to count the 'umms' Thomas would say when he spoke," Kelly Davis, his wife, once told me. "I'd say, 'Hey, you had 17 umms in that interview.' And now I don't have to do that anymore because it just comes to him so naturally."

In the pregame team huddles, head coach Ron Rivera said, "Thomas even gets me excited."

Rivera didn't get to Carolina until 2011, and by then Davis was considered damaged goods. He missed 39 of a possible 48 games from 2009 to 2011—a terrible series of "Groundhog Days" in which Davis would tear the ACL in his right knee, rehab it, finally get back onto the football field, and then tear it again.

There was a lot of angst surrounding Davis's comeback in 2012, but this time the knee held up. Three ACLs. Three strikes. And somehow Davis was still not out. "A straight warrior," Newton called him. Davis played in 15 of 16 games and played well. Rivera always was touched by Davis's long battle with his knee—Davis had thought hard about retiring after the third ACL tear, but decided to give it one more try. In 2012 Rivera got so choked up during a postgame news conference describing Davis's contributions to the team that the coach had to abruptly leave the podium.

"Thomas has a tremendous amount of pride in who we are," Rivera said that week, "and he gets that across to a lot of his teammates. His best characteristic as a player is actually his loyalty—how much he loves the organization and his teammates."

As the years between the surgeries had lengthened, Davis had seemed to become an even better player. His veteran craftiness had been there for a while, but now his speed had fully returned.

"The best way I can say it," safety Roman Harper said, "is that Thomas Davis is a work of art. And people around him need to appreciate him. Because like all of us, he's not going to play forever."

"We'll Be Ready"

Kuechly would freely admit to anyone who asked that Davis, in a pure foot race, was faster than he was. He first noticed it during

Jonathan Stewart (28) jumps for joy in pregame introductions before the Panthers' home playoff game against Seattle in January 2016.
Photo by David T. Foster III

Jerry Richardson (sitting), the Panthers owner and founder, shares a laugh with head coach Ron Rivera. Both men once played in the NFL.
Photo by Jeff Siner

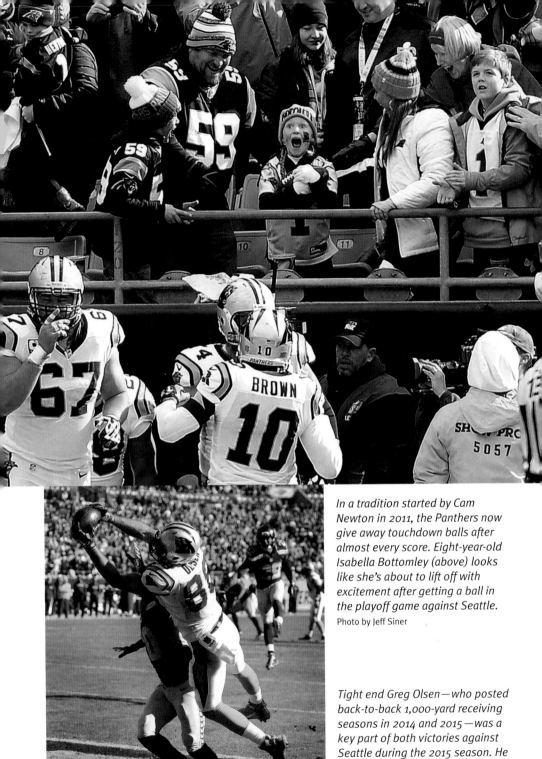

In a tradition started by Cam Newton in 2011, the Panthers now give away touchdown balls after almost every score. Eight-year-old Isabella Bottomley (above) looks like she's about to lift off with excitement after getting a ball in the playoff game against Seattle. Photo by Jeff Siner

Tight end Greg Olsen—who posted back-to-back 1,000-yard receiving seasons in 2014 and 2015—was a key part of both victories against Seattle during the 2015 season. He made one of the best TD catches of his career against the Seahawks in the playoffs, as Carolina sped to a 31–0 halftime lead. Photo by Jeff Siner

Luke Kuechly (59), after picking off Seattle QB Russell Wilson, takes it back for a touchdown in the playoff game against Seattle as Carolina jumped out to an early lead. Kuechly ended up taking two interceptions back for TDs in the playoffs, scoring against Arizona as well.
Photo by David T. Foster III

After Seattle scored 24 straight second-half points to cut Carolina's lead to 31–24, linebacker Thomas Davis (58) skies high to recover an onside kick late in the fourth quarter to secure the game. Davis was submarined on the play after making the catch but held on.
Photo by Jeff Siner

Panthers tight end Greg Olsen celebrates after Carolina's playoff win against Seattle.
Photo by Jeff Siner

Thomas Davis (58) and Luke Kuechly (59) combine on this tackle of Arizona tight end Darren Fells in the NFC Championship Game. Davis broke his forearm on this play but had it wrapped up and played with the injury during Super Bowl 50.
Photo by David T. Foster III

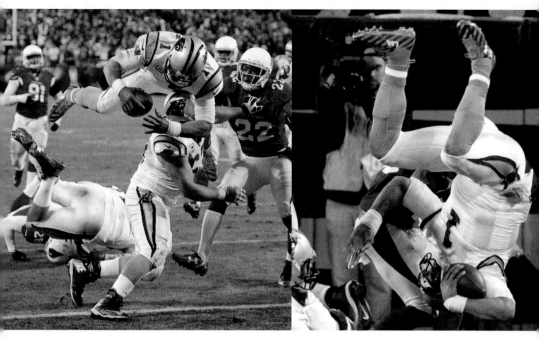

Cam Newton flips into the end zone (above) for a touchdown against Arizona in the NFC Championship Game in January 2016 and then celebrates with a dab (below). The Panthers destroyed the Cardinals 49–15 in the first NFC title game ever held in Charlotte. Above left photo by Jeff Siner; above right photo by David T. Foster III; bottom photo by Jeff Siner.

Jonathan Stewart (28, above) runs through a hole against Arizona. Carolina ran for at least 100 yards as a team in every game in 2015. The Panthers' six team captains of 2015 enjoy a picture with the Halas Trophy (below) after winning the NFC title. From left to right: Luke Kuechly, Charles Johnson, Greg Olsen, Thomas Davis, Cam Newton, and Ryan Kalil (who is mostly hidden by Newton). Photos by David T. Foster III

When the Panthers arrived in California for Super Bowl 50, spirits were high. Cam Newton photo-bombed a picture that included Greg Olsen (in toboggan) and Luke Kuechly (far right) as Josh Norman (far left, in orange pants) looked on. Photo by David T. Foster III

Carolina's most famous fan, two-time NBA MVP Stephen Curry, grew up in Charlotte. Prior to Super Bowl 50, he bangs the "Keep Pounding" drum, inspired by the iconic speech by the late Sam Mills.
Photo by Jeff Siner

Just before the start of Super Bowl 50 in Santa Clara, California, the Carolina Panthers line up for the national anthem. From left to right, Thomas Davis, Ted Ginn Jr., Cam Newton, and Ron Rivera stand at attention. Photo by Jeff Siner his rookie year, in 2012. "In a game against the New York Jets, he blitzed and sacked the quarterback," Kuechly said. "There was this burst I hadn't seen before. Everyone had said how fast he was, but he hadn't cut it loose yet. Then he did, and I saw what everyone was talking about."

Quickly, the two realized they were usually going to go one-two in tackles—they had the twin advantages of speed, a good defensive line, and great instincts. It was just a matter of who was first and who was second. "It's a competition to the ball," Kuechly said of Davis. "That has helped us both out."

Said Davis, "We're at different stages in life. I've been around here a lot longer. But it has been really big for me to have a younger guy come in, be energetic, and really push me to be the best I can possibly be. I use Luke's energy. He wins the tackle competition most of the time, but it makes us both better. And there are times I'm able to walk away with a victory, and I let him hear about it."

Kuechly has received far more national recognition. Davis didn't make the Pro Bowl until the 2015 season, an injustice his teammates had long railed against. Inside the Panthers organization, the contributions of No. 58 and No. 59 were considered roughly equal. The two had very different styles of playing, though. Said Panthers safety Kurt Coleman, "Luke is a little more reserved, although he's very fiery on the field. T.D. is raw emotion."

Said Rivera, "Luke has tremendous talent, but he also diagnoses plays very quickly. He relies on what he's learned and what he takes from all the meetings and the film study. T.D.? He's a natural 'feel' player. He plays off of true instinct."

By the time of the Arizona playoff game in early 2015, Davis was 31. Every year now, he was being asked how much longer he wanted to keep playing. He usually answered the question something like this: "Until my body tells me I can't play any more. And it ain't talking to me. So I'm going to keep going."

He was certainly going to keep going for the Arizona playoff game. Davis had his pregame speech lined up and was set on avoiding another home playoff loss. "The moment is almost here," Davis said. "I've been waiting a long time. And we'll be ready."

26

FIERY DEFENSE, SMOKY ENDING

ONCE LEFT FOR dead at 3–8–1, the Carolina Panthers instead were in the playoffs for the second year in a row. And the first 10 days of January would provide all sorts of drama—a record-setting playoff win, a disappointing playoff loss, and a scary fire that took 56 fire-fighters to control at the home of coach Ron Rivera.

It began with the Arizona game. As linebacker Thomas Davis promised, the Panthers were indeed ready. So were Carolina's fans, despite an all-day drizzle that saturated them on January 3, 2015. The game was soggy, but the Panthers defense was sensational. In a 27–16 victory, Carolina allowed Arizona's offense a paltry 78 yards—the fewest yards ever gained in more than 80 years of NFL playoff games.

It helped that Arizona's quarterback was Ryan Lindley, who looked exactly like the overwhelmed third-stringer he was. The Panthers intercepted Lindley twice, sacked him four times, and harassed him constantly. Unlike the following year, when Carolina would have to play Arizona in the NFC Championship Game with a healthy Carson Palmer at quarterback, this Cardinals team had been decimated at the game's most important position. Palmer was hurt, and then his backup Drew Stanton got hurt, and then Lindley had to play. Once 9–1, the Cardinals had limped to a 2–4 finish, and then had to travel to Carolina to face a Panthers team that was only 7–8–1 but had started to get healthy and good at the right time.

The game really shouldn't have been as close as it was, given that each time Arizona made a first down it seemed like a miracle.

Carolina's defense was extremely dominant, with Luke Kuechly and Davis flying all over the place. "Kuechly and Davis, those two hellacious players, they make plays all day for them," Arizona wide receiver Larry Fitzgerald said.

The Panthers struggled for some time to put Arizona away, however, because the Cardinals defense was also good, and the Panthers made some mistakes of their own. Arizona's two TD drives went for 30 and 17 yards—one after Brenton Bersin muffed a punt and another after Cam Newton threw an interception that was returned 50 yards. The Panthers actually were trailing 14–13 in the third quarter when Fozzy Whittaker made the best play of his young Carolina career, bouncing off four tacklers in the rain and taking a Newton screen pass 39 yards for a TD. That gave Carolina a 20–14 lead.

The Ted Ginn Effect

One theme that has been oddly constant throughout Carolina's rise has been Ted Ginn, the speedy wide receiver/kick returner who helps Carolina out every year. In the 2013 and 2015 seasons, it was with his big plays as a receiver. In 2014, however, Ginn was with Arizona. He had left the Panthers for more money with the Cardinals, but then had seen his role with the Cardinals receiving corps diminish to practically zero due to the emergence of John Brown. The Cardinals were only using him as a returner, and in that role he caught a kickoff in the third quarter with Arizona down by six points.

Certainly, it was by mistake, but Ginn helped the Panthers again. Hit on the kickoff by Melvin White, Ginn fumbled and Carolina recovered at the Arizona 3. Newton soon threw a one-yard TD pass to Mike Tolbert to put the Panthers up 27–14. A Kuechly red-zone interception sealed things. Arizona made its total-yardage statistic look worse by losing 23 yards on a desperate five-lateral sequence on the game's last play.

Rivera knew his history, and he sent the players back onto the field to celebrate with the fans after the victory just like the 1996 and 2003 teams had done after home playoff wins. This was only the third home playoff win the team had had in 20 seasons, so it made sense to savor the moment. "All the fans wanted was a lot of selfies and high fives," Panthers safety Roman Harper said. "And sometimes you have to give the people what they want."

The Panthers had outgained the Cardinals by an astonishing 386–78. Defensive end Charles Johnson was a disruptive force all day, and Jonathan Stewart had continued his hot streak with 123 rushing yards and a touchdown. Referee Ed Hochuli had provided a little entertainment, too, inadvertently leaving on his on-field microphone and twice referring to an instant-replay official as "Jungle Boy."

Fire at the Coach's House

About 36 hours later, Rivera's roller-coaster weekend would speed downhill. Two of his brothers and their wives were visiting, staying at the house the coach shares with his wife, Stephanie. They were watching more of the NFL playoffs on Sunday and using a first-floor gas fireplace while doing so. Rivera, a bit of a safety freak at home, made sure he was the one who turned off the fireplace before everyone went to bed.

About 4:00 AM Monday, Stephanie Rivera awoke and gasped. That gasp woke her husband, too. They both smelled smoke in the house. The coach grabbed a fire extinguisher and started running through the house, searching for the source. But he couldn't find it. Meanwhile, people were waking up and 911 was being called (thanks to the installed security system). The Riveras, their guests, and their dogs all grabbed coats and blankets and went out into the cold January morning while firefighters—ultimately there were 56 of them in all—started to pour into the south Charlotte neighborhood.

Fire investigators would later determine that the fire was due to the gas fireplace being installed incorrectly, without a baseplate. The fire had then crept through the inside walls of the house. No one was hurt, and much of the Riveras' memorabilia was recovered, but the blaze caused about $500,000 in damage. The Riveras would temporarily move into Panthers offensive tackle Jordan Gross's old house for about six months while their own house was being repaired.

On that Monday, though, Rivera knew that once he got his family settled he needed to go into Bank of America Stadium. The Panthers were about to have to travel to Seattle to play another playoff game. Rivera was hours late on Monday, and when he drove toward the stadium he started thinking about the old holiday movie *It's a Wonderful Life.*

"When things get a little bit hairy, a little bit tough, all of a sudden you realize the friends that you have," Rivera said. "You see things through a different set of eyes now."

Rivera used his first news conference after the blaze to repeatedly praise the firefighters and their teamwork, and to advocate home safety. "If you don't have an alarm system, folks, at least make sure you have smoke detectors," he said.

It was not your typical pre-playoff news conference. Less than a month after Cam Newton's car wreck and during a season where Greg Hardy's absence had hovered over the team, here was another case of real life weaving its way into the Panthers' world. Rivera had already called the season the strangest of his NFL career—and that had been before the fire. "I tell you, it has been different," the coach said. "You can't make this stuff up."

Season Ends in Seattle

As Stephanie Rivera took care of the insurance calls and everything else that had to be done after the fire, Ron Rivera and his staff hurriedly prepared for Seattle. The Seahawks had won the Super Bowl the year before, destroying Denver, and Seattle was the No. 1 seed in the NFC and favored to make it there again. Carolina had played Seattle pretty well in the regular season, losing 13–9 in Charlotte, but had not been able to get over the hump against the Seahawks. For three consecutive years, quarterback Russell Wilson had found a way to beat the Panthers in tight games in the fourth quarter.

This fourth meeting in three years would be very difficult for Carolina, with the game in Seattle's notoriously loud home stadium. If I saw one fan walking around in a No. 3 Wilson jersey drinking a Starbucks coffee in the hours before this Saturday night game, I saw a thousand. But the Panthers believed they matched up decently against the Seahawks. And until the fourth quarter, that was a correct assessment.

Wilson took advantage of both rookies in Carolina's defensive backfield, burning Tre Boston for a 16-yard TD and then Bene Benwikere for a 63-yarder in the first half. But Carolina hung in there—those TDs sandwiched a sweet Newton throw to Kelvin Benjamin on a slant. A Graham Gano field goal on the last play of the second quarter made the score 14–10 Seattle at halftime, as Carolina maintained a good striking distance.

The Seahawks had a little more talent than Carolina at this point in the two teams' history. It would be different a year later, but in this game Carolina would have needed a break or two to pull the big upset in the Seahawks' home. And they had a couple of chances. On the second play of the third quarter, Carolina's Wes Horton knocked the ball out of Marshawn Lynch's hands on a running play. A recovery would have given the Panthers the ball at Seattle's 23. Instead, Wilson jumped on the ball.

The third quarter ended scoreless, but Seattle got a field goal early in the fourth. Down 17–10, the Panthers had a third-and-11 on their own 19 when Newton came off his first read and checked the ball down to Tolbert. The fullback had room enough to make the first down, and the ball hit him in stride, but he dropped it.

The Panthers had to punt, and less than three minutes later Seattle scored when Russell Wilson found tight end Luke Willson for a 25-yard TD pass. That made it 24–10, and Carolina was almost done. The final coffin nail would soon be hammered in by Seattle safety Kam Chancellor. With the Panthers driving and facing a second-and-4 at the Seattle 13, Bersin fell down on a route where Newton was looking for him. Newton swung his head back the other way toward backup tight end Ed Dickson, but by this time it was too late. Newton threw the ball anyway. Chancellor stepped in front of it and ran 90 yards for a TD as the Seahawks' stadium reverberated with sound. That gave Seattle an insurmountable 31–10 lead.

Newton connected late with Benjamin for another TD to make the final score a more respectable 31–17. Seattle ended the game with Wilson kneeling down with the ball inside Carolina's 20, clearly the best player on the field on this day. He had thrown for 268 yards and three touchdowns and led a Seahawks offense that didn't commit a single turnover. "Impeccable!" gushed Seattle coach Pete Carroll.

Newton didn't get enough help, but he also made three turnovers (two interceptions and one botched handoff) in a game Carolina would have needed to play almost perfectly to win. "I'm very proud of this team," Rivera said outside Carolina's locker room.

For the second straight year, the Panthers had made it to the NFL's final eight teams, only to lose in the divisional round of the playoffs. Seattle remained a huge obstacle. Newton, for all his wondrous plays, had yet to reach his ceiling. The Panthers needed to fix left tackle—Byron Bell had been overmatched too many times during the season—and learn how to score some more points. They needed to cause more turnovers.

In the 2015 season, all of that would happen. And then some.

PART VI

THE RISE

The 2015 Season

27

THE WORLD ACCORDING
TO JOSH NORMAN

JOSH NORMAN WAS a football-playing Forrest Gump for the Panthers during the 2015 season—which would turn out to be his fourth and last in a Carolina uniform. The talkative, talented cornerback always seemed to be in the middle of big moments. He had a brief but heavily publicized fight with Cam Newton in training camp—a fight Norman talked about in his hour-long interview for this book in far more detail than he ever had before.

The player teammates call "J-No" also had four interceptions in the Panthers' first four games in 2015, including a game-preserving interception versus New Orleans and two pick-sixes. He goaded the New York Giants' Odell Beckham into losing his composure in December. He heatedly debated NBC Sports analyst Rodney Harrison. He made his first Pro Bowl and played in his first Super Bowl. After the Super Bowl, he got franchise-tagged by the Panthers; didn't sign the one-year, $13.95 million offer that came with it as a negotiating tactic; had the offer rescinded by Carolina in a shocking move; and only 48 hours later, signed a five-year contract with the Washington Redskins that could be worth up to $75 million.

All that action came from the Panthers' fifth-round draft pick of 2012, a lightly recruited player who grew up in Greenwood, South Carolina, and who spent a year out of football between high school and college. The Panthers were once so unsure about Norman's future with the team that, in 2013, after he allowed the winning touchdown in a road loss to Buffalo, he found himself in coach Ron Rivera's doghouse and almost never got out. But once he did, Norman became the best playmaking cornerback the Panthers have ever employed with two always sturdy and occasionally spectacular years in 2014 and 2015.

Although Norman is gone from the team now, his ascent was a key part of Carolina's rise, and is worth exploring in depth. Norman's original path to the Panthers can best be understood in context, starting with a young man in Greenwood who couldn't get a Division I scholarship anywhere coming out of high school. Courtesy of an exclusive interview with Norman, let's take a trip inside his mind.

"I Had the Couch"

Many Panthers fans wondered for years why Norman turned 25 during his rookie season for the Panthers in 2012, which made him two or three years older than the average NFL player beginning his career. Let him explain.

"I started school late," Norman said. "My birthday is in December [December 15, 1987]. My mom thought back in the day I needed to be one of the older ones in class, not one of the younger ones. And then she held me back again, so I did kindergarten twice. I was like, 'What is going on? I'm back in the same room, and now all my buddies are a year ahead of me.' But she thought that was best."

Norman would then lose another year after he graduated from Greenwood High, where he was a standout two-way player on a team that won a state championship his senior year. He had received some interest from the University of Georgia, he said, and that's where he wanted to go to school on a scholarship. But then he didn't get a high enough test score on the SAT the first time he took it to qualify for admission, Norman said.

"I flunked the SAT," Norman said. "Then I took it again and I passed it. I got ready to get all the information to the guy who was recruiting me at the time and he said, 'You know, we took someone else.' I didn't know, but they took somebody else because they didn't think I was going to make the grade. All these Division II schools were looking at me, but I didn't want to go there, I didn't feel like that was my path. So I sat out."

Norman had an older brother named Marrio Norman who was on scholarship and playing college football at Coastal Carolina in Conway, South Carolina, which is close to the resort town of Myrtle Beach. Worried that he might get in the wrong crowd in Greenville, Josh followed Marrio down to Coastal Carolina but did not play or enroll in school. He instead lived with his brother and two other friends in a three-bedroom apartment. "I had the couch," Norman said. He took classes at a local community college called Horry Georgetown Tech and also worked with at-risk kids at a psychiatric facility for adolescents as what he described as a "glorified guidance counselor."

"I was called a mental health technician," Norman said. "I would take them outside, to recess or to lunch, and if they got out of line, I had a piece of paper and a pad and I had to write them up. I tried to keep them in line."

After a year of community college, working and training on his own—Norman frequently ran sprints around Coastal Carolina while his brother was practicing—Norman was able to enroll at Coastal Carolina as a "preferred walk-on."

"So really, since I missed that year in between high school and college, you could say I was held back three years," Norman said.

From there, the gregarious cornerback became a starter as a freshman, grabbed eight interceptions as a sophomore, earned a scholarship, and eventually turned into one of the Chanticleers' best players ever, staying at the school through his senior season in

2011. He originally was going to major in theater—makes sense, right?—before realizing the time commitment involved.

There was an NCAA investigation into his eligibility before his senior year, Norman said, because there was a question about whether he had gotten some personal training benefits for free. Norman said he had paid for the training and that he was cleared, but the probe took several months. "It was all very hush-hush," Norman said. "Don't nobody know about that."

Norman's long arms, live-wire personality, quickness, and utter confidence impressed the Panthers. Defensive backs coach Steve Wilks called Norman on the phone a couple of picks before Carolina chose him at No. 143 overall in 2012. Norman was the 15th cornerback taken overall in that draft, having dropped some due to an official time of 4.66 in the 40-yard dash at the NFL scouting combine.

"Coach Wilks said, 'Congratulations,'" Norman remembered. "And I said, 'What took you so long?' I really did. Then I said, 'Okay, thanks, but somebody dropped the ball somewhere. And I'm going to make somebody pay.'"

From Rookie Starter to the Bench

Norman looks fondly back on the player he was for the Panthers in 2012—raw and unsophisticated, but with talent oozing from everywhere.

"I really wish I could go back sometimes to that player," Norman said. "Then it was just like: 'You don't know what you don't know.' I was trying to do everything the coach asked me to do. I had never played in a system where I was eight yards off somebody. I was used to freedom. I thought they had gotten me to be that lockdown guy, to take away a No. 1 [receiver], I mean off the face of the earth."

The Panthers, though, ran a more structured system. Norman was often asked to cover a certain zone on the field, and he struggled with a shift from left corner to right corner for a while. Still, he won a starting job, in part due to one extraordinary practice in which he had five interceptions. Norman did not set the world on fire but he played well enough for that 7–9 Carolina team and started 12 games.

The next season, though, would be different. While Carolina went 12–4 and made the playoffs, Norman was inactive for nine of the Panthers' last 13 games and still isn't happy about it. "That was the most trying time of my NFL career," Norman said. "It was freakin' bananas." His demotion followed the two-yard, game-winning TD pass he allowed against Buffalo on a missed assignment in the Carolina loss that indirectly sparked the birth of "Riverboat Ron" Rivera.

What people don't know about that game, both Norman and Rivera said, was that Norman was playing hurt throughout the fourth quarter. The Panthers had suffered a slew of injuries in the defensive backfield, and then Norman had gotten blasted on the thigh during the game.

"He had taken a pretty good shot in the leg," Rivera said. "He came to the sideline and wasn't sure he was going to play. I challenged him, and he went back out there and played."

Norman said on the sideline there was even some discussion as to whether to issue a battlefield promotion to backup running back Armond Smith and make him a cornerback because the Panthers' numbers were so depleted at the position.

"I was unable to run well, so I didn't think I was going to come back in the game in the first place," Norman said. "But we had nobody else. So I had to suck it up. I remember taking painkillers on the sideline. And I put everything I had out on the line. And then the communication between me and the other defensive back—he called 'Switch,' but I was locked in. I was trying not to let my man get inside on me, because I couldn't run. I didn't switch. EJ Manuel saw his receiver, and it was a touchdown. Everybody looked at me....What were they trying to say? That I lost the game? Obviously I didn't lose the game [by myself], but they put it on me, and I never saw the light of day."

For weeks, Norman brooded during and after Panthers practices.

"I always just worked out on the practice field, helping the other guys," Norman said. "I remember crying out there, and making picks and just throwing the ball down. I was a very, very disruptive force. I came to work *pissed*....I knew what happened. I had learned from what happened and I was ready to go out there. But they didn't trust me enough to put me out there....I was really ready to book it, to be honest with you. I was. That totally pissed me off to the point where I haven't forgotten about that. Everybody else may have, but I haven't."

For his part, Rivera said in our interview for this book that he believed Norman had lost his confidence after the Buffalo mistake and that it took him a while to get his groove back.

Said Rivera, "Josh and I have had some great conversations, and one of them was that....That Buffalo game broke him down. It stripped him down to the bare minimum, and then [he was] trying to build himself back up. I think that really did set him back."

Norman Emerges as Shutdown Corner

In early 2014, Norman still wasn't totally trusted by the Panthers. Carolina hired veteran cornerback Antoine Cason and started him in front of Norman along with Melvin White. Norman played in the first three games, but did not start. "They brought in Cason," Norman said. "Oh my gosh. First it was Drayton [Florence, another veteran cornerback the Panthers employed in 2013] and then Cason. I was like, 'Why are they bringing these guys onto this team?' The answers are here. But with God's help, I'll get there."

Then, in Week 4, Steve Smith torched his old team for 122 yards and two touchdowns in the first half during a blowout Baltimore win. "It was ridiculous," Norman said. "And in that second half,

I remember the coaches coming and saying, 'Josh, go in and you do not come back out. Get 89!' So I went in and I followed that son of a gun wherever he went. And that is what I was brought to Carolina to do, man—take out their best man. That's my specialty. And ever since that day, man? I've never freakin' looked back." For every game in which Norman was healthy for the next two seasons, he would always start. He made waves by shutting down Atlanta star wide receiver Julio Jones twice late in the 2014 season, and by then Norman's rambunctious personality was in full flower.

Said Rivera, "He got that crazy haircut that looked like a tread mark on the top of his head, and you could see the personality come back. It was kind of the rebirth of who Josh is, and that was very pleasing to see."

Rivera still remembers Norman's incredibly athletic interception against Cleveland. During the runback, he ended up losing the ball on his own fumble, but the interception itself was a play few NFL cornerbacks could have made.

Inside the Fight

The Panthers made Norman a substantial contract extension offer worth about $7 million per year in the 2015 off-season, but he turned it down—betting (correctly) on himself that he was worth far more than that to some NFL team. He entered Carolina's training camp in a contract year, clearly the Panthers' No. 1 cover corner and more confident than ever. He and similarly confident quarterback Cam Newton both liked to strut after big plays. They both understood each other's ability, but they weren't particularly close.

"Cam's a good guy, but we didn't really talk," Norman said, referring to the duo's relationship before their fight. "We had an admiring respect. A respect, like, a sniffing kind of respect. You know when two dogs sniff and they know what's good and then they go their different ways? And don't really play with each other? Like that. I just wanted to one-up him, and he just wanted to one-up me."

Both Newton and Norman were prone to flaunting their success during practice. With the No. 1 offense and defense going against each other often in training camp in Spartanburg, this was a pot that was about to boil over. On August 10, 2015, it did.

"Right before the play," Norman said, "Cam was just lighting up our defense. Whatever he wanted to do, he just did it. He was out there making a big show. Fans were going crazy, he was swinging his arms, doing a dance, and laughing. Being a big kid. I was like, *You know what? Freak this. Enough is enough.*"

Newton then tried to thread a pass into a receiver that Norman was guarding. Instead, Norman made a sliding interception, got up, and started running. By the unwritten rules of training camp, Norman could have stopped once he made the interception. By those same unwritten rules, quarterbacks are never supposed to try and make tackles due to injury risk.

Instead, Norman didn't stop, and Newton came after him. "I palmed the ball with one hand and I went back with it," Norman said. "Cam was in chase mode so I was like, 'Man, okay.' I juked one offensive lineman, and here he [Newton] comes. I stiff-armed him, but I didn't think I stiff-armed him that hard. I just thought I was going to score or whatever. And then I threw the ball. And here he is, all 6′5″ of him, and he was like 'Throw that ball at me again!' I was like 'Who do you think you are?' and then we were clutching each other. I grabbed his face mask, and then somehow his helmet came off. He grabbed me....It was mayhem."

The only photographer with any decent pictures of the scuffle was David Foster III of the *Charlotte Observer*, and the one that was published most widely showed Newton with his helmet off and a fierce smile, throwing Norman to the ground as the two headed toward the turf together.

"He had a piece of me, and I tried to sling him," Norman said. "I tried to hip-toss him. And they got that picture of him smiling and he's got me clutched up—of all pictures to get!"

"We're Both Better from It"

Norman can laugh about the incident now, because he believes it ultimately made the team better in 2015. Newton would say much the same thing the next day. "At the end of the day, we're both better from it," Newton said. "There's no hard feelings. I bring out the best in Josh, and he brings out the best in me."

But Norman wasn't laughing then in what he called a "mêlée." The two were separated after about 30 seconds, but not before both had fallen to the ground and briefly wrestled. The whole fight happened 15 yards in front of me—I was on the sideline, because reporters can get much closer to the action at training camp than at any other time during the season. I have never seen Newton madder, before or since. "Hit me like that again!" Newton dared.

Norman was furious as well. Linebacker Thomas Davis spoke for a lot of people right after the altercation had been brought to a halt when he screamed, "That's stupid!"

Safety Kurt Coleman was among those stunned at the break in the Panthers' routine. "I didn't know all that transpired," Coleman said. "All I saw was Cam going at it, and I thought, *Cam, what are you doing?* But when you see the whole thing, I totally get it, and I love both guys for it. I mean, it's who they are and it's why they are going to become so great at their positions. They really are one and the same with that never-lose mentality. Even though Cam had thrown a pick, it was, *They're not going to get the touchdown.* And for J-No, he got the pick and kind of flaunted it in Cam's face."

Practice eventually continued, and each man went back to his own huddle. Newton calmed down more quickly than Norman, addressing the team as a whole at the end of practice. Norman thought about doing that as well, but his emotions were still too high.

"I was mad the whole practice," Norman said. "I almost ended up crying. That emotion just spiraling—it just came out. And after we got that out of our system, he talked to the team. I wanted to say something, but I was still hot. So I just kept my words in and listened."

The two would talk shortly after practice, however, and that's when the healing began. Not long after that, Norman took a picture of himself and Newton together at a private movie screening in Spartanburg for the Panthers of *Mission Impossible: Rogue Nation* and posted it on his Twitter account. That was as effective as anything else in publicly defusing the incident.

Newton's teammates tried to downplay the scuffle—"just a little training-camp tiff," center Ryan Kalil called it—and Newton did the same thing.

"What regrets? Me practicing? It's football," he told reporters the day after the fight. "Emotions are going to flare. From the outside, you see scuffles. I see guys challenging each other."

Ready to Rip, Rivera Reconsiders

It was true that Newton wasn't the first NFL quarterback to get into a training camp fight—Dallas Cowboys Hall of Famer Roger Staubach had done so in 1976 with an erratic backup quarterback named Clint Longley. And Rivera told reporters he had seen quarterbacks fight before, reminding them, "Remember, I played with Jim McMahon."

In our 2016 interview, Norman said he and Newton were able to calmly talk about the incident within a couple of hours. Said Norman, "We talked in the showers and he was like, 'Look, we're going to fight every day. If it has to be like that to compete and to win, we're going to fight every day.' And I was like, 'You know what? I love that. I respect that 110 percent. You're darn right.... We're going to fight, and we're going to win. There ain't going to be no backing down. So we became close. Now we talk. I call him when I'm in town to see if he wants to go do something. And if anybody ever says anything bad about him, I say, 'I don't know what you're looking at. That's a competitive guy who loves to have fun. He's enjoying what he's doing.'"

Rivera, for his part, believed the fight's aftermath allowed the team to grow because the dispute was handled internally rather than from the top down. He planned to address the issue at length at the next team meeting. "I was ready to make a big speech," Rivera said in his interview for this book. "I was going to rip some people's asses, talk about team, all that type of stuff. And then in walks Ryan Kalil, and he says, 'Coach, I got this.' Thomas Davis— same. Charles Johnson—'Coach, I'm gonna get 'em straight.' So I ended up not M.F.-ing anybody. Cam said what he had to say, Josh said what he had to say, and that was it. We moved on....I think it kind of showed for Josh, that it didn't matter who I was going against, I'm challenging people. I think for Cam it was a little bit of a test of his humility, a 'Hey, you know what? You've got to fight and compete just like everybody else.' So in my weird way, I'm try- ing to justify it. And to a degree it did help out."

The captains taking over was a significant moment for Rivera. He was learning to trust his leaders more and more. Earlier in train- ing camp, he'd had to fly to the West Coast to attend and deliver the eulogy at the funeral of his beloved older brother, Mickey. Mickey had died of pancreatic cancer at age 57. (Six months later, Rivera would dedicate his 2015 NFL Coach of the Year award to Mickey.)

Before he left training camp, Ron Rivera had met with the cap- tains, asked them to make sure the players didn't slack off while he wasn't there, and was pleased with the reports he got when he returned. In his mind, the handling of Cam and Josh had been another locker room success and boded well for the future.

Benjamin Goes Down

Nine days after the fight between Newton and Norman, a far more damaging event occurred at training camp. The Miami Dolphins had come to Spartanburg for a couple of days of joint practices with the Panthers. Both sides had been warned not to fight, as similar joint workouts at other NFL training camps had led to some brawling.

But Kelvin Benjamin's injury had nothing to do with a fight. While running a route and trying to get open in a one-on-one drill against a Miami Dolphins defensive back, Benjamin planted his left leg into the ground and tried to cut. There was no contact, but Benjamin crumpled to the ground and let out a scream of pain.

Benjamin had been having a fine training camp. Wide receiver Jerricho Cotchery had called him the "lead dog" of the receiving corps. Benjamin had struggled a bit with his weight and hamstring injuries in the off-season. But when he drove into training camp in his big truck with the enormous "FSU" sticker and the vanity tag "KB13," you could see the extra weight was gone. He was in fine shape. Benjamin seemed poised to improve on the 1,008-yard, nine-TD receiving season he had posted as a rookie in 2014. At 6′5″ and 240 pounds, Benjamin was nearly the size of Newton and had become one of the quarterback's two favorite targets in 2014 (the other being sure-handed tight end Greg Olsen).

Dolphins and Panthers players gathered around Benjamin—some talking quietly to him, some in prayer. Benjamin was carted off the field. The diagnosis was public within hours—he had torn his ACL, meaning he was done for the year before he had even started it.

It was a startling blow and one that would reverberate throughout the season. Benjamin's injury meant that Newton would have to work diligently to develop some more receiving threats beyond Olsen, and it put a big question mark beside the offense.

The injury had the effect of ripping one of Newton's security blankets away, and in reality the quarterback seemed to get better because of it.

Panthers No. 19 in Power Poll

"One of the best things that ever happened to Cam Newton was Kelvin Benjamin going down in the 2015 training camp," said

Eugene Robinson, who played 16 years as an NFL safety and has worked as an analyst for the Panthers radio team since 2002. "He was throwing to Kelvin or Greg Olsen all the time. Now it was, 'Cam, you do what you do. Just throw it to whomever is open.'"

But on that sunny day in August, the Panthers had seen their second national story blossom in the span of 10 days—and neither one of them was positive. First, it had been the Newton-Norman fight. Then Benjamin went down for the season with a torn ACL. The news had not been good, and the Panthers seemed to be stumbling before they even reached the official start line.

Certainly, the Panthers were under the radar despite making the playoffs the past two seasons. After Benjamin's injury, modest national expectations dropped even further. ESPN has what it calls its "Power Panel," which is a group of more than 80 NFL writers, editors, and TV personalities. They rank the NFL teams 1–32 each week.

Before the 2015 season began, ESPN had Carolina ranked No. 19 in its weekly "Power Poll." Seattle was No. 1, New England No. 2, Green Bay No. 3, and Indianapolis No. 4. In *Sports Illustrated*, the Panthers were picked to go 9–7. (The magazine picked Baltimore to win the Super Bowl. The Ravens would finish 5–11.)

But negative thinking like that wasn't accounting for a couple of dynamics. For one, the Panthers themselves knew what they had. They saw it every day at training camp. Panthers defensive end Mario Addison proclaimed "I see a Super Bowl!" during camp to reporters. Numerous teammates quietly agreed.

Secondly, Newton and Luke Kuechly were having a tremendous training camp. Yes, Newton had gotten in the fight, but he was playing so well and running the offense so fluidly. Kuechly had taken another step up the ladder, too. And when you have the "Cam and Luke Show" on your side, anything seems possible.

28

CAM AND LUKE, TOGETHER

BEFORE THE 2015 season ever officially began, the Carolina Panthers scored twice.

In June, Cam Newton signed a five-year contract extension worth $103.8 million. At the press conference announcing his signing, both coach Ron Rivera and general manager Dave Gettleman said that the quarterback could lead the Panthers to the promised land.

In September, a few days before the opening kickoff, Luke Kuechly signed his own five-year extension worth about $62 million. It can't be overstated how important it was for the Panthers to make sure the franchise quarterback and franchise middle linebacker got locked into the long-term in Charlotte and that no other team had a chance to even get near poaching away Carolina's two most important cornerstones. The two players both justified the money by raising their own levels of play in the 2015 season. During the most successful season in Panthers history, the two most significant reasons were Cam and Luke.

Dave Gettleman, incidentally, made sure of one thing when he signed those two to extensions within months of each other. "I did not want Luke's and Cam's contracts ending in the same year," the GM said, "and I wasn't going to let that happen. Initially the length of the deal that [Kuechly's agents] wanted was going to finish the same year as Cam, and I said, 'That ain't happening.'...So Cam's last season under contract is 2020 and Kuechly's is 2021."

Gettleman also said in his interview for this book that the Panthers had honestly considered not re-signing Newton to an extension at one point. "We talked about it at length," Gettleman said. "What if you don't do it? What if you play it out? And all the distractions of him being in his UFA [unrestricted free agent] year, and all that crap."

That idea was dismissed. The Panthers had made a run at signing Newton to an extension during the 2014 season but couldn't get it done. But in the summer of 2015, the Panthers tried again, and this time the deal came together in about 72 hours, Gettleman said.

Dressing Like Cam

Newton and Kuechly have very different personalities—Newton once called themselves the "yin yang twins." Newton is African American, a paragon of style and the life of every party. Kuechly is white, admittedly un-stylish, and happy to stay on the sidelines everywhere except on the field itself.

"Cam walks into a room and lights it up," Carolina Panthers coach Ron Rivera said. "Luke has this ability to kind of sneak in."

But they have more similarities than you might think. They are elite players with superb study habits, immense talent, and fine senses of humor. They tease each other all the time. Newton either calls Kuechly by his middle name (August) or else pokes at him by using the "Captain America" nickname Newton once gave him. And Kuechly, although quieter than Newton, is no shrinking violet. He shocked everyone when he dressed up as Newton for a team meeting just before Halloween in 2015.

In a prank aided and abetted by linebacker Thomas Davis, Kuechly raided Newton's locker for some cleats and practice pants. "Then all you've got to do is find some headphones and a Gatorade towel, throw that on, smile, put the kneepads on and all that stuff, and you're good to go," Kuechly said.

The team's reaction was "hysterical," according to Rivera, although Newton wasn't laughing at first. "I think when he first saw me he was trying to act like it wasn't funny," Kuechly said, "but it was only a matter of time before his big smile came out."

The difference in size between the two is quickly apparent in the photo that Davis snapped of Kuechly in his Newton Halloween outfit (which Davis gleefully posted on Instagram). While Kuechly is listed at 6′3″, he's probably closer to 6′1″. In the picture he is standing on his tiptoes just trying to get close to the height of the 6′5″ Newton.

"Dang, He Gets It"

Each player has learned from the other. The No. 1 overall pick in 2011, Newton thought he worked hard as a rookie until he saw what Kuechly did to prepare after he got drafted No. 9 overall in 2012. "He put so much pressure on me when he first got here, staying late, watching extra film, making sure that everyone on the defensive side knows what they're doing," Newton said of Kuechly. "For me watching, it was a competitive enviousness that I grew, and I was like, 'Dang, he gets it.'"

That led to Newton staying later and coming into the stadium more often. The two have an unofficial competition now to see who is watching more film, and Kuechly likes to peek into the quarterbacks' meeting room when he leaves at night to see whether Newton is still in there.

"I want to see who's going to be the last to leave," Kuechly said. "It goes back and forth."

Rivera had to kick Kuechly out of the stadium on Christmas Eve. But Kuechly said that sometimes "Cam's in there with all the lights off and his headphones on, watching film."

Said Rivera, "They are opposites in some ways. But for the most part I think they are a lot more similar than people realize….Their commitment to whatever they do is tremendous."

Their style, on the other hand, is tremendously different. Newton has his own clothing line at Belk. He has posed for *GQ*. He wore black and gold Versace pants on the team plane to the Super Bowl (retail price $849), saying he picked the pants out because of the black and gold color theme that Super Bowl 50 had. Newton also has numerous foxtails that he wears as an accessory.

Kuechly wears jeans and T-shirts. He once joked that he was going to get some fashion tips from Newton, although he knew they would only go so far. "There are certain things he can wear that I can't," Kuechly said. "I don't think I can pull off the foxtail. I don't think I'm cool enough to pull off the Versace pants. I'm going to start with baby steps."

The likability factor of the two men is also somewhat different. Newton is much more well-known nationally, does far more endorsements and TV shows, and to me seems an ideal candidate to one day host *Saturday Night Live.*

Kuechly is not as well-known nationally, and even the pronunciation of his name (KEEK-lee) trips people up who aren't from the Carolinas. But unlike Newton, you would have a very hard time ever finding someone that says they can't stand him. Women either want to date him or mother him. Men want to be like him.

Newton has immense popularity among everybody 25 or younger, and his name recognition is through the roof. But he also has his share of detractors and knows it. Some people—often older than 45, but not always—don't like the dancing, or the photo ops, or the Superman pose, or the occasional petulance when he loses a game. Newton has described those two camps as the "Damn, Cam's cool!" faction and the "Hell, I hate Cam!" faction.

Newton said he doesn't understand why people dislike his on-field celebrations. "I don't know," Newton said. "But I guess you'll have to get used to it, because I don't plan on changing."

Kuechly's Concussion

In the 2015 season, though, both Newton and Kuechly were superb. Newton would ultimately become the NFL's Most Valuable

Player—the first time any Panther had received that honor. Kuechly had the most productive regular season of his career in terms of big plays and then became the first player in NFL history to return an interception for a touchdown in consecutive games in a single postseason. And, as always, he made dozens of tackles.

"He gets there very quickly," Rivera said of Kuechly. "And, as the old saying goes, he arrives in a bad mood."

Kuechly had an unusual start to his season, however. While Newton came back from an unusual 2014 season—one game missed due to cracked ribs, another due to a car wreck—to play in all 19 of the Panthers' games during the 2015 season, Kuechly sustained a concussion in the season opener against Jacksonville. In an otherwise forgettable win over Jacksonville, Kuechly ended up hitting a Jaguar helmet-first.

"I went in to hit a guy and I slipped a little bit," he explained later. "I moved and then he moved at the last second, and the way the contact happened, it was poor tackling form. That's really what it comes down to. I need to have my head up, and if I would have had my head up, that issue wouldn't have happened. I went down and knew there was something wrong, and it was something I had never felt before."

Kuechly would miss the rest of that game and the next three as well, as the Panthers put him through the concussion protocol and carefully monitored his progress. Carolina had once had a linebacker named Dan Morgan who could have been great, but his career was undone by a series of concussions. Morgan ended up staying in football and working in Seattle's front office. Every time I saw him, it reminded me of what might have been.

So the Panthers moved Kuechly out of the lineup after his concussion and then kept him out of it for the first month of the season. That was a testament to how careful the Panthers are with concussions these days. Rivera remembers having one as a player with the Bears and the team reacting far differently.

"I came from an era where you played," Rivera said. "I remember having a concussion and going right back on the field and playing."

Now, with much more research into concussions and their affect on long-term health, the NFL is much stricter on what sort of tests a player must take to return to the field. Like every NFL team, the Panthers have had their share of players who have debilitating health conditions once they leave the game. Rivera said he is fortunate in that he doesn't appear to have any memory loss, headaches, or other symptoms, but he knows that he's one of the lucky ones.

Defense Survives without Kuechly

It was quite a test of the defense to go without Kuechly for an extended period, and it showed how many good players the Panthers had. Cornerback Josh Norman, who returned an interception for a touchdown in that season opener against Blake Bortles (waving "good-bye" as he did it), added three more picks in the first four games of 2015. All of a sudden he was becoming a dominant NFL player. The same went for defensive tackle Kawann Short. Davis was excellent as usual. All three would make the Pro Bowl in 2015, which meant Carolina had a Pro Bowler at every position group on defense and two at linebacker once Kuechly returned. Backup linebacker A.J. Klein also did a nice job subbing for Kuechly.

With Kuechly playing less than two quarters of Carolina's first 16 quarters of the season, the Panthers still began 4–0. But the level of competition was questionable. And that was what all the talking heads on ESPN and the NFL Network harped on every time the Panthers' undefeated record came up. The Panthers beat Jacksonville, Houston, New Orleans, and Tampa Bay in that first month, which was not exactly a murderers' row (although Houston would eventually make the playoffs).

Carolina had a lot of trouble scoring in that first game against Jacksonville, netting only one offensive touchdown. But as Newton grew more comfortable playing without the injured wide receiver Kelvin Benjamin, he also started gaining more confidence in an unpredictable, flashy receiver who had been considered a moderate bust everywhere except Carolina.

His name was Ted Ginn Jr.

29

THE TED GINN EXPERIENCE

FOR MUCH OF his NFL career, Ted Ginn Jr. has been considered an "almost" sort of player. He would frustrate fans by almost doing this and almost doing that. The Miami Dolphins had taken him No. 9 overall in the 2007 draft, and their fans are still complaining about that pick. He stuck around the NFL because of his top-end speed and his elusiveness, but no one had ever confused him for a No. 1 wide receiver. He too often ranked dubiously high in the "drop percentage" statistic for wide receivers. He sometimes would run out of bounds to avoid big hits.

And yet, at Carolina, Ginn had flourished. In 2013, his lone year with the Panthers, he scored five touchdowns—more than twice as many receiving TDs as he had ever scored before in a single season. That had been on a one-year contract, and Arizona had lured him away in 2014 with a three-year deal.

But the Cardinals' crush on Ginn quickly dissipated. He was relegated to the bench as he got banged up, and rookie wide receiver John Brown instead gained Arizona's trust. All the Cardinals wanted Ginn to do once Brown emerged was to return punts and kickoffs—that was the other thing that had long kept Ginn in the league—and then he had managed to fumble the ball away inside his own 5 in Arizona's playoff game at Carolina.

Less than two months later, Arizona fired Ginn. "I felt like deep down inside that [the Cardinals] thought I couldn't do it," Ginn would later say, describing the experience. "They sent me back out to the wolves."

One wolf out there was friendly, though. Panthers general manager Dave Gettleman had wished he had signed Ginn to a multi-year deal in 2013 so he wouldn't have gotten away in the first place, and now here Ginn was—somewhat chastened for leaving in the first place and on the free-agent market again. Gettleman swooped him back up, this time with a two-year deal. The GM proclaimed that the 30-year-old Ginn—who would be entering his ninth NFL season—was still valuable because he could still run as fast as he always had.

In 2013 Ginn had been the Panthers' third receiver—a speedy change of pace who played behind starters Steve Smith and Brandon LaFell. That's about where Carolina saw him fitting in again. But then Kelvin Benjamin had torn his ACL in training camp in August 2015, and suddenly Ginn's opportunity had come.

"Not Just a Straight-Line Guy"

When Benjamin got hurt, Cam Newton went to Ginn and talked to him. Recalled Ginn later, "Once Kelvin went down, Cam told me, 'Come on, Ted, let's have the best you that you've ever had.' And we went out and we put work in. We changed a lot of things up because of the size of me. [Ginn is quite small for an NFL wide receiver, generously listed at 5'11" and 185 pounds and thus about half a foot shorter and 55 pounds lighter than Benjamin.] And we just went out and we wanted to be great, and it showed."

Wide receivers coach Ricky Proehl, along with offensive coordinator Mike Shula, was tasked with maximizing Ginn's output. "For me, Teddy's got all the tools to be great," Proehl said. "He can run. He can get in and out of a cut. He's not just a straight-line guy. He's got good hands, although at times he's inconsistent. It's just building that confidence and playing up to his ability where he can thrive and be successful. We know who he is and what he is, what he does well and what he doesn't."

In the Panthers' first game, against Jacksonville, Ginn had a dropped pass inside the 5 that would have been a touchdown. Fans cringed. This was part of the "Ted Ginn Experience"—that dizzying, frustrating, extraordinary thrill ride that was part of employing Ginn.

Then the next week, against Houston, Ginn dropped a pass on Carolina's first series and yet another shortly after that. Newton would not leave Ginn alone, though—he couldn't. No. 19 kept getting open, and the quarterback's options were limited.

So Ginn later caught a 25-yard touchdown pass that day—his first of the season. And from that point on, Ginn established that this would be the best NFL season he had ever had. The former high-school All-American from Ohio—he earned that honor at defensive back in football and as a sprinter and hurdler in track— was finally going to show his mettle as an NFL wide receiver. He was about to make his childhood friend LeBron James proud.

"My Heart Was in My Socks"

That Houston game was notable for another reason, too, as Newton made one of the most ridiculously athletic plays of his NFL life. It was only a two-yard run, but the degree of difficulty was out of this world. Newton scored on a two-yard quarterback draw by executing a full front flip into the end zone.

"My heart was in my socks," Newton said after the Panthers had won 24–17 to go to 2–0. "As I was flipping, I was like, *Hey, I wonder how this is going to end?* And then I'm coming down and said, *Hey, I can stick this!*"

"He's probably the only quarterback in the league who can do that," Olsen would say later. "That's obvious. When you have a quarterback run designed for the goal line, and you block everybody but the one guy you can't block, and then the quarterback jumps over him, it's hard to game plan for that."

Marveled Ginn, "You don't see a lot of guys 6′6″ who are that athletic who play football. You see them play basketball or run track or something. For a guy to be a quarterback and to do something I can't do is amazing."

Newton hopped up and went into his Superman celebration—especially apt this time, since he had just finished a short flight.

"Superman, huh?" Panthers cornerback Josh Norman said. "He went up and over and almost landed on his feet! Hey, that's our guy."

Said Olsen of Newton, "I told him the Russian judge gave him a 3, but everyone else gave him a 10."

Two More TDs Versus Tampa

The Panthers, Newton, and Ginn all stayed hot the next week as Carolina edged New Orleans 27–22. Ginn caught four passes for 93 yards, including a 55-yarder, although this time he didn't score. The victory was preserved by Norman, whose leaping end-zone interception on a pass intended for Brandin Cooks sealed it.

"I saw ball, got ball," Norman would say later. Norman's acrobatic pick was a huge play and helped Carolina avoid a New Orleans comeback that could have been devastating. The rest of the Panthers players had seen Norman pull off a very similar interception in practice Thursday against Cam Newton—this time there was no fight involved afterward, although Newton would admit to being "ticked off" that he had thrown the pick. So his teammates weren't as surprised as the rest of the stadium.

The Panthers had led 27–16 with five minutes left in the game, and the Saints had Luke McCown at quarterback because Drew Brees was injured. New Orleans had the ball on Carolina's 23 with 1:17 to go, so there was plenty of time for the Saints to take the lead. The headline in the next day's *Charlotte Observer* read "Norman Conquest."

Ginn would play a big part in Carolina's next win, too—a messy 37–23 win on a rainy day at Tampa Bay. For the first time in his

NFL career, he caught two TD passes in the same game. They were on short routes of 12 and six yards, showing again that the Panthers were going to run Ginn on more routes than just 50-yard fly patterns.

"You look two years ago at what he did," Proehl said, referring to Ginn's 2013 season, "and he went deep and he ran a lot of comebacks. Now he's running over the middle. He's doing a lot of different things that keep defenses off-balance....And he's as good as there is running after a catch. That's when the punt returner in him comes out. It's just a matter of getting the ball in his hands."

The excellent Panthers PR staff used those two TDs against Tampa as an impetus for this note: In 20 career regular-season games with Carolina (in 2013 and 2015), Ginn already had eight TD catches. In 104 career games with the other teams he'd played for (Miami, San Francisco, and Arizona), Ginn had six touchdown catches. "Ted is really evolving into that player he's capable of becoming," Newton said. In fact, Ginn would end the 2015 season with 10 TDs, becoming the first Panthers receiver with 10 or more TDs since Steve Smith hit double digits in 2005.

"This team knows what I can do," Ginn said. "It recognizes my speed and my talent."

Ginn also threw an important block—yes, a block—on a freak play against Tampa Bay when tight end Ed Dickson plucked Jonathan Stewart's fumble out of the air and rumbled 57 yards for a TD. "It's not pretty, but we're getting wins," Ginn said. "Ain't no game going to be just straight dominance, you know what I'm saying?"

The Panthers had not really dominated anyone yet—their largest win margin had been 14 points. But they were 4–0, and they had done that without Kuechly. He had missed three-and-a-half out of a possible four games with a concussion, but now he was ready and champing at the bit to return. It was a good thing, too. Now came the real test—the one they had failed, over and over, in the previous three years. It was once again time to go to Seattle.

30

SLAYING SEATTLE

CAM NEWTON HAD heard the questions ever since 2012, when he and Russell Wilson met on a football field for the first time. Why couldn't he beat the Seahawks? Why did Wilson—a third-round draft pick who was physically much smaller than Newton—keep beating him? How had Seattle and Wilson managed to go 4–0 against Carolina from 2012 to 2014?

Those questions would persist as long as Seattle kept getting the better of Carolina. The Panthers all knew that. It wasn't like Carolina was alone in getting beaten by the Seahawks, though. Seattle had represented the NFC in the past two Super Bowls, winning against Denver and then losing to New England on a last-second interception. Seattle was the NFC's elite. And though the Seahawks (2–3) had not started the 2015 season nearly as well as the Panthers (4–0), there was no doubt in any Panther's mind that this was a team Carolina had to go through to get to the Super Bowl.

Nine months after the Panthers had flown out to Seattle and gotten eliminated in the 2014 postseason, they made the same trip again. It was a better squad this time that Ron Rivera took on the team plane. Kelvin Benjamin was injured, yes, but the Panthers had made a substantial upgrade at left tackle. Michael Oher— whose life was the basis for the movie *The Blind Side,* although he had long ago tired of talking about that film—had washed out in Tennessee and been released. The Panthers, though, were convinced Oher could still play. Newton had contacted Oher during the recruitment process, telling him not only did he want him, but that he *needed* him. Oher signed up and quickly found the fountain of youth. No longer was pressure coming constantly from behind Newton, as too often had happened the year before when Byron Bell had manned the spot.

As Oher reemerged into a viable NFL starter, questions about the movie would persist. He liked the way it inspired people, but was not that happy with the way he was portrayed in the film. In real life, Oher was much smarter than the oafish character in *The Blind Side* and not nearly as much of a football neophyte in high school. He also had never met Sandra Bullock, either (who played his movie mom and won an Academy Award for her portrayal).

The Panthers hadn't made a huge number of other upgrades. Cornerback Charles Tillman had come aboard to play one spot and starting safety Kurt Coleman was just beginning to have what would become a very big year. But the Panthers' improvement was mostly from within—players like defensive tackle Kawann Short, cornerback Josh Norman, offensive guard Trai Turner and running back Jonathan Stewart were all well on their way to the first Pro Bowl seasons of their respective careers. And Newton was playing as well as anybody in the league at quarterback.

So Carolina entered the game with some confidence but also with a lack of sleep and a little trepidation. Some unknown person had pulled the fire alarm about 5:40 AM at the Panthers' hotel in Seattle, sending some players out into the lobby in the wee hours (Newton was among those who ignored the alarm). "I think it was an inside job; it had to be," Panthers rookie linebacker Shaq Thompson grumbled. "There was just no way it would just hit our floors."

The Panthers had lost by four, four, five, and 14 points in the previous four Newton-Wilson matchups, with Wilson seemingly able to make the biggest play of the game in every fourth quarter. "I hadn't been in Carolina in previous years," Coleman said. "But everyone had told me that was just a mental hurdle that we just needed to jump over. It wasn't so much that they were better than us in previous seasons, but they mentally just had an edge."

Seahawks Take a 13-Point Lead

Playing before the usual sellout crowd in Seattle, where the constant "12th Man" noise is a point of pride, Carolina's offense started horribly. It went three-and-out with a Newton sack on its first series and then made it even worse on the next series, when Newton was intercepted on third-and-14. Seattle took over at the Carolina 33, but the Panthers defense held the Seahawks to a field goal.

Then Newton began showing why this game was going to be different than the previous four. Carolina had always struggled to score against Seattle's vaunted defense with Newton at the helm, averaging only 11.2 points in his four losses against the Seahawks. But this game would be different, with Newton finally getting the best of Seattle's D numerous times. The first time came on a methodical 14-play, 80-yard drive that ended with Newton scoring from two yards out to give Carolina a 7–3 lead.

With Kuechly back and making tackles all over the field, the Panthers were doing their best to hold down old rival Marshawn Lynch. But they didn't on the next series. The Seahawks trumped Carolina's 80-yard drive with a 90-yard march of their own, ending it on a one-yard Lynch plunge.

That made it 10–7 Seattle, which would remain the score at halftime. Then the Seahawks threatened to pull away at the beginning of the third quarter. On a trick "double-pass" play in which Lynch got the ball and threw it back to Wilson, the quarterback then heaved it 40 yards into the end zone to Ricardo Lockette. Coleman was in decent position on the play, but Lockette out-jumped him for the ball. Seattle led 17–7 and quickly tacked on another field goal thanks to Newton's second interception of the afternoon.

At 20–7, the Panthers' situation looked somewhat dire. But Greg Olsen caught two different 22-yard passes from Newton on the very next drive, gaining more than half the yardage in Carolina's second 80-yard march of the day. Stewart finished it off with a one-yard TD, slicing Seattle's lead to 20–14 late in the third quarter.

Seattle made it a two-possession game again with Steven Hauschka's third field goal of the game, increasing the lead to 23–14 with 11:51 to go. Again, the Panthers offense came up with an answer, and it once again heavily involved Newton and Olsen. The quarterback found his tight end for 12 yards and then 32 yards on the same drive, Stewart rammed it in from one yard out, and it was 23–20 with 3:58 to go.

Graham Gano then made what could have stood as one of the worst kicks of his career. To make life more interesting, the NFL had changed the length of extra points to 33 yards on an experimental basis in 2015. Gano picked this moment to miss his first extra point at the new distance, meaning if Carolina got the ball back the Panthers could no longer win with a field goal.

It would all be academic, of course, if Carolina's defense couldn't get the ball back. Seattle coach Pete Carroll and his staff was well-known for trying to be aggressive and throwing the ball in tight situations: witness Wilson's interception from the New England 1 that had lost the previous Super Bowl.

This time, Wilson hit Jimmy Graham (long a thorn in Carolina's side while at New Orleans) on the first play. But then Lynch was called for offensive holding on another pass play, and Seattle couldn't dig its way out of a third-and-20 hole when Short sacked Wilson. It was a huge stop. Carolina's defense didn't have its best game of the season in this one—for the only time during the entire season, the Panthers never forced a turnover—but it had one of its grittiest. At one point, linebacker Thomas Davis had to pop a dislocated finger back into place—during the middle of a play!—and still made a tackle on Lynch on a screen pass.

So Carolina ended up with the ball again—first-and-10 from its own 20, with 2:20 left in the game and one timeout left in its pocket. One of the most famous drives in Newton's career was about to begin.

"All Hell Was Breaking Loose"

Newton had made some fourth-quarter comebacks before, but never one with quite this degree of difficulty. He had beaten New England and New Orleans with big-time, last-minute drives in 2013, but both those games were at home. He had converted a late fourth-and-10 to help win a game that same year, but that was in a relatively placid fan environment in Miami.

This was Seattle, home of one of the best home crowds in any sport. And here came Newton. He quickly completed three passes—eight yards to Jonathan Stewart, 18 to Ted Ginn, and 14 to Ed Dickson. That got Carolina to Seattle's 40, but Newton was quickly sacked. That made it second-and-19, and Carolina used its last timeout with 1:20 to regroup. This was the moment in the past when the Panthers might have panicked, gone for it all, and then turned it over.

Instead, Newton was steady. "That whole drive really sticks out in my mind," Rivera told me later, "and not just for the touchdown. On a play leading up to that one, Cam signified to me that he got it. All hell was breaking loose. We were trying to get personnel in and get the play call right. And he just stuck his hand up in the air to tell everybody, 'I got it. Relax. Calm down.'"

Newton then fired a 16-yard strike to rookie Devin Funchess, who had dropped three passes on the day but made this catch. On third-and-3, he threw in tight coverage to Jerricho Cotchery, and "Cotch made a one-handed catch to keep the drive going," Newton would say later.

The clock was still running as Carolina huddled at the Seattle 26, with Newton trying to yell out the play call amid the din. A delay-of-game penalty seemed possible. "That's the fastest we've ever gotten a play off," Olsen would tell center Ryan Kalil later in a moment captured by NFL Films. "We broke the huddle with seven seconds [on the play clock]."

Kalil snapped it barely in time, and Olsen—in the play his teammates would later vote as the No. 1 most important of the regular season in a poll I took before the playoffs—lined up on the quarterback's right and ran hard toward the end zone.

The Seahawks, normally so seamless on defense, had a problem. Two defensive backs each thought the other was going to be covering Olsen, so the end result was that no one covered the Panthers' most reliable receiver. Newton's 26-yard throw to a wide-open Olsen was his easiest of the day. It gave Carolina a 27–23 lead with 32 seconds left.

Seattle cornerback Richard Sherman would call the last TD a "fluky play" because the Seahawks got confused on their coverage. Sherman played one type of coverage, fellow Pro Bowl safety Earl Thomas played another, and the two looked at each other in exasperation after the play. But there was nothing fluky about what Newton did on that last drive. He completed six passes to six different receivers. He led his fourth 80-yard TD drive of the game. He proved to himself—and his teammates, and the Panthers' fans—that Seattle wasn't always going to have Carolina's number.

Said Newton after the game of the winning TD drive, "I don't want to make this about me. It was a great team win, and an unbelievable catch by Greg. Just an unbelievable game by him, being there when I needed him the most."

The quarterback went into a screaming celebration right after Olsen's TD. "When you get a late touchdown like this in a hostile environment, it just puts everything into perspective on why you play so hard, why you play through injuries," Newton said. "When you look in the huddle and see 10 guys looking back at you, and you can't let those guys down. When Greg caught that ball, there was so much that was bottled up inside of me."

After the game, though, Newton was somewhat subdued. Businesslike, even. "Well, we were just doing our job," Newton said. "Nothing special. They're a good team. We're a good team, too."

But it was more than that. This was the sort of game that made Carolina believe and Seattle understand that if a rematch came in the playoffs, the Panthers would be more than ready. Concurrently, Newton had removed a troublesome albatross from around his neck.

Following the win, Davis said about Newton, "I think he's going to start getting some of the respect that he deserves as one of the best quarterbacks in the league, a guy who can flat-out lead the team and go out there and get it done. He's going to erase some of the doubters that he has. We're excited to have him as our quarterback."

"To me, they were the elite of the NFC," Rivera said later of Seattle. "And going there and being able to win really helped validate who we are as a football team. We still have a long ways to go. But the best part about it, more than anything else, is we've proven to ourselves we can do it."

31

BANNERS, TENNESSEE MOM, AND THANKSGIVING DAY

THE PANTHERS' WIN over Seattle was like a 60 mph wind gust, pushing Carolina through the next five games like a sail. In order, Carolina beat Philadelphia, Indianapolis, Green Bay, Tennessee, and Washington—and only one of those games was within a seven-point margin. The Panthers were starting not just to beat teams but to humiliate them. In a 44–16 thumping of Washington, the Panthers' key number was five. Cam Newton threw five TD passes, while Carolina's defense caused five turnovers and produced five sacks.

The only game Carolina came close to losing in this stretch was to Indianapolis at home, when Andrew Luck nearly led the Colts to victory in a rainy *Monday Night Football* thriller. The Panthers were ahead 23–6 with less than 11 minutes to play. At that point a lot of fans thought the game was sewn up and instead were talking about the four protesters who had sneaked climbing gear into the stadium and rappelled down to hang a huge banner that read "Dump Dominion." Two of the protesters dangled in the air for about 30 minutes just below the stadium's upper level before firefighters safely got them down (after they refused to come back to the stands on their own). The protesters were calling on Charlotte-based Bank of America to stop financing Dominion Resources, which was building a liquefied natural gas facility in Cove Point, Maryland, on the Chesapeake Bay.

But then the Panthers started to collapse, Luck got hot, and everyone's attention reverted to the soggy field. The player the Panthers likely would have selected if he had been available in the 2011 draft, Luck threw two quick TD passes and then got the ball back for a third time as Carolina's offense couldn't make a first down to seal it.

Luck directed the Colts into Carolina territory, where they ran four plays inside Carolina's 20 in the last 30 seconds. If any of them hit for a TD, Carolina's undefeated streak would be over. Instead, the Colts had to settle for a field goal and overtime. Indianapolis got the ball first in OT and scored on a field goal. The Panthers would have a shot at one possession to tie, however, because Indianapolis hadn't scored a TD. Carolina got a "make it or lose" 42-yard field goal from Gano—who had again missed an extra point—to tie it. Then the Panthers defense finally made a play. After allowing points on four possessions in a row, Carolina snatched an interception when Roman Harper deflected a pass and Luke Kuechly grabbed it. Another Gano field goal, this one a 52-yarder, provided a 29–26 victory.

A Banner Day

By the time Carolina got to Green Bay and Aaron Rodgers, Ron Rivera knew something special was brewing. Just before the Packers game, the head coach instructed the Panthers' video crew to intersperse some of the team's best highlights of the 2015 season with clips of Kurt Russell's speech from the hockey movie *Miracle*. Russell portrays hockey coach Herb Brooks in the movie about the U.S. team's upset of mighty Russia in the 1980 Winter Olympics.

"Hey, the Russians had had their time," Rivera told me. "They had been world champions, Olympic gold medalists and all of that. And I kind of related it to we're the new team, the new kids on the block, going up against the older team that has got the history."

The Panthers had trailed Green Bay 21–0 in the first quarter the year before, although four of the five secondary starters (counting the nickel back) that Aaron Rodgers had carved up in that game were no longer with the team. Carolina had upgraded its secondary substantially, and it showed.

This time, the Panthers pulverized the Packers in the first two quarters and went into halftime with a 27–7 lead. The second half wasn't as impressive, as the Panthers allowed a couple of late TDs to make it scary for their fans once again, but Carolina held on for a 37–29 win. Thomas Davis made a game-saving interception at his own 4 on a play in which Kawann Short hurried the throw. Rodgers would later fire a computer tablet to the ground in disgust after seeing a replay of a wide-open Randall Cobb that he hadn't been able to locate during the play because of Short's pressure.

That Green Bay home win was not without controversy, mainly because Newton had taken down a banner during pregame warmups from some Green Bay fans that read "North Carolina Cheesehead." Newton, who had four total TDs in the game, said it was a matter of respect and that he just didn't like seeing other teams' banners inside the Panthers' home stadium.

Said Newton when I asked him following the game about the incident, "There was a Green Bay banner in Bank of America Stadium. It just doesn't match....I was passing, the sign was dangling. Either somebody was going to have to take it off or I'd take it off. And it's no disrespect to nobody, it's more of a respect to the stadium."

Newton also said that he had seen no Panthers banners in Green Bay in 2014 when the Packers had lambasted Carolina. "You're not up here about to sell a Whopper at a McDonald's, you know what I'm saying?" he said. The Panthers had a duplicate banner made for the Green Bay fan and shipped it to his house. The Panthers then revised their banner policy to allow only smaller, handheld signs, but did still allow signs supporting the opposing teams to be taken into the stadium.

Tennessee Mom's Letter Goes Viral

Carolina's 27–10 road victory against Tennessee was thorough and forgettable, mostly remembered now for the aftermath. A woman from Nashville named Rosemary Plorin took her fourth-grade daughter to the game and was disturbed at Newton's gesticulations after good plays. She wrote a critical open letter to Newton and sent it to the *Charlotte Observer*. We printed it, and the letter quickly went viral, with lines like: "Because of where we sat, we had a close up view of your conduct in the fourth quarter. The chest puffs. The pelvic thrusts. The arrogant struts and the 'in your face' taunting of both the Titans' players and fans. We saw it all."

Newton had broken out his version of "the dab" after a rushing TD, a dance born in his native Atlanta and eventually destined to be imitated by everyone from entire elementary school classes to Charlotte's mayor. (Pretend you are suddenly sneezing into the crook of your arm, and you're already doing a bad version of it.)

Tennessee players didn't like Newton's extended celebrations and took exception to them, which only made Newton dance more. He didn't do a throat-slash. He didn't drop to one knee. He didn't taunt. That's why none of his actions were penalized; Newton was acting more like Michael Jackson in the old "Beat It" video than a gangbanger. But the comments of "Tennessee Mom" did expose some of the tension around Newton. She was part of the backlash to his celebrations. Then came a backlash to the backlash (Tennessee Mom would later make nice, saying she was unaware of all the good community work Newton did for children. Newton, for his part, said she was entitled to her opinion.)

In the meantime, Carolina kept winning, and the Panthers' first-ever Thanksgiving Day game in their 21 seasons was looming.

A Thanksgiving Day Feast

While the Panthers had played in nearly every conceivable time slot during the franchise's history—including Sunday nights, Monday nights, Thursday nights, and Saturday nights—they had never been selected for a Thanksgiving Day game before. Thanksgiving had long been the exclusive province of the Dallas Cowboys and the Detroit Lions, with each playing a high-profile opponent that would help draw huge TV ratings. The time slot with the Cowboys traditionally drew the best TV rating of the NFL regular season, and that was the one the Panthers were slated for on Thanksgiving Day 2015.

Carolina entered the game 10–0. Dallas was 3–7. The Cowboys had gotten no uptick from their controversial acquisition of Greg Hardy—even though his NFL-mandated suspension had been reduced from 10 to four games—and were on the verge of another seriously disappointing season. But Dallas was Dallas, and Carolina was Carolina, and there was no doubt which team had the most name recognition. Las Vegas odds opened with the Cowboys, somewhat inexplicably, a one-point favorite over Carolina.

"It is a little disrespectful, but apparently they know something we don't," Rivera said, sarcastically referring to oddsmakers.

As money poured into the casinos on Carolina, that opening line quickly changed into the Panthers becoming the slight favorite. But Rivera and his players conveniently ignored that part. Much more compelling to them was the idea that the Panthers had been disrespected—again!—by the oddsmakers who had dared to make a 3–7 team a favorite over a 10–0 one, even briefly, and even if that 3–7 team did have its oft-injured but ballyhooed quarterback Tony Romo back for this game.

Panthers center Ryan Kalil, a five-time Pro Bowler who had played for Carolina since 2007 and was one of the most thoughtful men in the locker room, had declared this the most talented

Panther team he had been on (including the Carolina playoff teams of 2008, 2013, and 2014 on which he also started).

"And there's a lot of young talent in this group," Kalil said, "that a lot of people haven't heard of. That's why we get a lot of criticism, a lot of 'They do more with less'—which I don't think is fair."

Respect was slow to come, but certainly the Panthers were getting noticed. I got to know coach Don Shula in the early 1990s as the *Miami Herald's* beat writer covering the Miami Dolphins, and so now I called him up to ask him what he thought of the Panthers. His son, Mike Shula, was the Panthers offensive coordinator—a mellow, underrated coach whose play-calling had been superb all season. The elder Shula told me he really hoped the Panthers would become the first team to go undefeated in 43 years since his Dolphins did in 1972. The story made some national news, since members of the 17–0 Dolphins are widely known for cheering when the last undefeated team loses each season.

But to hear the oddsmakers tell it, Carolina might just go ahead and lose on Thanksgiving Day. "To come into this game as underdogs, that's a true sign of disrespect," grumbled Thomas Davis.

As part of an NFL promotion, the Panthers wore all-blue uniforms. The Cowboys looked vaguely medical in their all-white uniforms. A sellout crowd of 90,909 packed themselves into AT&T Stadium in Arlington, Texas, hoping to see the Cowboys finally get back on track in what had been a desultory season.

"Look for the Cutback"

In pregame warmups, defensive backs coach Steve Wilks and safety Kurt Coleman always have a talk. This time, Wilks wanted to tell Coleman about a dream he had the night before.

"He said, 'I had a dream last night that you were going to get a pick,'" Coleman recalled in an interview for this book. "And he said, 'When you get that pick, look for the cutback. It will be there.'"

The Cowboys had the ball first and quickly faced a third-and-six from their own 24. Let Coleman pick up the story from there: "You know, whether you're a player or a fan, that Tony Romo is going to go to Jason Witten a lot of the time in that situation," he said. "This time they ran Cole Beasley on a little pivot route underneath, and I knew they were going to try to throw the ball to Witten against our guy Luke Kuechly. So I read Romo, and I picked it."

Coleman had never scored an NFL touchdown before, although he had come close a couple of times. This time only two Dallas players had much of a chance at him. One was Cowboys receiver Dez Bryant, but he was too busy jawing with cornerback Josh Norman during the play to put up much of a chase. The other player with a chance was Witten. But Coleman cut back at just the right time and found the end zone. Wilks' dream had come true. Coleman's 36-yard pick-six stunned the crowd and made it 7–0 Carolina with only 59 seconds gone.

Coleman celebrated with his teammates. Norman said of his issue during the play with Bryant, "Me and him were having choice words. Then I pointed at Kurt as he scored, and I said, 'Look at that. Now take that back to your huddle and come back again!'"

Dallas would try to come back, certainly, but to no avail. Hardy was a complete non-factor against his former teammates, not registering a sack or a tackle. Romo threw two TD passes in the first half—but both went to the Panthers. Kuechly grabbed the other one, picking off a pass and going 32 yards for a TD in the second quarter. On the very next Dallas offensive play, Kuechly intercepted another pass with an even more athletic play when he grabbed another ball that Romo tried to force into Witten. If anyone had debated leaving Kuechly off the Pro Bowl team because of his missing three-and-a-half games early in the season, there was no debate anymore.

Newton said after the game that Kuechly was "a little fire-cracker" with a "dark side." Added the quarterback, "A person who plays like that is not just a nice guy. He has the smile, the charisma, the lawyer look, but a demolition mentality....In my eyes, though, he'll always be Captain America."

For once, Newton really wasn't the headliner in a Panthers win. Carolina's defense was—it intercepted Romo three times before knocking him out of the game with another injury. "I would like to think I am a good enough player not to just give touchdowns to the defense," Romo said. And oftentimes he had been—Romo's career record was 4–0 against Carolina until that Thanksgiving Day.

Newton didn't have a TD throwing or running until late in the third quarter. Then he ran it in from four yards and danced again—you knew he wasn't going to miss a dance on Thanksgiving Day. Again, he changed things up. Instead of the new-school "dab" that he had broken out against Tennessee, this time he went with the old-school, Chubby Checker "Twist" and also did a swim move. Newton would say later he has "diverse dance ability" and, on this occasion, decided to use some dance moves that he breaks out when he wants his grandmother to get up and dance with him.

Norman, meanwhile, said he was in a "dark place" the entire game. He said Bryant had "disrespected" the Panthers with some pregame chatter. Norman didn't have an interception—in fact, after grabbing four in the first four games of the season, he never had another one. But he shut down Dallas' Bryant completely and batted down anything that was going to be a big play on his side.

"Give thanks for thievery!" Norman proclaimed later. "Best secondary in the league, bar none!"

On days like this, it sure looked like it. The Panthers had completed their third consecutive undefeated month of the season, and would enter December with an 11–0 record.

On to Lucky 13

The Panthers won their next two games, as well—one of them close, one of them not close at all. The first one was another thriller, as Carolina turned the ball over three times in the first half at New Orleans. The Panthers trailed 14–0 in the first quarter, 16–13 at halftime, and 38–34 with 5:21 left in the game. Carolina had all sorts of problems it had to overcome—Norman got beat for a TD pass on a clever fake by Drew Brees; Ted Ginn dropped two would-be touchdown passes; and Carolina had an extra point blocked and returned for a two-point conversion (the first time in NFL history that has happened).

Newton had also taken some big hits, and one was totally his fault, when he had slowed down near the end zone to more thoroughly enjoy the moment and instead got blasted by a linebacker. The quarterback told a team doctor later, "I deserved to get hit like that, taking that foot off the gas. I was so shocked. The guy came out of nowhere it felt like."

But Newton, who had been checked for a possible concussion after that play, wouldn't let Carolina lose this one. On a fourth-and-4 at the New Orleans 46, he scrambled left and flicked a pass to Greg Olsen, who had to dive to get it. Olsen did—barely—and the play gained 16 yards. Three plays later, Newton hit Jerricho Cotchery for a 15-yard TD pass. The Saints couldn't get past midfield on their last drive, and Carolina had survived again. Ginn had made up for his two drops with two other TD catches, while Newton had thrown for 331 yards with five TD passes.

"We missed some today," Rivera said later. "We threw a couple long…and we did drop some. It's going to happen. The thing you have to do is go in and make plays, and that's what happened."

In the next game, the Panthers made far more plays and had a near-perfect 38–0 home rout of Atlanta. It was only Carolina's seventh shutout in its 21-year history. The Panthers led 28–0 at halftime after Ginn snagged TD passes of 74 and 46 yards from

Newton, and the Panthers' defense stopped Atlanta and Matt Ryan cold. The first quarter alone was a game's worth of work for some offenses. Carolina gained 260 yards, which was the most the Panthers had ever gained in any quarter. In the meantime, the Panthers had five quarterback sacks. Atlanta coach Dan Quinn called the whole afternoon "unacceptable," while Ryan labeled it "ugly."

The only real downside for the Panthers was when valuable nickel cornerback Bene Benwikere fractured his leg on an attempted tackle in the fourth quarter. Carolina already had some injuries at cornerback—this one would ultimately necessitate the Panthers playing Cortland Finnegan and Robert McClain a lot in the playoffs, even though neither had been on the team's roster midway through the season.

But the Panthers didn't worry too much about that. They were 13–0, riding their wave for all it was worth. "It's our moment," Newton said, "and we want to seize it as much as possible."

Carolina's sheer dominance was the news in that 38–0 whipping. The next week against the New York Giants, the headlines would be far different after the game—and a lot of them would have to do with Norman and a Giants wide receiver named Odell Beckham.

32

THE ADVENTURES OF ODELL AND JOSH

ON ONE OF the strangest days of the 2015 season, the Carolina Panthers played a thriller that was eclipsed by a personal battle. Normally, Carolina rising to a 14–0 record by winning a game 38–35 on a field goal with no time remaining—after blowing a 35–7 lead against the New York Giants in the final 17 minutes of the game—would have been the headline.

But not on December 20, 2015, when Carolina cornerback Josh Norman and New York Giants wide receiver Odell Beckham engaged in a private war on the field that just went on and on and on. Beckham would end up with three personal-foul penalties and Norman with two. Beckham really should have been thrown out of the game—his most egregious offense was the time he attempted to take Norman's head off from the blindside by turning himself into a missile with a 10-yard running head start. Beckham wasn't ejected, although the NFL tacitly admitted the wide receiver should have been by suspending him without pay for the next game. Norman certainly was an instigator that afternoon, too, although of the two he was the more clear-headed.

In our interview for this book in 2016, Norman had plenty to say about Beckham and said he will never forget a day that most Panthers fans will remember for years as well. Because Norman signed a monstrous five-year contract with Washington in April 2016 that could be worth up to $75 million, he will now face

Beckham twice a year as a division rival in the NFC East. Is he looking forward to it? You could say so.

"I'll be honest," Norman said of Beckham, "I don't care for the guy at all....Now don't get me wrong, he's a good player or whatever, but he's not what he thinks he is. If you hit guys like that, if you completely jam them and shake them up, they can't relate to that. So they start making excuses like, 'Oh, he touched me.' They don't know how to respond because they never got hit like that. So me, every time I see him, I'm going to hit him in the mouth. I don't care. Until he stops crying and bitching."

The confrontation was the talk of the NFL for the entire next week. And the residue from "The Adventures of Josh and Odell" continues to be felt into 2016 with an NFL rules change specifically designed to eliminate personal confrontations that go on for long periods of time during games.

A Rodney Harrison Appetizer

Norman always made things interesting around the Panthers, and he had been fired up for much of the week leading into the game. His matchup with Beckham was receiving national notice. Norman was by then widely perceived to be having the best season of any cornerback in the league, and Beckham was an explosive player who was making his fantasy football owners very happy with six straight 100-yard receiving efforts.

After Carolina plastered Atlanta 38–0, I spoke with former NFL safety Rodney Harrison about Norman and the Panthers. Harrison was now a high-profile NFL analyst for NBC, who had been dismissive of the Panthers and Norman on several occasions on national TV. I had originally scheduled the interview to talk about the difficulties of going undefeated—Harrison had played on a New England team that came very close to doing so—but it quickly veered off into Norman territory. Harrison had opined before the Atlanta game that Julio Jones would have the advantage on Norman in that game, and Norman had written after that on Twitter that Harrison was "horrible at his job."

So both men were mad at each other—which, as you know by now, is wont to happen to happen with Norman sometimes. He seems to thrive on a little controversy in his life. (And Harrison, often on the edge of hitting wide receivers late, was the same way as a player.)

So I talked to Harrison, who stuck by his statement about Julio Jones and added that Jones is "physically more superior than Josh." Harrison also bristled about Norman that "he needs to shut up!" about Harrison's job performance.

I texted Norman to see if he wanted to respond to those comments. He quickly texted back, saying, in his words, he would like to "indulge." Norman then said in our conversation, "You can insult my intelligence if you like. You can even insult my little puppy. But please, whatever you do, don't insult my talent level." Norman also called Harrison a "bitter old guy."

So that was Norman's pregame Rodney Harrison appetizer. But the main course, on Sunday, was still to come.

"A Field Full of Alpha Males"

Before the game, Beckham and some of the Panthers defensive backs had some words. The DBs had brought a black baseball bat onto the field to symbolize hitting a home run, they said, as well as in tribute to injured cornerback Bene Benwikere. Beckham didn't like the bat, though, and there was some controversy about whether he felt threatened by it and how much brandishing or threatening the Panthers did with the bat in hand. (The Panthers, under orders from coach Ron Rivera, would not bring the bat to any more games after this one.)

In any event, Beckham began the game in a highly emotional state. On New York's very first drive, he sprinted right past Norman, ran under a perfectly thrown deep pass from Eli Manning—and dropped what should have been a 52-yard TD. Beckham would have another drop later and would end the half with zero catches for the first time in his career.

Norman and Beckham were jawing at each other throughout the game, and for a while it seemed like they were getting locked up on nearly every play. The officials allowed it to continue for far too long, flagging maybe every third incident.

"You got a field full of alpha males, they're not going to be playing 'patty cake, patty cake' out there," Cam Newton said about the multiple incidents.

Panthers coaches would later go through the film frame by frame and count 14 incidents involving Beckham. Twelve, they would say, were instigated by Beckham and two by Norman.

"I hope I pulled back the mask on who this guy really is," Norman said shortly after the game.

Said Panthers safety Kurt Coleman in his interview for this book, "There are times in a game where I had to tell J-No to calm down and get his emotions under control. But I thought that in that game he was pretty in check and for the most part defending himself."

In the meantime, the Panthers were rolling. Newton was having a field day against a poor Giants defense, throwing for five touchdowns, no interceptions, and 340 yards. Ted Ginn Jr. had a couple of those TD catches, with Greg Olsen, Philly Brown, and Devin Funchess all contributing one. Ginn's final TD came with 5:32 left in the third quarter and made the score 35–7. For all intents and purposes, the game appeared to be over.

But Manning was still on the other sideline, and he started to play like he did when he won two Super Bowls with the Giants. The Panthers suddenly couldn't move the ball anymore, and the Giants couldn't be stopped. A 38-yard run for a TD by the Giants was sandwiched between three Manning TD passes—the last one a 14-yarder to Beckham over Norman on a fourth-down play with 1:46 to go.

That made it 35-all. But Newton got the ship righted, moving the Panthers downfield one more time to position Graham Gano for a 43-yard field goal with 0:05 left. Gano had seen a 34-yarder blocked that had helped the Giants comeback—the fifth field goal he had had blocked that season—and so it was no sure thing.

Two-Second Delay Seals the Victory

The Giants, in a last-ditch effort, brought Beckham in to try to jump over the line and block the kick. Smartly, long snapper J.J. Jansen and holder Brad Nortman altered their pre-snap routine. They figured the Giants might be keying on Nortman's head movement—a common tactic in the NFL is for the long snapper to snap the ball just after he sees the holder move his head. Jansen and Nortman have the authority to alter the snap count however they like within reason. This time they decided to have Nortman turn his head early but for Jansen not to snap it immediately, holding the ball for about two extra seconds.

Gano, meanwhile, went onto the field "extremely confident." The last block had not been his fault, for the Giants had somehow figured out the cadence. Gano, who would eventually set a Panthers team record in 2015 with 146 total points, had drilled five straight extra points during the game and had buried his kickoffs out the back of the end zone. He had not missed a field goal during all of warmups. And he was kicking to the side of the field at Giants Stadium that he preferred. The timeout Giants coach Tom Coughlin called to ice him had no effect but did allow Jansen and Nortman to perfect their snapping strategy.

As the stadium roared and Nortman turned his head, Beckham started running full tilt toward the Panthers' offensive line. But Jansen didn't snap the ball. The slight delay completely messed up the Giants' timing. A flag flew. Jansen then snapped the ball, relying on Nortman to be ready to catch it as always. Nortman caught it and put it down. Gano hit the kick so perfectly he didn't even look up to watch it go through the goalposts.

"I saw the line it was on and the trajectory," he said, "and then I just started celebrating."

The flag was against the Giants for an illegal formation—a penalty caused by the Panthers' slight delay. If Gano had missed the kick from 43, he actually would have gotten another chance to make it—this time from 38 yards.

But there was no need. Carolina was 14–0. And Beckham's behavior was in the crosshairs of the national sports media.

"Bad Santa"

Maybe it would have been different had the Giants won a game that had been played five days before Christmas. As it was, though, New York's tabloid newspapers eviscerated Beckham—usually one of the kings of New York—the next day. The *New York Post* headline read, "GIANT JERK! Odell's Private War Helps Torpedo Big Blue."

The *New York Daily News* headline said, "BAD SANTA: Odell Hit with 3 Personal Fouls in Embarrassing Meltdown." Golfer Jordan Spieth had even chimed on Twitter during the game, tweeting during one of Beckham's displays: "OBJ is embarrassing himself right now."

Norman certainly wasn't blameless—he ended up getting fined $26,000 for his part in the whole charade—but he came out the better of the two in terms of reputation. The one-game suspension of Beckham was big news for the next week. It stayed in the news for several more cycles because Beckham unsuccessfully appealed.

Looking back on the incident, Coleman said, "It's unfortunate things escalated the way they did, because that's not the game of football. That's not why anybody plays this game. You never want to disrespect the game of football like that. But I think both guys are learning as this thing continues to move on. As they get older, they'll understand, and they'll look back and say it was probably a little silly. But sometimes in the game of football you get caught up. It's emotional."

Beckham did himself no favors when, after the game, instead of answering any questions about Norman, he kept petulantly repeating, "It is unfortunate that we lost." To his credit, after being suspended, Beckham did issue an apology that read in part, "Sportsmanship and respecting the game are as important as blocking, running routes, and catching the football. I dropped the ball on sportsmanship on Sunday. I apologize to my teammates, the Giants organization, and to all fans of the NFL."

The game's long shelf life also contributed to a rules change. NFL commissioner Roger Goodell proposed—and the NFL owners voted for—a one-year trial of the "automatic ejection rule," which means that any player getting two unsportsmanlike-conduct penalties in the same game would be ejected.

Norman and Beckham also continued their feud on and off through Twitter in 2016. In March 2016, Beckham "subtweeted" Norman—referring to him without mentioning his name—on Twitter as Norman made a national TV appearance. "That boy should thank me for all I've done for you!!!" Beckham wrote.

This made Norman seethe when we talked for this book, as he made a reference to Beckham's amazing one-handed catch in 2014 on a Sunday night game, giving Beckham more publicity than he deserved. "He's yapping over there," Norman said of Beckham. "And [Beckham doesn't] even sound like he's making any sense. He just went [in the draft] in the first round and everything is handed to him. He gets to New York....He catches one stupid little ball, and everybody in New York [loves] this guy, because that's the biggest amount of media in the world....So all that went to his big old head, and for some odd reason he thinks he's somebody that he's not."

The Panthers, on the other hand, knew exactly who they were. They were a 14–0 team playing for history—but about to find themselves on the wrong side of it.

33

14–0 FADES AWAY AT ATLANTA

ON CHRISTMAS EVE 2015, Cam Newton had a secret. He rushed out of the Panthers' practice, missing the final five plays, and toward Atlanta. His longtime girlfriend, Kia Proctor, was about to have his first child.

Chosen Sebastian Newton was born later that day, although his father wouldn't reveal the birth until the following week when he broke the news via Twitter. The quarterback did give a big hint, though, when he pretended to rock the football like it was a baby after scoring a TD on the opening drive of the game at Atlanta.

At that point, the Panthers had outscored the Falcons 45–0 in their last 66 minutes of football. The Panthers were already one of only four teams in the Super Bowl era that had begun the season 14–0, joining the 2007 New England Patriots, the 2009 Indianapolis Colts, and the 1972 Miami Dolphins (the only team that stayed undefeated the rest of the way). Now it appeared that the journey to 15–0 was imminent and that the undefeated season would still be alive.

But as any new parent knows, things don't always go according to plan. The Panthers wouldn't score another TD the rest of the afternoon, losing 20–13 to the team they had blasted just two weeks before.

It had been 392 days since Carolina had lost a regular-season game, but this one was no fluke. "We got our ass kicked today," Newton said, "and to a degree we deserved it."

Both offense and defense shared the blame for the Panthers. Newton and Atlanta quarterback Matt Ryan each attempted 30 passes, but Newton gained only 142 yards with his throws while Ryan had 306. The most damaging play was Ryan's 70-yard Hail Mary to Julio Jones, who took the ball off the top of Luke Kuechly's helmet and ran in for the score. Panthers safety Kurt Coleman had fallen down on the play, leaving Kuechly one-on-one with Jones 40 yards downfield.

Carolina had the ball twice in the game's final 2:23, but never mounted a serious threat to the disappointment of about 30,000 Panthers fans who had snapped up tickets and filled almost half the seats in the Georgia Dome. On the last offensive snap of the game, Atlanta defensive end Vic Beasley beat Mike Remmers around right end and caused a sack-fumble of Newton that Atlanta recovered. It was a play that would be repeated almost exactly in the Super Bowl by Von Miller on the strip-sack for Denver that provided the game's first touchdown.

Newton called the offense's performance "lethargic" and "unacceptable." He grumbled, "We lost the game by seven points, and there were seven points out there to be made." It was the first time all season that Carolina had not scored at least 20. Two weeks before, the Panthers had taken a big sideline picture orchestrated by Newton with two minutes left in their 38–0 victory. This time, Falcons owner Arthur Blank did the "dab" in the Atlanta locker room.

The loss was a blow to the Panthers, and it also meant that their final game of the season would mean something. At 14–1, with Arizona snapping on their heels at 13–2, the Panthers needed to win at home versus Tampa Bay to secure homefield advantage.

The Chosen One

The loss rankled the Panthers, but not for that long. They knew that all of their goals except for the undefeated season were still out there to be had. And Newton, as a new father, couldn't stay down long. He talked publicly about Chosen—a name he had picked out—for the first time the next week. The baby had been a healthy nine pounds and six ounces. Said Newton, "It's pretty cool....When you see life coming into existence, it's a wonderful thing."

The quarterback also then began what would be a running joke about Chosen's advanced maturity. "I took him out for a jog yesterday," Newton said. "He was running alongside me. He has a couple of scholarship offers already on the table." Newton would joke within the next few days that Chosen was soon going to get a driver's license, had learned how to dunk, and was accepting invitations to the prom.

As for the name, Newton said he had leaned toward an unusual one and had not wanted to saddle his son with the name "Cam Newton Jr." Said the quarterback, "Every person that I've had this conversation with, I say I didn't want him to have the pressure of being a junior. And then they reply with, 'What the hell do you think Chosen is going to bring?'" Newton showed a somewhat charming naïveté about what fatherhood would entail. "Nothing has pretty much changed besides our record, and the focus now is still the same," Newton said. That, of course, was patently untrue. Once you become a father, many things change. But Newton did have a role model in mind. He said he wanted to be "the same father my dad was to me....I'm going to be the same way—but cooler."

Tampa Trouncing

The first loss of the season did allow Rivera to play the "no respect" card he was so fond of laying on the table. He said before the Tampa Bay game about the NFL season in general, "I just don't think we were invited to the party. I think we crashed the party. I think people were expecting 8–8, 9–7, I guess. It took people a long time to pay attention to us."

While Tampa was only 6–9, the win wasn't a sure thing. Carolina would be without its leading rusher (Jonathan Stewart) and leading receiver (Ted Ginn) due to relatively minor injuries that the Panthers did not want to take a chance on with the playoffs looming.

It turned out not to matter, though. Tampa Bay took a brief 3–0 lead, and then Carolina stormed away with the game with a 24-point second quarter. Newton would end up rushing for two TDs, throwing for two more, and unofficially clinching the NFL MVP. Thomas Davis became the Panthers' all-time leader with 954 tackles, surpassing safety Mike Minter (although it's likely one day that Luke Kuechly will pass them both). And Tampa Bay receiver Mike Evans became the latest player to lose his cool against Carolina's defense, getting thrown out of the game after two straight unsportsmanlike conduct penalties after he thought Josh Norman had interfered with him. Norman said Evans' behavior during the game amounted to "a peasant throwing rocks at a giant."

It was another entertaining quote from the Panther most known for providing them. But the bigger picture was that Carolina had secured its first-ever No. 1 playoff seed in the NFC. The Panthers were 15–1, but not close to done. The most successful regular season in history was history. The playoffs were about to begin.

34

SEATTLE—ONCE MORE, WITH FEELING

THE PANTHERS RECEIVED two real rewards and one fake one for their 15–1 season and No. 1 NFC seed. They would get a bye during the first week of the playoffs, which was important and would allow players like Jonathan Stewart to heal his sprained foot more fully. They would also get to play at home until the Super Bowl, if they got there, which was very significant since Carolina had won 11 straight games in Bank of America Stadium.

Those things they knew. Their opponent they didn't, because the NFL automatically gives the No. 1 team in the conference the lowest remaining seeded team as an opponent after the first-round games are completed. Most of the Panthers would be watching closely to see whom they would play, although Cam Newton claimed he was not among them. Newton channeled his inner Yogi Berra when he said before the bye weekend, "I'm not a big football fan outside of football."

The fake reward turned out to be Carolina's opponent. Seattle was seeded No. 6 and last among the NFC playoff teams, but the Seahawks had just blistered Arizona by 30 points in the final week of the regular season. Seattle was hot at the right time, and a matchup between the Seahawks and Carolina seemed likely to produce the NFC champion.

It wouldn't occur in the NFC Championship Game, however. Seattle went to Minnesota and survived a day of minus-25 wind chill to edge the Vikings 10–9. The Seahawks were lucky to win—Minnesota kicker Blair Walsh missed a 27-yard field goal in the final seconds—but sometimes you need some playoff luck. So after edging Seattle in October on Greg Olsen's late TD catch, the Panthers would have to do it again.

"We'll both hit each other in the mouth," Seattle cornerback Richard Sherman said. "Then we'll see who's standing at the end."

A Shocking Early Lead

Although Carolina had won the first matchup in Seattle 27–23, the Panthers were determined to do better in a couple of phases. One was turnovers. Carolina had led the NFL in interceptions with 24 and in takeaways with 39, but the game against Seattle was the only time all season the Panthers had not forced a single turnover. Third-string quarterback Joe Webb—one of the best athletes on the team and a special-teams standout—would play the role of Seattle quarterback Russell Wilson in practice, trying to replicate Wilson's talent for extending plays.

Second item: Carolina had to get off to a better start. Carolina had only won in Seattle after making a herculean comeback after trailing 20–7. This time, the Panthers wanted to try to play from ahead early. They had set a team record with 59 TDs, after all—a far cry from the 2–14, Jimmy Clausen–led Panthers that had scored only 17 TDs in 2010, just before the Panthers renaissance began. Even against Seattle's vaunted defense, the Panthers thought they should be able to score more.

As always, Carolina would also try to run the ball. The team had rushed for at least 100 yards in every game during the 2015 season—that was one of Ron Rivera's favorite statistics because he believed it spoke to how controlling the line of scrimmage really won games. Stewart and fullback Mike Tolbert had both made the Pro Bowl and decided to give the offensive linemen a gift in appreciation. In one of the gestures that helps explain why the Panthers have such a good locker room, Stewart and Tolbert split the cost and bought all of the starting offensive linemen, as well as the reserves, new 49-inch flat-screen TVs for about $600 apiece.

The gift looked like a good investment on the very first play from scrimmage. Stewart took a handoff, popped out of a hole created in part by Pro Bowl offensive guard Trai Turner, and suddenly was in the secondary. With fresh legs after not playing football for a month (Stewart had missed a 1,000-yard season by 11 yards due to sitting out the final three games), the running back sped past everyone he thought had a chance to catch him. As he ran, he dared a look up onto the huge scoreboard video screens, where he could see himself blazing toward the end zone.

"I shouldn't have looked at it," Stewart said, "because when I looked up, I slowed down a bit." Sherman, the only Seahawk with any shot, chased Stewart down at the Seattle 16 after that wayward glance. It turned out not to matter much, though, as Stewart ended up scoring on a four-yard run three plays later. Quickly, it was 7–0.

The day soon got even more shocking. On Seattle's second offensive play, defensive tackle Kawann Short slipped a block and was immediately in Wilson's face. Wilson, who hardly ever makes a decision you could truly label as terrible, did this time. Rather than take a sack, he hurried a throw that was well behind intended target Marshawn Lynch. Luke Kuechly picked the ball off on the fly at the Seattle 14 and sped into the end zone for a touchdown. In less than four minutes, before Cam Newton had even thrown his first pass, it was 14–0. A day that had started with snow flurries suddenly felt warm due to the combined body heat, as the upper deck at Bank of America Stadium literally shook in surprise and delight. Carolina had accomplished both its goals already—getting a turnover and grabbing an early lead—and the Panthers were not done by a long shot.

31–0 at Halftime

Carolina scored the next time it got the ball, too, on a methodical 15-play, 86-yard drive. Stewart ran it in from a yard out, and it was

21–0. And it just kept getting more lopsided. Cortland Finnegan intercepted Wilson on the very next play from scrimmage. The Panthers couldn't move the ball this time, but Graham Gano's 48-yard field goal made it 24–0.

The landslide continued as Seattle went three-and-out in its next series. Carolina got the ball back, and on third-and-14 from the Seahawks 19, Newton threw a high dart toward tight end Greg Olsen. Olsen was running the same pattern that he did for the game-winning TD pass against Seattle in October. "Only this time they covered me," Olsen said later with a grin.

It didn't matter—Olsen leaped to make one of the most gorgeous catches of his career, and it was 31–0. That, remarkably, was the score at halftime.

"We made a mess of it in the first half," Seattle coach Pete Carroll said afterward. "We just couldn't get started well. Carolina took advantage of all the opportunities. It was a terrible start."

A Nerve-Tingling Comeback

The first half was the magic for the Panthers. Then came the misery.

Wilson is one of the NFL's best players, and there was no way to keep him down forever. He walked up and down the sideline incessantly in the second half, urging teammates on, telling them that Seattle could still win this game.

The tide turned on the very first play of the second half when Seattle's Tyler Lockett returned the opening kickoff 50 yards. Wilson turned that into a TD pass 90 seconds later, and it was 31–7. Panthers fans didn't mind that one too much. But then Wilson hit Lockett for a 33-yard TD—Lockett beat Kurt Coleman on the play after Josh Norman didn't get home to Wilson on a corner blitz— and it was 31–14 with 7:40 still left in the third quarter.

Panthers fans stirred in uneasiness. The Seahawks couldn't come all the way back—could they? Carolina's sideline also was getting nervous. As Newton memorably put it later, "There were a lot of guys playing with their butts tight. Coaches with their butts tight. At one point, the fans and myself with butts tight, too, but you just have to find ways to get your groove back."

The Panthers couldn't move the ball at all—they would not score a point in the second half—as they kept trying to control the ball on short, safe plays. It didn't really work. "Our philosophy at times was just to play keep away," Newton said.

The Seahawks got it to 31–21 midway through the fourth quarter on Wilson's third touchdown pass. Carolina picked up one first down, punted again, and the Seahawks drove inside the Panthers 20 before stalling. A Steven Hauschka field goal made it 31–24 Carolina with 1:12 to go.

Said Wilson, who had once starred at N.C. State, three hours from Charlotte, "They were up 31–0. We had no doubts in our minds that we could win the game...if we could have one more drive."

So it was time for an onside kick. Everyone in the stadium knew that. That meant it was time for Carolina's "hands" team. As Panthers special-teams coach Bruce DeHaven would say later, you don't need your "hands" team much. But when you do, much like when you need a parachute, you *really* need one.

Carolina organizes its "hands" team differently than most NFL teams. Most teams put a number of blockers up front and a wide receiver or tight end behind them. The players behind are the "catchers," while the blockers are supposed to keep the kick-off team's guys away long enough to field the ball cleanly. New England, for instance, has tight end Rob Gronkowski as one of its catchers.

The Panthers used tight end Greg Olsen in the middle of the field in case Hauschka bunted the ball 10 yards straight ahead and tried to pick it up himself. But their catchers were linebacker Thomas Davis and Norman, which shows how much trust the Panthers have in those two players.

Hauschka's kick was pretty good and bounced high to Davis's side. He sprang into the air to get his hands on the ball and then got submarined by a Seattle player. Davis held on, though, securing the ball and, finally, the game.

Later, Carroll would wish that Hauschka's kick had gone slightly higher. "The ground is so soft, it is such a soft field, it just didn't elevate," Carroll said. "Thomas Davis made a great play on the ball."

Seattle couldn't stop the clock, and Carolina jubilantly ran it out. The Seahawks—the NFC representatives in the past two Super Bowls—had finally been dethroned.

NFL Films cameras caught an exchange between Newton and Seattle safety Earl Thomas after the game as they embraced. "About time," Thomas said, referring to the fact that Newton and Carolina had advanced to the NFC Championship Game for the first time in the quarterback's career.

"You're right!" Newton yelled. "I gotta get mine! Y'all can't be greedy! I need mine too!"

The Panthers took their now-traditional playoff victory lap around the stadium. Players and fans looked equally exhausted. Everyone had been put through the emotional wringer. But the Panthers had survived. They were set to host the NFC title game in Charlotte for the first time in franchise history. And this time the opponent would be their old foe Arizona—a team that was much improved from the Cardinals team that Carolina had beaten in the playoffs one year ago.

35

RAZING ARIZONA

FOR A LOT of the Panthers players and their fans, what happened January 24, 2016, was a mountaintop experience. Five years removed from 2–14, Carolina had ascended to the NFC Championship Game and also got to host it. And then came one of the most comprehensive beatdowns the Panthers had ever laid on any team, much less on a stage that big. After the nail-biting second half against Seattle in which Carolina had lost almost all of a big lead yet again, the Panthers finally put two dominant halves together. The result: Carolina 49, Arizona 15.

Everything the Panthers had prepared for came to fruition on that one miraculous Sunday. Arizona committed seven turnovers—the most in any NFL playoff game in 15 years. Cam Newton had yet another four-TD game, this time getting two via pass and two via run. Luke Kuechly took back an interception for a TD for the second straight game. Ted Ginn Jr. had a monster night against his old team. The offensive line did such a good job on a first-quarter blitz pickup that Newton had all day to find Philly Brown, who hauled in a pass and took it 86 yards for a TD.

It was one of those days where everything worked—and one that is perhaps even sweeter in retrospect, given what was in store for the Panthers at the Super Bowl two weeks later.

Coach Ron Rivera had banned hoverboards—the self-balancing, two-wheeled scooters—from the Panthers facility after they had started to become too prevalent. "I caught them drag-racing in the hallways one time, too," Rivera said.

But against Arizona, it seemed every Panthers player was riding a hoverboard, and that all of them were floating a few feet in the air. The Cardinals looked slow, out of sorts, and shell-shocked, right from the beginning. A game that most observers felt would be far closer than the playoff matchup a year before wasn't close at all. On a brisk, clear night under a full moon, Panthers fans stood for much of the night—partly for warmth, but mostly due to excitement.

The Heisman Matchup

Oddly, the game marked the first time that two Heisman-winning quarterbacks would meet in any NFL playoff game. Palmer (36) and Newton (26) were a decade apart in age, but they had both thrown exactly 35 TD passes in the regular season. Palmer was a far more adept triggerman than Ryan Lindley, the backup quarterback thrust into a starting role in Charlotte the year before because Palmer was out. Those Cardinals had only gained 78 yards all day—an all-time NFL playoff low—and the Panthers won by a modest 27–16 only because Carolina's offense had some trouble moving the ball, too.

This Panthers offense was much more explosive, having led the NFL in points. But Arizona had finished No. 2 in that category, and the Cardinals had beaten Green Bay in overtime the week before because ageless wide receiver Larry Fitzgerald had taken over the game.

It snowed late in the week before the game, and the Panthers practiced in it on Friday. Newton made a few snow angels before the practice and then started heaving snowballs at teammates. Then he directed a crisp practice where the receivers, according to Rivera, never dropped a ball. The stadium itself was cleared of snow by Sunday, in part due to workers from Charlotte Motor Speedway who came over to help.

Although much about this game would be a surprise, Carolina's first play was not. The Panthers had developed an unwritten rule during the course of the season that Jonathan Stewart must get the ball on a first-play handoff if he was healthy. It helped the Panthers' most physical back get going early. The Panthers had done it 11 times in a row entering the game, and Stewart's three-yard run on first down this time made it 12.

Carolina earned a field goal out of that drive, made Arizona punt, and then got a 32-yard punt return from Ginn. The fleet wide receiver had never been more primed to play in a game, still angry at the way the Cardinals had signed him and then released him in 2014. On second-and-3 from the Arizona 22, Ginn started left and then circled all the way back right on a crowd-pleasing reverse. It looked like a high school play when one player simply was able to outrun everyone else, and Ginn scored standing up to make it 10–0. The only player near Ginn at the end of the run was Newton, who came up from Ginn's blindside and, the receiver said, "scared me."

After another Arizona punt, here came Newton's 86-yard strike to Brown, who shucked off one tackle and was gone. It was 17–0 Carolina, and the first quarter wasn't even over yet. For the second straight playoff game, Carolina had leapt to an enormous lead.

The teams traded second-quarter TDs to make it 24–7, and then Ginn made another sterling play. With Newton looking for more points near the Cardinals end zone, the quarterback made his one really bad throw of the game. He overshot tight end Ed Dickson and threw it directly into the hands of Arizona cornerback Patrick Peterson at the Cardinals 6.

As fans gasped, Peterson started sprinting the other way. He looked uncatchable and about to score a 94-yard TD that would cut Carolina's lead to 24–14 in the second quarter. But here came Ginn, running like he was in the 100-meter dash at the Olympics and closing the gap. He raced down to catch Peterson at the Arizona 22 to save a TD.

On the next play, Palmer was intercepted at the goal line by Carolina safety Kurt Coleman, who jumped high to get it and made a circus catch. Carolina took its 24–7 lead into halftime. Newton addressed the team then about the importance of not letting the Cardinals come back like Seattle had, and that never happened. The Panthers led by at least 17 points throughout the second half as, for once, fans breathed easily and enjoyed the ride.

The critical pickoff just before halftime was one of Coleman's two interceptions on the day, bringing his season total to nine. Carolina would not allow Palmer and Arizona's powerful offense to complete a single pass of more than 21 yards. Fitzgerald, normally so sure-handed, dropped a couple of passes. Arizona defensive players were yelling at each other on the sideline. It turned out that Philly Brown (113 yards) had more receiving yardage than Fitzgerald, Michael Floyd, and John Brown put together (90 yards).

"That was my favorite game of the season," Coleman said in his interview for this book. "Not for my personal stat line, but because it meant we were going to the Super Bowl and that we did it as a team. People had said our defensive backs couldn't hold up against Arizona and its high-powered offense. There was such a feeling of euphoria on the field. It was so great to do it with those guys. And after the game I was able to see my wife and my kids, and to celebrate that moment with them was irreplaceable."

"Long-Cooked Collard Greens"

There were a lot of irreplaceable moments in the game. Team owner Jerry Richardson was the surprise banger of the "Keep Pounding" drum before kickoff. Safety Tre Boston not only had a fumble recovery but also an interception. Rookie wideout Devin Funchess—who had been steadily improving and had 120 yards receiving in the season finale against Tampa Bay—scored his first postseason TD. Cornerback Josh Norman proclaimed that the Panthers could have "put a 50-burger" on the Cardinals—referring to the number of points Carolina scored—but that the coaches had held them back. That was true.

Richardson was presented the Halas Trophy (given to the NFC champions) after the game and then passed it around. When Kuechly stepped up to make a brief speech to the fans, it was completely drowned out by the familiar cries of "L-u-u-u-uke."

It wasn't all great, though. The most troublesome part: linebacker Thomas Davis broke his forearm on a tackle. He reappeared on the sideline with the arm in a sling, but his status for the Super Bowl was in doubt—at least to everyone but No. 58. "I wouldn't miss the Super Bowl for the world," Davis said.

But for the most part, the day was celebratory. Newton likes to make a colorful analogy in a press conference when he's feeling good, and so he brought up a new one Sunday night after the victory when asked a question about the five years it took him and the Panthers to get to the quarterback's first Super Bowl. Said Newton, "It wasn't going to be...instant grits, quick grits. It was going to be a process like long-cooked collard greens. I think those collard greens are brewing right now. You can smell it from 100 miles away."

Meanwhile, 1,562 miles away, Denver had edged New England 20–18 to advance to the Super Bowl, as well. The Broncos had overwhelmed New England's offensive line, hitting quarterback Tom Brady close to 20 times. Denver linebacker Von Miller had been the biggest star with 2½ sacks, two more tackles for loss, and an interception. Teammate DeMarcus Ware had hit Brady seven times on the day.

This, then, would be the Panthers' biggest challenge—their offensive line was going to have to try and hold up against the team that had led the NFL in sacks. But the Panthers had made it. For the second time in their 21 years, they were going to the Super Bowl.

PART VII

THE SUPER BOWL ...AND BEYOND

2016 and a Bright Future

36

STAR AND KK

WHILE THE PANTHERS' record scoring output gained most of the attention in the NFC Championship Game in early 2016, the contributions of two defensive linemen up front were a hidden pivot point on which the game turned.

General manager Dave Gettleman's first two draft choices ever for Carolina—Star Lotulelei and Kawann Short—had continued to pay dividends throughout the playoffs. Gettleman remained convinced that "big men allow you to compete," as he often quoted former New York Giants coach Tom Coughlin. And in the players known inside the locker room as "Star and KK," he had two rocks upon which the Panthers could build the rest of their defense. As Gettleman had said right after he drafted the two in 2013, "You look historically at the Super Bowl champions, and you show me one that's had a bad defensive front. Doesn't happen—I'm telling you."

When the Panthers flew to California for Super Bowl 50 a week before the game, it was Cam Newton's black-and-gold Versace pants (which retailed for $849) that made all the news. No one remembered what Star and KK wore on the team plane, which was just fine with them. They were content making plays for a defense that had ranked in the top 10 for four straight years—or, more exactly, Lotulelei would often occupy two blockers and allow Short more room to make plays.

Short had led Carolina with 11 sacks during the regular season and made his first Pro Bowl. His first step was almost as good as Kuechly's. Short had been the best pure pass-rushing defensive tackle in his draft class, and even when he didn't get to the quarterback he caused all kinds of havoc. Against Green Bay, his harassment forced Aaron Rodgers into a late interception to preserve a victory. Against Seattle in the playoffs, it was Short's pressure that had made Russell Wilson throw the ball hurriedly and right into the hands of Kuechly, who had returned it 14 yards for the TD. "KK gets absolutely all the credit for that one," Kuechly said.

Lotulelei on the other hand, was the steamrolling, run-stopping strong man. He rarely got to the quarterback, but he had a big hand in helping Kuechly and Davis run free because offensive linemen had to block him for so long. "He does probably 90 percent of the dirty work," Short said of Lotulelei.

Lotulelei (the No. 14 overall pick of 2013) and Short (No. 44) had entered the NFL together in 2013. "We came in the same draft class and we made a pact that we were going to try to be the best defensive tackles in the league," Short said. "We've still got room to improve, but we've made a big jump from year one to year three."

"Quality Three-Down Guys"

There has been speculation that the Panthers will have a tough time re-signing both No. 98 (Lotulelei) and No. 99 (Short) because they will cost so much. Gettleman helped postpone that call by picking up Lotulelei's fifth-year option in 2016, meaning that Star will be a Panther at least through 2017 and quite likely longer. The Panthers are definitely going to try to sign Short to a lucrative extension to keep him in the fold, and an extension for Lotulelei seems quite likely too.

As for the Super Bowl, both KK and Star could believe they were there. What they found hard to believe was that they would be facing 39-year-old Peyton Manning, a player who had already been an NFL star in their formative years. "When Peyton Manning was with Indianapolis for the longest time," Lotulelei said, "the

Colts were my favorite team on 'Madden' because of him. Marvin Harrison, Dallas Clark, Peyton—I always played as the Colts."

The two Super Bowl–winning teams Gettleman was involved with for the New York Giants included superb pass rushers like Michael Strahan, Justin Tuck, and Osi Umenyiora. To Gettleman, that just emphasized the value of a strong defensive line. "If you don't get in second-and-long and third-and-long situations, you can't rush the passer," Gettleman said Monday. "You can't do it. You only get there if you stop the run. And Star and KK are both quality three-down guys [who can play both the run and pass]."

While they play the same position, all Panthers opponents quickly find out that Short and Lotulelei don't play it the same way. "Star is just a powerful space-eater with good athletic movement," Gettleman said. "KK—and I said this to the scouts in the draft room [in 2013]—was the most natural pass rusher of all the defensive tackles in that class. He had things he did naturally that you can't coach." Short's work ethic was thought to be a bit questionable, however, which is why he dropped into the second round. (The Panthers had a first-round grade on him, however.)

Lotulelei averaged less than two tackles a game in the 2015 season, but all that space-eating meant he should get an unofficial assist in many of the tackles by the Panthers linebackers. Short has never been quite as good of a run-stopper, but his pass rushing gets him in the highlights more.

Short had four multiple-sack games in 2015, second only to Houston's J.J. Watt, and was the NFC's Defensive Player of the Month in both October and December. That latter honor meant he was the first defensive tackle in NFL history to be named defensive player of the month twice in the same season. His 11 sacks tied him with two other players—Aaron Donald and Geno Atkins—for most in the NFL among defensive tackles.

"KK is ascending, for sure," head coach Ron Rivera said. "But Star does a lot of the dirty work."

And because there is a lot of dirty work to be done in football, the Panthers would like Lotulelei and Short to anchor the defensive line for many seasons to come. At the moment, though, like the rest of their teammates, they were focused on preparing for the biggest game in which they had ever played.

37

SUPER-SIZED LETDOWN

AFTER THE BEST season in franchise history, the Carolina Panthers played their worst game in a long time in Super Bowl 50.

There are no two ways about it—Denver just flat-out beat Carolina, 24–10, on February 7, 2016, in Santa Clara, California. The Broncos did it with a defense that overwhelmed Carolina's offense, which suddenly looked frail in the face of the most fearsome pass rush it had seen all season. Carolina hurt its own cause with four turnovers, a special-teams miscue that resulted in a 61-yard Denver punt return, a missed 44-yard field goal, and three drops from Jerricho Cotchery, who hadn't dropped a single ball the entire season.

The Panthers defense played plenty well enough to win, allowing Denver only 194 total yards and stopping the Broncos 13 out of 14 times on third down. But it was still only the second-best defense on the field. The Panthers had averaged an extraordinary 40 points per game in their two playoff wins and 31.25 in the regular season, but in this game scored only 10—easily their lowest point total of the season. Quarterback Cam Newton really didn't have a signature positive play the entire game, but he did get sacked six times. And on two of those sacks, he lost fumbles that led directly to 15 of Denver's 24 points.

Even now, when people ask me, "How was the Super Bowl?" I always answer, "Great—until kickoff." California and its San Francisco Bay Area was a wonderful host. The weather cooperated. Panthers fans who were lucky enough to score tickets had fun touring San Francisco's various attractions. But the game itself? Not much fun.

"Don't Be a Vampire"

In 2012 center Ryan Kalil had raised a lot of eyebrows with a full-page ad that he took out in the *Charlotte Observer*. In the ad, placed just before Cam Newton's second season and just after Carolina had gone 6–10, Kalil guaranteed that the Panthers would win the next Super Bowl. It was a bold prediction, and quite incorrect—the Panthers would finish 7–9.

But it turned out Kalil was sort of right...eventually. The Panthers had a lot of talent in 2012, and even more now. Newton, Luke Kuechly, tight end Greg Olsen, running back Jonathan Stewart, linebacker Thomas Davis, and Kalil himself were all there already and were all Pro Bowlers for the Super Bowl Panthers. (All but Stewart were also team captains.)

Much of the pregame talk for Super Bowl 50 centered around the Panthers' celebrations, like Newton's first-down pointing and touchdown dabbing and the team pictures before the game was over.

"We're not trying to gloat or taunt," safety Tre Boston insisted. "We just want to have fun while we're playing the sport that we love."

As for the team's joyous nature, Boston said, "In the defensive backs room, we call it, 'Don't be a vampire.' You can't suck the life out of others, you know?"

The question some asked was how the Panthers would react when there wasn't much to be happy about. Deion Sanders, a Hall of Fame cornerback, was one of the most flamboyant players in NFL history. Sanders told me a few days before the game about the Panthers, "I applaud them for seizing the moment and having a lot of fun while they are seizing it....It's easy to have joy when you're winning. But you've got to keep that joy when you're getting your butt kicked, too."

Boomer Esiason was Cincinnati's quarterback on January 22, 1989, when the Bengals were edged 20–16 by Joe Montana and San Francisco when Montana threw a touchdown pass with 34 seconds left. I asked him a couple of days before Super Bowl 50 what the difference between winning and losing a Super Bowl ultimately was.

"Joe Montana and I go make an appearance somewhere, and he gets 500 grand for it and I get five grand," Esiason cracked. "And then I have to sit there and suffer the slings and arrows of how great he was."

So that was all at stake, and a whole lot more. The Broncos had been to the Super Bowl only two years before, but had gotten creamed 43–8 by Seattle. They wanted redemption. Carolina was trying to earn a place among the best teams in NFL history—only a handful had ever lost just one game and won a Super Bowl title. The Panthers would have Davis. He would indeed wrap up his broken forearm and play for Carolina, just as he had promised he would.

Finally, after a two-week break following the NFC and AFC Championship Games, the Super Bowl arrived. Panthers general manager Dave Gettleman had seen six of the teams he worked for make the Super Bowl over the years (three had won it), but he still never quite got used to the hype.

"When you get to the game, it's almost like the game's a damn afterthought," Gettleman said. "It's like, 'Does anybody know there's a game going on today?'"

Early Errors Dig a Hole

In a first quarter that would be emblematic of the game at large, the Panthers began poorly. Denver got the ball first, and the Broncos moved it more effectively than they would the rest of the day— Denver's only third-down conversion of the entire game came on its first drive. Quarterback Peyton Manning's arm wasn't that strong anymore, but it was good enough to complete a 22-yard pass on third-and-4. Denver stalled in the red zone but got a 34-yard field goal from Brandon McManus to lead 3–0.

When I talked to Panthers coach Ron Rivera about the Super Bowl in our interview for this book, he didn't mention that field-goal drive at all. Rivera said he has watched the Super Bowl "at least six, seven times by now, trying to learn from it." What sticks in his craw are the errors the Panthers offense made in its own first two series. Let him explain:

"Opening series for us," Rivera said. "On first down, we needed to press the hole a little longer [Stewart ran for two yards]. On the next play, we had a safety fall down. We had a receiver wide open and we missed the throw [Newton threw incomplete]. On third down, he throws a bit high, but he should have caught it for first down [Olsen caught the ball one yard short of a first down]."

Carolina punted. Then Denver punted. The Panthers then had Cotchery open for what could and should have been about a 25-yard gain. But Cotchery bobbled the ball, then appeared to have caught it just before it hit the ground. The officials ruled "incomplete." Rivera challenged, but the call stood. NFL Films caught a moment with Rivera and one official in which an angry Rivera made the point that if the ball had been ruled a catch to begin with it would not have been overturned, and the official agreed with him.

Instead of first-and-10 at about the 40, Carolina had a second-and-10 at the 15. Stewart ran for no gain. And then came arguably the biggest play of the game. On third-and-10, Newton dropped back. Denver linebacker Von Miller, single-blocked by Mike Remmers, destroyed the right tackle with a speed rush to the outside—almost the exact same move that Atlanta's Vic Beasley had beaten Remmers on during the fourth quarter in the Panthers' lone previous loss. Miller stripped the ball from Newton on a sack, and Denver's Malik Jackson pounced on it in the end zone for a touchdown.

This play, more than any other, put Miller on *Dancing with the Stars* later in 2016 (a show Tolbert said he had to turn off every time he saw Miller on it.) Miller would end up with another huge strip-sack later, in the fourth quarter, as part of his 2½-sack, Super Bowl MVP performance. But it was this first sack that set the tone and showed the Panthers just how difficult blocking Denver really was going to be.

In hindsight, the Panthers never should have blocked Miller with just one person the rest of the game. In reality, that's not what they did.

"So Many Glitch Things"

Down 10–0, Carolina clawed back in the second quarter with its lone touchdown march of the game. After scrambles of 11 and 12 yards by Newton and several mid-range passes that found the mark, Stewart scored from a yard out. The Panthers were down only 10–7.

But again, Carolina made a key mistake, and Denver capitalized. While covering a Carolina punt by Brad Nortman, two Panthers players both thought that Denver returner Jordan Norwood had signaled for a fair catch on a short punt.

Norwood hadn't called for one, though. Instead, he had decided to take a risk on catching the ball in heavy traffic and running it back. As Panthers gunners Colin Jones and Teddy Williams both backed off, worried about getting a penalty, Norwood burst through the gap and found lots of daylight. He would have scored except for the speed of Panthers defensive end Mario Addison, who ran him down at the Carolina 14.

"There were so many glitch things that happened," Rivera said. "But I'm not taking anything away from Denver. The Broncos played very well."

Carolina's defense held. The Broncos got another field goal, though, so it was 13–7 at halftime. The Panthers were within a score, but had not been able to move the ball with what had been the NFL's best offense. Denver had three good cornerbacks, and too often all of Newton's primary options throwing the ball seemed to be well-covered.

On the second play of the third quarter, the Panthers did get someone open. Ted Ginn grabbed a pass that ended up being a 45-yard gain, with 27 of the yards coming after the catch thanks to Ginn's speed. But Carolina stalled out at the Denver 26. Then Graham Gano missed a 44-yard field goal—a play on which it appeared Denver's Aqib Talib had been offside.

The Broncos made an adjustment at halftime, trying to throw away from Josh Norman and toward Robert McClain (who had only joined the Panthers in the last two months of the season after injuries had depleted the secondary). Emmanuel Sanders caught passes of 22 and 25 yards on Denver's next drive to set up a third field goal from McManus, and it was 16–7.

To say the Panthers never moved the ball against Denver would be incorrect—they just didn't do so consistently, and the big "chunk" plays Carolina loved never netted any points. On Carolina's next possession, in fact, Newton hit Philly Brown for a 42-yard strike. But the drive short-circuited later when Ginn had a ball bounce off his hands and into the waiting arms of Broncos safety T.J. Ward.

The Fumble Cam Let Go

In the meantime, Carolina's defense kept the Panthers in the game. The unlikely star was reserve defensive end Kony Ealy, who had the best day of his career. He set up a 39-yard field goal from Gano early in the fourth quarter with a strip-sack of Manning at midfield. With three sacks, one forced fumble, one recovered fumble, and one interception that he yanked in with one hand, Ealy would have been a good candidate for Super Bowl MVP had Carolina won.

After the Gano field goal, the Panthers were trailing by a single score, 16–10, when they got the ball back the next two times—the first with nine minutes to play and the second with 4:51 to go. The first resulted in a punt. The second was even worse.

On another play that will haunt the Panthers, Newton had Devin Funchess breaking open deep down the field for what could have been another 40-yard gain. Or more. But as he took an extra split second to allow Funchess to get deep and to wind up for a big throw, he was again strip-sacked by Miller—who had beaten Remmers again inside Carolina's own 20.

Unlike the first fumble, this time the ball was on the ground long enough for Newton to think about jumping toward a pile and attempting to grab it. Instead, inexplicably, Newton pulled away. Denver recovered at the Carolina 4. Newton would say two days later that he didn't dive because his leg could have been "contorted in some way" had he done so. It was a business decision, basically—Newton decided that the risk wasn't worth the reward.

It was probably a decision Newton would like to take back, too. Newton had the only real chance of recovering the ball. Denver did so instead. The recovery did come after Miller illegally batted the ball toward the goal line in an eye-blink instant too quick for the officials to see. Denver then quickly scored a touchdown and a two-point conversion. That turned into the game's final score of 24–10. The Broncos got to be the ones who earned the right to brag, and they certainly did.

"We don't have to say nothing," said Denver safety T.J. Ward, who had recovered the critical fumble. "We let them do all the talking. We let our pads talk. We talk with our helmets and our shoulder pads. They could do all the media talking, you know what I'm talking about? We're not about that flashy stuff. We're about that grind, putting in that work. Grind it. Work. That's how you get the 'ship. They want to be famous. We want to be champions.

They want to be rappers and backup dancers. We want to play football."

It's important to note that Newton sacrifices his body on a regular basis more than any quarterback in the league. He will soon be the quarterback with more rushing TDs than any other QB ever. And he wouldn't have had to make this decision if the Panthers had devoted two (or even three!) people to Miller and not allowed him to make his second game-changing play. Nevertheless, the fumble he didn't jump on is now part of Newton's narrative—a blemish on an MVP season. And what happened right after the game is part of his personal narrative, too.

Cam's Press Conference

When the Panthers lose, reporters like me who have covered the team during Newton's entire tenure know what to expect. He will often sit in the locker room with most of his uniform still on, facing the locker, for 15 or more minutes. He doesn't like being consoled by teammates during those situations, and mostly people just let him alone and give him time to process the loss. He has said numerous times, "I'm a bad loser." And while he has improved a little bit in that respect compared to when he was a rookie, it's only an incremental improvement.

It is often close to an hour after the game ends that Newton is actually made available to the media, by which time he has showered, put on a suit, and gotten his mind wrapped around the loss enough that he can discuss it calmly. He has never skipped the mandatory postgame press availability that every NFL quarterback is required to have, but he certainly enjoys them more after wins.

The Super Bowl is different. By rule, players are required to be available to the media after a brief cooling-off period. They don't generally have time to shower. This is how it has been for decades, and players who have lost the Super Bowl have dealt with it with varying degrees of public frustration.

Newton did not deal with it well, and his attitude during his press conference quickly became the predominant day-after story of a Super Bowl that had not been filled with too many dramatics. In two minutes and 29 seconds, Newton answered 13 questions. Eleven of his answers were three words or less. A sample of the full transcript:

Q: Can you put into words the disappointment you feel right now?

A: We lost.

Q: On that fumble, were you trying to extend the play and that's why you didn't hit the deck for it?

A: I don't know.

Q: Did Denver change anything defensively to take away your running lanes?

A: No.

Newton, who was wearing a black hoodie pulled over his head during the interview, was obviously bothered by the fact that Denver cornerback Chris Harris could be heard nearby, answering his own questions and crowing about the way the Broncos had stopped the NFL's MVP. After less than three minutes, Newton abruptly left his own press conference, announcing, "I'm done, man," and walking off.

It was a jarring end to the press conference, and a jarring end to the season for a quarterback used to winning in the biggest moments. Newton did not apologize for it when he met with reporters two days later, repeating that he was a "sore loser."

Rivera defended his quarterback in our interview for the book.

"It was almost like a mourning process he was having to go through," the coach said. "That's what I think people missed.... Everybody forgets the circumstances of what happens. You lose the biggest game of your career, okay, you're trying to get over it. You walk into the locker room, and everybody is either crying, or they've got their head in their hands, and they're down. And, you have a coach who's trying to cheerlead everybody to refocus and get past it already. Then, you take him, and you put him into a room, and 10 feet from him is the guy who's boasting about winning, talking about, 'We knew we could do this, we could shut it down, you see what happened.' And that thing was very hard on him."

Many other athletes have handled similar situations better, though, as Rivera knows—including 2015 Masters winner Jordan Spieth, who choked away a lead at the 2016 Masters and ended up having to put a green jacket on the man who beat him at a public ceremony only minutes later. Said Rivera, "People want to go, 'Oh, look at Jordan Spieth.' No! That's apples and oranges. Because professional golfers are taught to deal with their emotions. They know they can't play that way....Every shot, they control their emotions. That's why Jordan Spieth was able to do it the way he did it. I wish people would get past that, cause Cam has already come out and said, 'I am a bad loser. I know that. I'm going to work on that.' But we're going to move forward."

And forward was the only direction worth going, really, after the Panthers' 17-win season ended on such a sour note. But 2016 and beyond held great promise for a team that returns almost all of its core—with the notable exception of Josh Norman—and added several more key players in the 2016 off-season.

38

ONWARD AND UPWARD

THE PANTHERS UNDER Dave Gettleman and Ron Rivera are never going to be the team that "wins" the off-season. They don't go in for splashy, high-dollar, free-agent signings. Their draft picks are often fairly nondescript. But since they became a tag team in 2013, they have made mostly correct choices. Now they are striving to move beyond Super Bowl 50 and toward another future Super Bowl.

Still, Rivera planned to not sweep under the rug the many accomplishments of the 2015 season while he and Gettleman assembled the rosters for 2016 and beyond. Said the coach, "Going 17–2, winning the NFC championship—that's something we are going to revel in, because I think it's important that we don't diminish the fact that we won the NFC and that we got to the Super Bowl. And yes, we did lose, but guess what? Thirty other teams didn't even come close. So that, to me, is important."

Josh Norman's Departure

Every NFL roster changes every season, even the ones that win 17 games. And so it was with Carolina. The biggest national news the Panthers made in the months following Super Bowl 50 came in April, when they rescinded the franchise tag on star cornerback Josh Norman and allowed him to walk away from the team. When Norman hurriedly said he would sign the Panthers' one-year, $13.95 million franchise tag offer after all—he hadn't done so in order to increase his leverage—Carolina didn't budge.

Gettleman basically decided there were better ways to spend that $14 million, given that he believed it was going to be impossible to sign Norman to a long-term contract based on his salary demands. (Norman and his agent wanted around $15–16 million per season. The Panthers didn't want to go higher than $11 million.) After a bad experience using the franchise tag on Greg Hardy, Gettleman didn't want to rent Norman for a year—despite Norman's four interceptions in 2015 and the fact he gave up the lowest quarterback rating of any cornerback in the NFL for passes thrown in his area.

"Football is the truest of all team sports," Gettleman said. "You need 53 guys, bottom line. And the more we thought about it, the more flexibility that $14 million would give us. We just kept talking and talking. In order to get to the right answer, you have to ask the right questions....You have to understand that you can't keep everybody. It's impossible. And so now you have to decide who you're going to allow to graduate....This is a business decision, folks. At the end of the day, you can't have your cake and eat it, too. We'd all like to, but you can't."

Less than 48 hours later, Norman had gotten the sort of money he wanted—a five-year contract that could be worth up to $75 million with the Washington Redskins (including $36.5 million in guaranteed money). It was hard to blame either side for the parting. Norman had made relatively little money in his first four years in the NFL and needed to maximize his value for what will undoubtedly be the biggest contract he will ever sign. But Gettleman and the Panthers don't put as much value on the cornerback position as they do, say, middle linebacker—and they certainly didn't plan on paying Norman more than they paid Luke Kuechly.

Like all coaches, Rivera doesn't like to see talented players get in their cars and drive away from the stadium for good. But the coach had paid close attention as Gettleman had traded away Jon Beason and released Steve Smith and DeAngelo Williams—all popular and productive players for the Panthers—since 2013.

"We've done some good things the last three years," Rivera said. "And some of the things that we've done have been very hard. I think Dave's had to make a couple of tough decisions that have proven to be the best as we've gone forward. And quite honestly, I'm going to trust him on this one, too."

So money talked, and Norman walked. But the Panthers quickly moved to try and fill that gap by drafting three cornerbacks in a row in the 2016 NFL Draft in the second, third, and fifth rounds. Samford's James Bradberry, West Virginia's Daryl Worley, and Oklahoma's Zack Sanchez will all have a chance to win a starting job on a team that is radically rebuilding its defensive secondary yet again. Only Bene Benwikere remains among the top four cornerbacks of 2015, with Norman leaving for Washington and both Charles Tillman and Cortland Finnegan not being re-signed. Norman exited with some class, running a half-page ad in the *Charlotte Observer* in June 2016 that served as a thank-you letter to his fans and teammates. "Your support made it easy to wake up each and every morning to grind for the battle ahead," he wrote in the section where he thanked the fans.

Of the new "conners," as Gettleman calls them, Bradberry and Worley are both 6′1″ and have long arms like Norman did—those are characteristics that the Panthers prefer for their outside cornerbacks. Sanchez, known as a high-risk, high-reward player, is not quite as big and will likely fit better as a nickel cornerback.

As usual for Gettleman, a number of the players he drafted were ranked lower on other draft boards—especially those of the so-called draft experts. "I don't worry about the pundits, I don't," Gettleman said in a post-draft press conference. You guys know that....I've been doing this a long time, so I'm going to go with my ample gut."

More Hog Mollies

Gettleman prefers not to spend a lot of money on the cornerback position and instead devote more of it to the defensive line and linebackers. He took another of his beloved "hog mollies" in the first round of the 2016 draft, grabbing Louisiana Tech defensive tackle Vernon Butler. Butler, who Gettleman and Rivera believe has untapped pass-rushing ability that didn't show up in his modest college sack totals, will be inserted into the rotation of an already deep position. Gettleman also signed free agent defensive tackle Paul Soliai in the 2016 off-season and re-signed veteran Kyle Love to join starters Kawann Short and Star Lotulelei (whose contract the GM extended through the 2017 season by picking up Lotulelei's fifth-year option). It is thought to be only a matter of time before the Panthers give Short a big contract extension, given Gettleman's love for defensive tackles, although Short wants very big money and sat out a couple of days of voluntary workouts in June 2016 to make that known. "When you can roll guys in and out like we can," Gettleman said, speaking of the defensive linemen, "and there's no drop-off, it makes for a long day at the office for offensive linemen."

The Panthers also benefited from signing veteran defensive end Charles Johnson for one more year in 2016, with this happening only days after Carolina released him. Carolina first cut the team captain, nullifying the final year of a long-ago contract extension that had become financially prohibitive. Johnson received then at least one other offer in the $6-million-a-year range, but turned it down to play one more year with the Panthers—the only NFL team for which he has ever played—for $3 million.

Carolina also should get a major boost from the return of 2014 first-round draft pick Kelvin Benjamin, the wide receiver who will once again become one of Cam Newton's favorite targets as soon as he gets back on the field. Benjamin missed all of the 2015 Super Bowl run with a torn anterior cruciate ligament in his knee. The Panthers—who in 2016 will try to become the first Super Bowl loser in 23 years to return to the championship game the very next season—consider the return of the player whose vanity plate reads "KB13" to be almost like having an extra first-round draft pick.

No "Dumb Guys"

Through all those roster moves and all those that are to come, Gettleman promised he was going to make sure the players in the locker room had enough intelligence to get their jobs done.

"We're not bringing in dumb guys," Gettleman said. "We're not going to do it. I don't care how talented they are. Because, by the time they figure it out, Ron and I get fired....There are certain positions where you don't need to split an atom [to play well]. But you take an offensive lineman who is dumb, your quarterback is going to end up in the hospital—and maybe two or three different ones."

Speaking of smart offensive linemen, the Panthers extended the contract of left tackle Michael Oher for three years shortly after the Super Bowl, ensuring that Oher will protect Cam Newton's blind side for years to come. Rivera also received a contract extension after leading Carolina to three straight playoff appearances, as he put his days of almost being fired further in the rear-view mirror.

The 2016 season will see the retirement of one recent Panthers tradition, according to Cam Newton: his celebratory "dabbing" will be a thing of the past. Newton promised to find something new to do in the end zone, but with the "dab" being co-opted and performed at every turn (even Charlotte's mayor was doing it at one point), it was probably time for Newton to move on to the next big thing.

As for the locker room's reaction to Norman's departure, it was similar to when Smith and Williams were released. Every NFL player is aware of the adage that the league's initials really could stand for "Not For Long." They also realize that they better be fully committed to getting the Panthers to another Super Bowl quickly, because nobody is guaranteed tomorrow. As Gettleman said about the 2015 team, "Our culture was terrific....Everybody was all in. We want people that are all in."

They want that, yes, but the Panthers do not want an arrogant team that thinks the NFC South and a playoff berth will now simply be handed to it every season. "The second you think you've arrived, the second you think you've got it, you're done," tight end Greg Olsen said. "I've seen that play out on an individual basis my whole career, and I don't want to see that happen to us this year collectively as a team. I don't think it will. I haven't seen signs of it....Overconfidence and thinking you've arrived has ruined a lot of careers in the NFL."

No, the Panthers haven't arrived. But they are getting very close. And by building a team that finally appears sustainable for the long haul, there is little doubt that one day they will get back to the Super Bowl.

And this time, they will win it.